From a Cornish Study

Essays on Cornish Studies and Cornwall

by
Bernard Deacon

Published by CoSERG, Redruth, Cornwall
https://bernarddeacon.wordpress.com/

ISBN: 978-0-9513918-3-9

Printed by Create Space

Contents

Preface

Those of a literary bent may recognise the allusion in the title to Arthur Quiller Couch's *From a Cornish Window*, published in 1906. Of course, it would be invidious in the extreme for me to claim any status remotely akin to that of Cornwall's great Edwardian man of letters. So let me immediately hasten to assure readers that that is certainly not my intention. Nevertheless, this modest volume has one or two points of similarity with Q's book.

First, five of the eight chapters here were, as were the chapters in *From a Cornish Window*, 'written at intervals, and in part for recreation'. Chapters four to eight of this book have seemingly been haunting my computer for years, begun well before retirement, chopped, changed, submitted to journals, abandoned, restored, revised, retitled over the years. Rather than continue to rewrite them in order to fit the requirements and word limits of obscure academic journals I felt that they might be more accessible if published in one volume.

Q was keenly aware of the state of his early twentieth century world, the coming catastrophes of which lay ominously on the horizon beyond the rather light and witty essays that made up *From a Cornish Window*. During the years of writing the essays of his book Q had 'striven to maintain a cheerful mood while a popular philosophy which he believed to be cheap took possession of men and translated itself into politics which he knew to be nasty'. For Q this 'nasty' philosophy was 'sham-imperialism'. However, although Q's dedication mentions his dislike of this nostrum, only one or two chapters in his book refer to it, instead discoursing on varied subjects, including Oxford University, cricket, the Mediterranean, sailing, the Cornish mystery plays, and 'strangers who take up their residence in Cornwall', but with an overall focus on poetry. For 'sham-imperialism' now read 'neo-liberalism'. In similar fashion, in the pages below neo-liberalism makes fleeting appearances but is not addressed directly. Q also warned his readers to expect the occasional 'dull page'. I'm sure many dull pages may well be encountered below, although I trust not too many. So what does this volume contain?

From a Cornish Study makes an obvious reference to the academic field of Cornish Studies, one in which I've toiled for most of my life. Almost two decades backalong, I became entranced by the possibilities of an over-arching Cornish Studies methodology that would be a fitting partner in the 'new Cornish Studies' that was then enthusing some of us. Three contributions duly appeared in *Cornish Studies* containing various methodological speculations. While the *Cornish Studies* series is fairly easily obtainable (in Cornwall at least) it seems a good time, with institutional Cornish Studies now entering its third phase under the leadership of Garry Tregidga, to bring these together in one place as Chapters 1-3 below. I've resisted the temptation to update their content comprehensively, merely revising some stylistic gaucheries, correcting a few typos and removing some redundant and repetitive phrases and sentences. But for each I've added a short postscript, reflecting on them from a distance of 15-20 years. The fourth (and longest) chapter of the book contains a critical review of work on Cornwall in the humanities and social sciences since those initial methodological reflections appeared in print. This will hopefully provide a useful bibliography for students and others attracted to Cornish studies, while relating the recent corpus of work back to the methodological musings.

While the theory and method of Cornish Studies is the subject of the first half of the book, the second moves on to the practice of Cornish Studies, with chapters that are either published here for the first time or (in the case of Chapter 7) in an extended and redrafted form. Chapter 5 considers the possibilities of microhistory, taking as its cue Charles Barham's survey of the working conditions of Cornwall's miners and bal maidens in 1841. Barham's report, along with the other reports buried in Victorian 'blue books', are still an under-quarried source and would merit a lot more attention.

Chapter 6 overlaps with the period of Barham's survey and is a major re-assessment of Chartism in Cornwall. Hitherto relegated to a footnote in histories of this first working-class struggle for democratic rights in Britain, Cornwall is revealed as deserving more respect than previously granted. Small but determined groups of Chartist activists maintained a presence in Cornish towns throughout the 1840s, doing much to lay the ground for the Liberal-Radical 'nexus' that emerged after the mid-nineteenth century. It is hoped that this chapter might stimulate more work on the under-researched area of working-class politics in nineteenth and twentieth century Cornwall.

While Chapters 5 and 6 make up the first pair, the second is provided by Chapters 7 and 8, which turn to identity politics in Cornwall. Chapter 7 looks at the campaigns for a Cornish diocese in the mid-nineteenth century and the less well-known, but equally significant, struggle for a Cornish Sunday Closing Act in 1881-83. This latter provides one of those 'what might have been' moments of Cornish history, when acquiring an act for Sunday closing specifically for Cornwall would have been a symbolic expression of Cornish difference and a bridge to Wales and the other Celtic nations. But it was not to be, largely because the discourse of difference remained trapped within other discourses that ultimately subverted Cornish claims for special treatment. A more theory-orientated version of this chapter appeared in the *International Journal of Regional and Local Studies* in 2016 but the extended version here does more to consider the lessons for campaigners for Cornish rights in the early twenty-first century.

Prominent in those campaigns since the 1950s have been the men and women of Mebyon Kernow, Cornwall's own nationalist or autonomist party. Struggling against the condescension and/or ignorance of the Great British Public and the indifference of the majority of their fellow Cornishmen and women, MK activists have stubbornly maintained a presence for over half a century, but signally failed to make a breakthrough. The final chapter of this book examines the party in the context of the academic literature on ethnoregionalism. It argues that the academy has unduly ignored its presence for too long. The combination of persistence and durability with poor electoral performance provides a relatively unusual example and one that needs explanation. In Chapter 8 I try to explain it.

It only remains to provide some acknowledgements. With their genesis stretching back over two decades the chapters of this book have benefited from diverse direct and indirect assistance. Some of that, without whom they would probably not have been written, came from those who are no longer with us, giants of Cornish studies and Cornish history, such as F.L.Harris, Ronald Perry, John Rowe, John Rule and Charles Thomas, whose writings and encouragement were much appreciated in my younger days when teaching and writing about Cornwall. In what now in retirement seems like another world, I owe an equal debt to many students, from the old extra-mural and WEA classes of the 1980s through to the postgraduate students at the Institute of Cornish Studies (ICS) in the 2000s. Their ideas and responses often made me re-think assumptions and explore new avenues, as did my colleagues at Exeter University, in particular of course at the ICS. There, Philip Payton's thinking about Cornwall's recent past developed in close reciprocity with mine, while Garry Tregidga carries the baton of Cornish Studies onwards to fresh fields. I have also greatly benefited from the ideas of Allen Buckley, Neil Kennedy, Alan Kent, John Probert, Ella Westland, Malcolm Williams and Peter Wills among others. Thanks are also due to the University of Exeter Press for publishing the original versions of Chapters 1 to 3 and to Kim Cooper and the staff at the Cornwall Centre, who were unfailingly helpful over many years. More anonymously, the comments of referees of early versions of Chapters 6 and 8 opened up some new questions and improved the analysis contained in those chapters.

Bernard Deacon, Redruth,
August 2017

Chapter One

In search of the missing 'turn': the spatial dimension and Cornish Studies

(First version published in Philip Payton (ed.), *Cornish Studies Eight*, (Exeter: University of Exeter Press, 2000), 213-230.)

Over the past two decades the social sciences are said to have embraced a 'turn' to culture.[1] This brings with it a greater awareness of the role of language, meanings and representations in our understanding of the social world. Material reality is not transparently represented by language, which is no longer viewed as unproblematically carrying its own meaning. Instead, meanings crystallise at the moment that things are named.[2] The 'cultural turn' is thus intertwined with and accompanied by a 'linguistic turn'. In Philip Payton's argument that 'the elucidation and analysis of [the Cornish identity] is perhaps the prime task of Cornish Studies as an academic discipline' we might see the local influence of this 'cultural turn'. Furthermore, work on 'Celtic Cornwall' by Amy Hale and the influence of cultural studies approaches in articles in *Cornish Studies 7* indicate that the cultural turn is now firmly established in the mainstream of work on Cornish Studies.[3]

But what about another 'turn', also widely touted as having influenced the social sciences over the past couple of decades? This is the 'spatial turn', the explicit consideration of the spatial dimension of social or historical explanations. At a meta-level, postmodernist theory has been

---

1   For an example see David Chaney, *The Cultural Turn: scene setting essays on contemporary cultural history* (London: Routledge, 1994).

2   A convincing articulation of this case can be found in Miguel A.Cabrera, 'Linguistic approach or return to subjectivism? In search of an alternative to social history', *Social History* 24 (1999), 74-89.

3   Philip Payton, 'Introduction', in Philip Payton (ed.), *Cornish Studies Six* (Exeter: University of Exeter Press, 1998), p.1; Amy Hale, 'Rethinking Celtic Cornwall: an ethnographic approach', in Philip Payton (ed.), *Cornish Studies Five* (Exeter: University of Exeter Press, 1997), 85-99; Catherine Brace, 'Cornish identity and landscape in the work of Arthur Caddick', in Payton (ed.), *Cornish Studies Seven*, 1999, 130-146; Jim Hall, 'Maximilla, the Cornish Montanist: the final scenes of *Origo Mundi*', in Payton (ed.), *Cornish Studies Seven*, 1999, 165-192; Patrick Laviolette, 'An iconography of landscape images in Cornish art and prose', in Payton (ed.), *Cornish Studies Seven*, 1999, 107-129.

implicated in this 'turn'. Krishan Kumar informs us that 'post-modernity traffics ... in synchronic rather than diachronic time. Relations of nearness and distance in space, rather than in time, become the measure of significance'.[4] The devaluation of time and the elevation of space noted by Kumar was prefigured by Foucault who claimed that, whereas the 'great obsession of the nineteenth century was history ... the present epoch will perhaps be above all the epoch of space'.[5] Speculations such as these have a less abstract echo in the growing interest on the part of some sociologists in the spatial formation and the flows of modern society and in the insertion of place into discussions of politics and power.[6] However, we should also be aware that the apparent spatial 'turn' has been questioned by some geographers, who point out that an absence of explicit geographical and spatial contextualising or geographical analysis means that talk of spatial 'turns' is little more than 'hubristic overstatement'.[7]

The intention of this contribution is to stimulate some thinking about the spatial aspect of the Cornish Studies project and to suggest some research agendas that might emerge from an explicit engagement with spatial concepts, and in particular the concept of scale. To some extent of course, by privileging a level of explanation different from that of the nation-state, Cornish Studies and other 'area' studies already have their own implicit geographies. But Cornish Studies, 'new' perhaps more than the 'old', prefers to concentrate its analysis on a Cornwall-wide scale, driven by a concern to unpack those factors that produce and reproduce 'Cornwall' and its overall unity. This can lead to a down-playing of analysis at a lower spatial scale, at the levels of communities and districts within Cornwall. Pondering this, Malcolm Williams has proposed a three-stage model of research under the banner of Cornish Studies.[8] First, there are studies concerned with overall constructions of 'Cornwall'. Second, there are studies that disaggregate Cornwall and look for similar and contrasting patterns within it. Finally, his third stage, presumably one that co-exists with the second, includes a more explicitly comparative approach, defining and

---

4   Krishan Kumar, *From Post-Industrial to Post-Modern Society: new theories of the contemporary world* (Oxford: Oxford University Press, 1995), p.146.
5   Michel Foucault, cited in E.W.Soja, *Postmodern Geographies: the reassertion of space in critical social theory* (London: Verso, 1989), p.10.
6   See Scott Lash and John Urry, *Economies of Signs and Space* (London: Sage 1994); John Urry, *Consuming Places* (London: Routledge, 1995); Michael Keith and Steve Pile (eds), *Place and the Politics of Identity* (London: Routledge, 1993).
7   John Agnew, 'The hidden geographies of social science and the myth of the "geographical turn"', *Environment and Planning D: Society and Space* 13 (1995), p.379.
8   Malcolm Williams, New Cornish Studies Seminar, Truro, July 2nd 1999.

explaining differences and similarities within Cornwall and comparing these with places elsewhere. The second and third stages are less well represented than the first in Cornish Studies. This is despite the fact that a Cornish Studies perspective offers a clear opportunity to work, for example, with more traditional local history procedures in building on the latter's focus on discrete places and communities and placing them in a broader and more comparative framework. Nevertheless, Cornish Studies as a discipline has produced relatively few studies of differences, for example of identity or class or gender, within Cornwall.

In the following discussion I wish to pick up on Williams' insight and further explore the issue of different levels of scale through three brief case studies, suggesting possible research questions at three scales. First, I intend to interrogate some recent work on issues of identity in early modern Cornwall to show how pursuing intra-Cornish differences can raise some unsettling questions. Second, I will suggest that spatial factors and a comparison with other places at a regional scale shed new light on issues of class and community in the industrialising Cornwall of the late eighteenth and early nineteenth centuries. Finally, I wish to include the global scale by proposing that re-visiting questions of diaspora and identity through the lens of post-colonialist theory both adds another set of research questions to the familiar and well-trodden field of emigration studies and raises questions about social relations in contemporary Cornwall.

A transitional period: ethnic identities in early modern Cornwall

In a series of path-breaking articles Mark Stoyle established the case for the 'war of the three kingdoms' of 1642-46 to be seen instead as a 'war of five peoples' – the English, Irish, Scots, Welsh and Cornish.[9] As a by-product of this work he also constructed a narrative of the period from 1497 to 1648 that explains the Cornish risings of those years as part of a single continuum, as a 'struggle to preserve a separate identity'.[10] His argument is that, by the late fifteenth-century, pressures on the culture centred on the Cornish language had produced a communal cultural defensiveness. A 'visceral sense of difference', provides the underlying cause for the

---

9   Mark Stoyle, '"Pagans or Paragons?": images of the Cornish during the English
     Civil War', *English Historical Review* CXI (1996), 299-323; '"Sir Richard
     Grenville's creatures": the New Cornish Tertia, 1644-46', in Philip Payton
     (ed.), *Cornish Studies Four,* (Exeter: University of Exeter Press, 1996), 26-44;
     'The last refuge of a scoundrel: Sir Richard Grenville and Cornish
     particularism, 1644-6', *Historical Research* 71 (1998), 31-51.
10   Mark Stoyle, 'Cornish rebellions, 1497-1648', *History Today* 47 (1997), 22-28;
     'The dissidence of despair: rebellion and identity in early modern Cornwall',
     Journal of British Studies 38 (1999), 423-444.

explosions of violence that punctuated the following century and a half. By the end of the 1640s the struggle was effectively lost, marking the 'end of the line for the Cornish as a "puissant" people'.[11]

In making this case Stoyle has developed a gradually more sophisticated spatial awareness. In 1997, in the first appearance of his argument, he acknowledged that the 'Cornish speaking district of west Cornwall ... was the storm centre of popular protest'.[12] But spatial nuance tended to be elided by a more general description of 'Cornish' hostility to assimilation into the British state. Cornish distinctiveness was constructed on a Cornwall-wide level and the differences within Cornwall became obscured. However, by 1999 he had unfolded a more complex spatial typology. In his most recent article he proposes a three-Cornwall model; a Cornish speaking western part, a formerly Cornish speaking middle part of people of 'Celtic descent', and a far eastern part where the population was of Anglo-Saxon descent. On institutional grounds and in terms of myths of common descent "even the anglicised inhabitants of eastern Cornwall possessed many of the characteristics that were thought to denote a people ... but only the Cornish speaking westerners possessed them all".[13] It was the western Cornish who 'truly deserved the name of "a people"', displaying the characteristics that qualified them as one of A.D.Smith's 'ethnies', or proto-national groupings.[14]

Prominent, indeed dominant, among these characteristics was language. In the medieval period language was the principal definer of 'nations' in the medieval sense. Thus, for Hastings, Cornish 'ethnicity' remained culturally separate even as it was institutionally and politically absorbed into the early English kingdom. 'The fate of this identity in ethnic-national terms was ... finally decided by the Reformation' and the rapid decline of the language after the sixteenth-century paralleled a decline of the 'singularity of the Cornish ethnic identity within England'.[15] While noting other, institutional markers of difference such as the Stannaries and the Duchy, Stoyle also ultimately privileges the Cornish language and the culture that was associated with it as the core of an early-modern Cornish ethnicity.

If language was the principal marker of ethnicity, and if Cornish ethnicity was most marked in the west, how did those English-speaking Cornish of east Cornwall identify themselves? What was their ethnicity?

---

11 Stoyle, 'Dissidence of despair', 1999, p.441.
12 Stoyle, 'Cornish rebellions', 1997, p.26.
13 Stoyle, 'Dissidence of despair', 1999, pp.428-429.
14 Anthony D.Smith, *The Ethnic Origin of Nations*, (Oxford: Basil Blackwell, 1986).
15 Adrian Hastings, *The Construction of Nationhood: Ethnicity, Religion and Nationalism*, (Cambridge: Cambridge University Press, 1997, pp.66/67.

Stoyle lists a whole series of cultural differences – family structure, naming customs, sports, agricultural practices among them – between east and west in the sixteenth-century but nevertheless insists that, 'despite these divisions ... the ordinary inhabitants of the English-speaking districts of Cornwall clearly felt a greater identification with their western brethren than with the English proper'. This claim is supported by the evidence of tin-mining, which he argues provided an economic distinctiveness, binding the inhabitants of Cornwall together despite other divisions.[16] But, even in the economic sphere things were not so clear cut. First, tin mining was not a distinctively Cornish industry at this time. At the beginning of the sixteenth century around a quarter of tin production came from Devon, a proportion that remained above 10% until the early seventeenth-century.[17] Moreover, in his economic history of seventeenth century Cornwall, James Whetter drew an economic dividing line between Padstow and Fowey that closely matched the linguistic 'boundary' of late sixteenth-century Cornwall. East of this line the economic focus was the cloth manufacturing centres of mid-Devon and the port of Plymouth; to the west it was the rapidly developing mining industry of mid and west Cornwall.[18] If anything, therefore, economic divisions actually tended to mirror and perhaps reinforce cultural ones, especially by the mid seventeenth-century.

The evidence for the identification of the English-speaking eastern Cornish with their western cousins is sparse, as is any 'hard evidence about the underlying motivation of the Cornish peasantry' in this period. On the one hand we find the eastern observer Carew around 1600 specifically singling out 'some of the western people' as,

> together with the Welsh, their ancient countrymen ... fostering a fresh memory of their expulsion long ago by the English, they second the same with a bitter repining at their fellowship; and this the worst sort express in combining against and working them all the shrewd turns which with hope of impunity they can devise.[19]

But, in working these 'shrewd turns', did they distinguish the English speakers of east Cornwall from the English beyond the Tamar or did they draw the boundary around language alone?

---

16 Stoyle, 'Dissidence of despair', 1999.

17 G.R.Lewis, *The Stannaries: a study of the medieval tin miners of Cornwall and Devon,* 1908, (reprinted Truro: D.Bradford Barton, 1965), pp.252-255.

18 James Whetter, *Cornwall in the 17th Century: an economic history of Kernow* (Padstow, Lodenek Press, 1974), pp.173-174.

19 Richard Carew, *Survey of Cornwall* (London: J.Fauldner, 1811), p.184.

On the other hand, the risings of 1497 and 1549, while focused on the west - Ian Arthurson concludes that as many as two thirds of the 'major rebels' in 1497 were from the Cornish-speaking Penwith and Kerrier hundreds – did draw in many participants from east Cornwall.[20] Parishes such as Lawhitton, on the Tamar, were fined after these events as well as Cornish-speaking parishes such as Breage and Illogan.[21] To an even greater extent in 1549, identifiable leaders of the Cornish rising came from east Cornwall as well as from established centres of turbulence such as Penryn.[22] However, did these eastern 'rebels' join from a sense of identity with the cultural grievances of the west Cornish or were their motives more akin to that (significantly described by Stoyle) 'motley collection of English malcontents' who also attached themselves to the cause?[23] Alternatively, while the social and cultural situation in the Cornish-speaking west may have provided a potentially more inflammable fuse for the risings, perhaps the involvement of the easterners suggests multiple economic and religious causes that transcended ethnic fault lines. Could it be the case that ethnicity was not actually so important in the early modern period as early twenty-first-century historians, embedded in a world of nation-states and ethnic tensions, might be inclined to believe? Indeed, Colin Kidd concludes that ethnic identities were of only 'second-order importance' before the nineteenth-century and that applying the word 'identity' to the early-modern period is itself anachronistic.[24] Nevertheless, it might still be the case that ethnicity was of 'first-order' importance to some groups at some times and one of those groups may have been, as Stoyle argues, the 'western Cornish', whereas ethnicity was of less importance for the eastern Cornish.

The problem of explanation becomes most acute in respect of the 1640s. By this time the Cornish-speaking heartland was shrinking generation by

---

20 Ian Arthurson, *The Perkin Warbeck Conspiracy 1491-1499* (Stroud: Alan Sutton, 1994), p.181.

21 Philip Payton, '"a … concealed envy against the English": a note on the aftermath of the 1497 rebellions in Cornwall', in Philip Payton (ed.), *Cornish Studies One*, (Exeter: University of Exeter Press, 1993), p.7.

22 See Julian Cornwall, *The Revolt of the Peasantry 1549* (London; Routledge & Kegan Paul, 1977), pp.55-62; Frances Rose-Troup, *The Western Rebellion of 1549* (London: Smith, Elder & Co, 1913), pp.100-104 and pp.497ff; Helen Speight, 'Local Government and Politics in Devon and Cornwall, 1509-49, with special reference to the South Western Rebellion of 1549' (unpublished doctoral thesis, University of Sussex, 1991), pp.190-198; Joyce Youings, 'The South Western Rebellion of 1549', *Southern History* 1 (1979), 99-122.

23 Stoyle, 'Dissidence of despair', 1999, p.436.

24 Colin Kidd, *British Identities before Nationalism: ethnicity and nationhood in the Atlantic world, 1600-1800* (Cambridge: Cambridge University Press, 1999), p.291.

generation. Yet the evidence of the 1640s war – the symbolic role of the Tamar, the reaction of the common people in east Cornwall to Essex's Parliamentary army in 1644, the events around Richard Grenville's doomed scheme in 1645 to create an autonomous zone that largely respected the Cornish border – all point to a sense of Cornish particularism matching the geographical extent of Cornwall rather than the shrinking geo-cultural space occupied by the Cornish language. Stoyle explains this through asserting that 'the old Cornish dream of a national revival ... had resurfaced amongst the common people'; this was 'the old Cornish sense of difference' and 'the old Cornish desire for autonomy'.[25] Here, Stoyle's explanation is least convincing. Was all this old? Or was it in fact new?

Taking greater account of the internal diversity of the geography of Cornishness might suggest that two different processes were at work by the mid-seventeenth century. First, there was that familiar from the earlier risings, the culturally based resistance that found its strength in the west. This explains aspects of the 'commotion' of 1642, which was most profoundly felt in the west, and the final despairing rout at the Gear in 1648, both of which might well be seen as part of an 'ancient pattern of ethnic antagonism'.[26] However, new levels of print propaganda and literacy were allowing new imaginations of 'Cornwall' to emerge in the seventeenth century. As Stoyle has pointed out, both Parliamentarian and Royalist propagandists actively produced negative and positive stereotypes respectively of the 'Cornish' as a homogenous group, drawing the border of differentiation around all that named group of 'Cornish', those living within the territory of Cornwall. The impression that 'the Cornish were fighting as a people' was one assiduously reproduced both by their Parliamentary enemies and their Royalist allies and no doubt internalised at the least by those Cornish men who engaged in military activity.[27]

These representations might be tied to a discernible new shift in attitudes to 'national' identity in the late sixteenth and seventeenth centuries. As Steven Ellis points out, by 1600 English identity was being 'more closely tied to the national territory' rather than to a cultural grouping.[28] This shift from culture to territory as the basis of 'national' imaginings might also be seen in the references to the Cornish as a group in the 1640s. There was nothing 'old' about this. Such an interpretation implies a too fixed and essentialist approach to ethnicity. In contrast, what marks ethnic identity

---

25 Stoyle, 'Last refuge', 1998, pp.47/48.
26 Stoyle, 'Last refuge', 1998, p.36.
27 Stoyle, 'Pagans or paragons', 1996.
28 Steven G.Ellis, 'Civilizing Northumberland: representations of Englishness in the Tudor state', *Journal of Historical Sociology* 12 (1999), p.104.

construction is its plasticity and fluidity.[29] What we see in the 1640s is a transition period, one in which the older ethnic antagonisms associated with divisions between Cornish-speaking culture in west Cornwall and English-speaking culture elsewhere still plays a role, but is overlain by newer representations of identity that put greater emphasis on territory. Given the shrinking cultural heartland of the language these newer territorial representations provided the space for a sustained sense of Cornish ethnicity despite the supposedly final defeat at the Gear in 1648. Rather than being a resurgence of the 'old' they prefigured the more 'modern' imaginings of Cornishness that had emerged by the late eighteenth-century. And, paradoxically, these were more able to unite all the Cornish, east and west, than the older more linguistically based divisions.

Class formation and 'dispersed paternalism' in industrial Cornwall

The previous discussion implies that the internal geography of Cornwall in the sixteenth and seventeenth-centuries might be viewed as containing two culture regions divided fundamentally by language.[30] The core zone of the Cornish-speaking culture region was that 'revolutionary triangle' bounded by Penryn, Helston and St.Keverne, the epicentre of the risings of 1497, 1548 and 1648. By the late eighteenth century this Cornish culture region had been superseded. No longer a region marked by linguistic difference, the Cornish culture region had become, by the 1790s, one dominated by metal mining and Methodism.[31] Its core zone had been displaced from a rural-agrarian district bounded by three small urban communities to a larger rural-industrial district including the small but dynamic and urbanising communities of Redruth, Camborne and Hayle and bounded by the towns of Penzance, Helston, Falmouth and Truro. Cultural and economic differences between west and east Cornwall before 1650 had been augmented by their demographic experience from 1650 to 1750. In these years, while the population of the Penwith and Kerrier hundreds grew by 89% and 79% respectively, the five most easterly hundreds lost from 7% and 26% of their people.[32] This stark divergence accompanied the genesis of a unique rural-industrial society in the west of Cornwall.

---

29 See Richard Jenkins, *Rethinking Ethnicity: arguments and explorations* (London: Sage, 1997).

30 For the concept of culture region see Terry G.Jordan-Bychkov and Mona Domosh, *The Human Mosaic: a thematic introduction to cultural geography* (Harlow: Longman, 1999), pp.7-14.

31 Bernard Deacon, 'Proto-regionalisation: the case of Cornwall', *Journal of Regional and Local Studies* 18 (1998), 27-41.

32 Jonathan Barry, 'Population distribution and growth in the early modern period', in Roger Kain and William Ravenhill (eds), *Historical Atlas of South-West England* (Exeter: University of Exeter Press, 1999), p.117.

This society was made up of relatively homogeneous communities dominated by the mining industry. Hitherto, the labouring people of those communities have been viewed by historians as a problem of labour history, as a group with an absence of class consciousness and a limited labourist consciousness. John Rule's work is prominent in this respect. He noted that single factors such as Methodism or the tribute system of wage payment in the mines, cited as causes of a lack of trade unionism or collective action, in other places often coincide with these very same phenomena. Therefore, rather than emphasising single variables, he suggests that a combination of factors in Cornwall made up a 'configuration of quietism'.[33] The tribute system, an ambiguous employing class as a result of the organisation of mining, a landlord paternalism that wove a web of deference and dependence, Methodism, distance and isolation all came together, reinforcing each other to produce a particular configuration of social relations in Cornwall. This mix was inimical to the 'working-class' industrial and political movements associated with the early nineteenth-century. Thus Chartism failed to take root in Cornish mining communities in 1839 and the Cornish miner showed no desire to organise trade unions until 1866, a 'weakness' explained by the configuration of material factors. Leaving aside the problems associated with this approach, for example the narrow way it defines 'working-class' collective activity or its expectations of a 'normal' trajectory of class formation from which the Cornish deviated, through adding the neglected spatial dimension we can revise and deepen our understanding of social relations and class formation in Cornwall's rural-industrial communities before the 1840s.

Michael Savage notes how the social history influenced by E.P.Thompson, among which we must include Rule's work, focuses upon the temporal but not the spatial aspects of class formation. For Savage space is important in two ways.[34] First, particular places can become 'habitats' for certain social groups, bases for a strong sense of community cohesion and collective identity. These gave rise to dense local networks that in turn sometimes helped to create a sense of class consciousness but, just as often, did not 'in themselves appear to be enough to sustain class formation at the level of political mobilisation'.[35] What was required for this latter was the second kind of network identified by Savage, one stretching across space to

---

33 John Rule, 'A "Configuration of Quietism"? Attitudes towards Trade Unionism and Chartism among the Cornish Miners', *Tijdschrift voor Sociale Geschiedenis, achttiende jaargang* 2/3 (1992), 248-262.

34 Michael Savage, 'Space, networks and class formation', in Neville Kirk (ed.), *Social Class and Marxism: defences and challenges* (London: Routledge, 1996), 58-86.

35 Savage, 'Space, networks and class', 1996, p.74.

link members of a class in different localities. However, this second kind of extensive inter-locality network could be in tension with the first. 'Dense ties of localism may work against the construction of wider ranging ties' and individuals' 'involvement in wide ranging networks may preclude them from the dense local world of the neighbourhood'.[36] For such reasons class formation was always problematic and difficult to sustain.

If we argue back to the Cornish case from this we might suggest that the strength of kinship and neighbourhood links in industrial communities in west and mid Cornwall before the 1840s inhibited the range of network links to other communities in Cornwall and elsewhere. In mid and west Cornwall there was a cohesive social group that showed a high propensity to establish some types of collective organisation, such as friendly societies, and displayed what Thompson called "an irascible consumer consciousness", willingly and regularly engaging in crowd action to defend the 'moral economy of labour' in the years from 1729 to 1847.[37] But, crucially for political mobilisation, it did not build up the necessary range of extensive network ties. As an example of this Charlesworth compares the food 'riots' in Cornwall in 1795 and 1801 with those of Devon. In the latter county there was a clear geographical pattern of unrest centred on Exeter, indicating a conscious effort to organise the protest, one that reflected a 'network of labour clubs and combinations centred on Exeter'. In Cornwall, in contrast, crowd actions were more haphazard and confined to market days. Charlesworth concludes that 'rather than taking matters fully into their own hands, the miners followed the rhythms of the periodic marketing system'.[38] For him, this suggests the absence of the type of network that facilitated trade union organisation.

Cornish mining communities, therefore, while producing dense networks of mutual aid, a factor that may well explain lower than expected levels of resort to the Poor Law in west Cornwall, were weakly linked both to other mining communities in neighbouring districts and to communities in other industrial regions. This was particularly critical in the period from the 1790s to the 1830s, when a more 'economistic' critique of capitalism and a sense of class identification began fitfully and episodically to emerge in industrial regions elsewhere. In this vital period, Cornish working class communities remained focused on their neighbourhood networks. Furthermore, this was in marked contrast to the more extensive spatial networks developed by

---

36 Savage, 'Space, networks and class', 1996, p.69.
37 Martin Gorsky, 'The growth and distribution of English friendly societies in the early nineteenth century', *Economic History Review* 51 (1998), 489-511; E.P.Thompson, *Customs in Common*, (London: Penguin, 1993), p.213.
38 Andrew Charlesworth, 'The spatial diffusion of riots: popular disturbances in England and Wales, 1750-1850', *Rural History* 5 (1994), p.10.

other classes in Cornwall. Thus the landed class and the merchant capitalist elite had, before the 1780s, forged Cornwall-wide networks. And, in the period from the 1810s to the 1850s, the urban middle classes followed suit by establishing a range of contacts between the small towns, particularly of west Cornwall, facilitated by the provincial press and the network of lecturers travelling the circuit of the county learned societies and emerging small town literary and philosophical societies. In contrast, when Chartism appeared in towns such as Truro in 1838, the impression we gain is of only tenuous links to sympathisers in the mining towns of Camborne and Redruth.[39]

Why was this? Why had Cornish mining communities not engendered the extensive network ties conducive to political and industrial mobilisation? The simple answer is that they had not needed to. In order to explain this we might again point to a combination of historical and spatial factors. In Cornwall industrialisation was early. By the 1780s, the increasing capitalisation associated with deep copper mining had produced a scattered series of rural-industrial working class communities in a geographically concentrated district of west Cornwall. These were communities created in conditions of merchant capitalism, where the focus of the dominant social group, merchant families and landlords, was on exchange rather than production. Because the owning class was not too concerned with the details of controlling production, a space was maintained both for relatively autonomous work relations formalised through tribute and tutwork and for the emergence of equally autonomous village communities. These were enmeshed in a loose hierarchy of landlord paternalism, but this was a paternalism mediated by agents and, in the majority of cases, by distance. People in such communities displayed a vigorous sense of 'independence', buttressed by some non-market access to food and fuel resources and reproduced by the cottage religion of Methodism, the first mass revivals of which in the 1780s help us date the coming to maturity of this rural-industrial society, one largely restricted, as the geography of revivalism indicates, to west and mid Cornwall.[40]

39 See Alf Jenkin, 'The Cornish Chartists', *Journal of the Royal Institution of Cornwall* NSIX (1982), 53-80; John Rule and Roger Wells, *Crime, protest and popular politics in southern England 1740-1850* (London: Hambledon Press, 1997), 66-80.

40 Charles Barham, 'Report on the Employment of Children and Young Persons in the Mines of Cornwall and Devonshire, and on the state, condition, and treatment of such children and young persons to the Royal Commission on Children's Employment', *British Parliamentary Papers* (London: HMSO, 1842), xvi, p.759; Seymour Tremenheere, 'Report on the State of Education in the Mining Districts of Cornwall', *Minutes of the Committee of Council on Education, 1840-41* (London: HMSO, 1841), p.93; Bernard Deacon, 'Proto-

Cornwall was thus the site of a relatively early, 'negotiated' compromise between community and capital. The details of this compromise differed from those reached at a later date in other industrial regions. For example, it was unlike that in the coal mining communities of mid nineteenth-century north east England, where traditions of autonomy in the labour process accompanied dependencies and paternalist social control above ground via truck payment, tied housing and employer-provided schools. And it was also different from that in north Welsh slate quarrying communities, where the payment system was similar to the Cornish but where the influence of a single landlord was dominant in securing consent from the quarrying communities through a mix of charity, sick and pension clubs and residential and political favouritism.[41] In Cornwall the earlier compromise between community and capital is best described as one of 'dispersed paternalism'. Three life leases and housing tenancies did tie working families to landlords and relations of dependence were created between these families and the agents of those owners. But a key disciplinary role both at work and in the community was fulfilled by another group, the mine captains. Additionally, the dispersed geography of the mining districts enhanced the autonomy of working class communities and the self-sufficient and dense social ties that developed within them.

These social relations also carried their own implications and meanings, harking back to the free tinner-husbandman of the early eighteenth century and earlier, helping to reproduce a particular discourse of independence that provided little immediate space for the later discourses of Chartism and trade union solidarity. The continuing efficacy of the social relations of dispersed paternalism and the discourse that accompanied them help to explain their durability. It was only the social changes that came with the onset of mass emigration, together with changing agricultural practices and perhaps also rising literacy and growing links with other localities, that began finally and fatally to undermine this compromise in the 1840s.

---

industrialization and potatoes: a revised narrative for nineteenth-century Cornwall', in Payton (ed.), *Cornish Studies Five*, 1997, 60-84; Damaris Rose, 'Home ownership, subsistence and historical change: the mining district of West Cornwall in the late nineteenth century' in Nigel Thrift and Peter Williams (eds.), *Class and Space: the making of an urban society* (London: Routledge & Kegan Paul, 1987), 108-153. David Luker, 'Revivalism in theory and practice: the case of Cornish Methodism', *Journal of Ecclesiastical History* 37 (1986), 603-619; Peter Isaac, *A History of Evangelical Christianity in Cornwall* (no place of publication, no date (1999/2000?)), p.112.

41 For the idea of 'negotiated' local compromises between community and capital see Richard Price, *Labour in British Society: an interpretative history* (London: Croom Helm, 1986), pp.77-78.

However, the more explicitly spatial approach sketched out above also raises a number of outstanding research questions. Assumptions have been made about working class community networks in industrial Cornwall. But exactly how 'dense' were these networks? How far were occupational groups 'bounded' or did they interact, both geographically and socially, with other groups? Micro-studies of the marriage registers of Cornish parishes in the first half of the nineteenth-century and nominal linkage of these with the first available Census Enumerators Books in 1841 and other records might provide a better picture of the networks of working class communities on the ground. More research on social and geographical mobility within Cornwall and overseas would also help to trace the ways in which individuals and families within communities interfaced with other groups. This might help us to answer the question of whether we should imagine occupationally bounded communities or, rather, communities that transcended occupational boundaries in the early nineteenth century and, by implication, in eighteenth-century Cornwall. Finally, how did the patterns of network interaction in Cornwall compare with those of other industrial and non-industrial regions?

Race, colonialism and contemporary Cornwall
It is generally agreed that the Cornish experience of emigration and diaspora in the nineteenth and early twentieth centuries was a crucial component in the making of modern Cornwall.[42] In moving to this experience we move to another, global, scale that links Cornwall and its people to other peoples and to places around the world. Searching for an equally global framework for understanding the effects of these links, we inevitably confront the broad theory of postcolonialism. In reality postcolonialism is more of an expanded (and contested) umbrella term for a hybrid collection of perspectives than a single homogeneous theory.[43] Indeed, the definition of the postcolonial in what is regarded as its classic text - *The Empire Writes Back* - is remarkably broad, 'all the culture affected by the imperial process from the moment of colonisation to the

---

42 Philip Payton, *The Cornish Overseas* (Fowey: Alexander Associates, 1999) provides the long-awaited synthesis of the different Cornish emigration streams.

43 For causing me to think about the possibilities of applying postcolonialist theory to Cornwall I am indebted to a student on Exeter University's MA programme in Cornish Studies, Cheryl Hayden of Australia. For an introduction to postcolonialist theory see Peter Childs and Patrick Williams, *An Introduction to Post-Colonial Theory* (London: Prentice Hall, 1997); Anna Green and Kathleen Troup, *The houses of history: a critical reader in twentieth century history and theory* (Manchester: Manchester University Press, 1999), pp.277-296.

present day', and thus provides more of a framing context than an explanatory theory.[44]

Nevertheless, we can identify two varieties of writings from a postcolonialist perspective. The first is a normative resistance to colonialism and to the often taken for granted narratives of cultural superiority and a belief in 'progress' that ideologically underpinned nineteenth and twentieth-century imperialism.[45] Postcolonialist writings that focus on this dimension strive to forge a voice for colonised peoples, deconstructing colonial discourses and reconstructing interpretations of the world through the eyes of the colonised, thus transcending and inverting colonialist assumptions. The second type of postcolonialist approach appears to revolve around a recognition of the fundamental role of the colonial experience for both coloniser and colonised and the interconnections and transfers between these categories. Such connections as revealed by postcolonialist writings thus undermine binary conceptions of 'us' and 'them' as well as 'colonised' and 'coloniser'.

Identity is central in this. According to Said, ideas of the Oriental 'Other' say as much about self-representations of people in the West than they do about the East.[46] And, with the process of decolonisation and onset of migration flows from the former colonies to the European colonial heartlands, we see the 'Other' coming home.[47] In the British case, while bringing more sharply into focus the consequences of an imperial past, these 'postcolonial' migrations also unsettle binary notions of identity and further problematise the 'fuzzy frontiers' of British identity.[48]

What might a postcolonialist perspective say about Cornwall? It has been pointed out that Australians can be simultaneously colonisers, colonised and post-colonial.[49] However, in Cornwall's case we only have the first two possibilities. Payton has already drawn attention to similarities between the categories of 'Celt' and 'Aborigine' as externally generated constructs that have powerful impacts on the groups so named.[50] The

---

44 Bill Ashcroft, Gareth Griffiths and Helen Tiffin (eds.), *The Empire Writes Back: theory and practice in post-colonial literatures* (London: Routledge, 1989), p.2.

45 See Beverley Southgate, *History: What and Why?: ancient, modern and postmodern perspectives,* (London: Routledge, 1996), p.101.

46 Edward Said, *Culture and Imperialism* (London: Chatto & Windus, 1993).

47 Homi Bhabha, *The Location of Culture* (London: Routledge, 1994), p.6.

48 For these 'fuzzy frontiers' see Robin Cohen, *Frontiers of Identity: the British and the Others,* (London: Longman, 1994), pp.5-36.

49 Aijaz Ahmad, 'The politics of literary postcoloniality', *Race and Class* 36 (1995), p.9.

50 Philip Payton, 'Introduction', in Philip Payton (ed.), *Cornish Studies Three,* (Exeter: University of Exeter Press, 1995), p.2.

revisionist 'post-Celtic' literature of writers such as Chapman and James deconstructs the role of the 'colonising' centre in producing this category.[51] But what postcolonial theory might introduce would be the way in which the 'colonised' have appropriated and used centrally defined categories for their own purposes in attempts to empower themselves.[52] Nevertheless, this sort of research agenda remains on a binary level of colonised/coloniser or centre/periphery. The promise of the postcolonial perspective is sometimes seen as the breaking down of such meta-narratives and the re-capture of the fragmentary, the subjugated and the local.[53]

For this we perhaps need to turn to the second aspect of the Cornish colonial experience, the role of the Cornish as part of a colonising process and their relations with the colonised overseas. The discussion of indigenous peoples in the classic texts on Cornish emigration has been limited. They appear as 'hostile' or 'fierce', 'friendly' or 'helpful' in turn, occasionally causing 'trouble' or comprising a 'problem' to be solved.[54] But, however described, their role is secondary to the dominant narrative of economic development and community formation that underpins these texts. Here, there appears to be room for more work that explores the ambiguities of contact between Cornish settlers and indigenous peoples. Is there an equivalent of the Irish Gaelic writer Mici MacGowan, who wrote an account of his sojourn through North America at the end of the nineteenth-century? On the way he recorded his empathy with the native Americans' loss of land and culture, which he compared to the situation in his home county of Donegal, but at other times his writing betrays ideas of white superiority that were deeply inscribed into the dominant ideology of European emigration.[55] Philip Payton's account of the complex attitude of William Whitburn to the Cubans in the 1830s hints at similar attitudes

51 Malcolm Chapman, *The Celts* (London: Macmillan, 1992); Simon James, *The Atlantic Celts: ancient people or modern invention?* (London: British Museum Press, 1999).

52 For a hint of what such a perspective might involve see Amy Hale, 'Foot in the mouth, or foot in the door? Evaluating Chapman's *The Celts*', in Philip Payton (ed.), *Cornish Studies Four* (Exeter: University of Exeter Press, 1996), 158-170.

53 c.f. Philip Payton, 'Introduction', *Cornish Studies Four,* 1996, p.1.

54 A.L.Rowse, *The Cornish in America* (London: Macmillan, 1969), pp.44 and 253; John Rowe, *The Hard Rock Men: Cornish immigrants and the North American mining frontier* (Liverpool: Liverpool University Press, 1974), pp.135, 140, 178, 224.

55 *Rotha Mór an tSaoil*, a film produced by Sylvia Stevens for Faction Films/Mondial TV, London, 1999.

among Cornish emigrants, but these significantly refracted through the lens of Methodism.[56]

When the interactions between colonising and colonised groups are explored, for example in Richard Dawe's treatment of the Chinese labour question in South Africa from 1900 to 1910, a complex picture of inter-ethnic divisions and attitudes is exposed.[57] Moreover, in this example, we are reminded of the way ethnic interactions at the frontiers of Empire impinged back onto Cornwall. Local papers such as the *Cornubian* carried cartoons demonising the Chinese labourer and drawing on wider contemporary stereotypes of the 'Yellow Peril'; the issue was a major factor in the politics of the Mining Division and return migrants re-imported attitudes of racial superiority, modified by their actual experiences of contact with the 'Other'. All this helped to produce a local discourse of 'race' in Cornwall in the early twentieth-century. But did this differ from racist discourses elsewhere in the British Isles? What overall effect did the large scale Cornish emigration have on this local discourse? Similarly, how had the great popularity of overseas missions among Cornish Methodists in the early nineteenth-century affected the ideas that Cornish emigrants took overseas with them?[58]

Aspects of domestic Cornish society thus affected peoples in the imperial periphery. At the same time the experience on that periphery was reflected back into Cornish society. In the 1950s and 60s the cultural nationalists of the young Mebyon Kernow certainly found it difficult to break with an imperialist discourse. Attitudes such as those of MK member, Robert Dunstone, who wrote in 1962 that 'a greater Cornwall must mean a greater Britain', or J.R.Finlayson, who stated in 1967 that 'both Smiths – Michael Joseph ... in 1497 and Ian in 1967 – share the dream of recognition of full independence' might suggest that the imperial experience had become an intrinsic part of their Cornish consciousness, etched deeply into their identity.[59]

Moreover, in a development that further complicates attitudes to race and racism in contemporary Cornwall, local discourses of race, to some degree constructed through direct contact with the 'Other' during the process of imperialism, have been added to through another process of indirect and imagined contact. Since the 1960s counterurbanisation has inserted a new

56 Payton, *The Cornish Overseas*, 1999, p.123.

57 Richard Dawe, *Cornish Pioneers in South Africa: "gold and diamonds, copper and blood"*, (St Austell: Cornish Hillside Publications, 1998), pp.193-224.

58 See David Luker, 'Cornish Methodism, Revivalism and popular belief, c.1780-1870' (unpublished doctoral thesis, Oxford University, 1987), pp.296-299. My thanks to John Probert for reminding me of this aspect of Cornish Methodism.

59 *West Briton*, 28 April 1962 and 21 September 1967.

population into Cornish society, the majority from south-east England and the Midlands. While this population contains some diverse strands and includes 'back to the land' enthusiasts, Celtic romantics and new pagans as well as retired stockbrokers, anecdotal evidence suggests that a proportion of these migrants also bring with them virulently racist attitudes towards the black population they have left behind in the metropolitan areas.[60] The racist attitudes of some 'counterurbanisers' are then slotted into subtle status perceptions within Cornwall concerning migrants and non-migrants, Cornish and non-Cornish. What effects do these status hierarchies have on the reception of racist ideas in contemporary Cornwall? And how do imaginings of race and racial difference interlock with popular europhobia and with contemporary attitudes towards Cornishness? A rich potential research agenda is thus opened up, one where attitudes of colonised and coloniser collide and intermingle.

Conclusion

The brief and necessarily speculative case study of postcolonialism and Cornwall indicates that, in order to explain aspects of historical and contemporary Cornwall, we have to be aware of processes simultaneously operating at a number of differing scales. Cornwall's location in a global process as part of the experience of imperialism interacts with its peripheral status in state-wide processes of demographic change and cultural imaginings to produce complex and shifting discourses of race and racism in contemporary Cornwall. At the same time these local discourses may well contain subtle distinctions from wider racist discourses, distinctions explained by the particularities of Cornish history. Pursuing these distinctions calls for a comparative approach, investigating Cornwall in parallel with other places at a similar scale on an inter-regional level. But, in addition, there may well be differences within Cornwall, on an intra-Cornish scale. To explore these, investigations at a micro-scale are required. Ideally, therefore, the Cornish Studies researcher must stay alert to processes that operate at different scales: the global, the Cornish and the local. The inter-connections between these different scales then need teasing out. In doing this new research questions and new issues will no doubt emerge. Recognising the role of space is, therefore, fundamental to the Cornish Studies project.

---

60 Interestingly, a report produced by the Commission for Racial Equality on racism in south-west England failed to note this link between racist discourses and counter-urbanisation. See Eric Jay, *"Keep them in Birmingham" challenging racism in south-west England* (London: Commission for racial Equality, 1992).

Postscript

This first excursion into the methodology of Cornish Studies has aged relatively well on re-reading. Its call for a sensitivity to connections and relations at contrasting spatial scales remains relevant. Moreover, since its publication, it's not been difficult to encounter work addressing intra-Cornish difference. Archaeologists in particular have been innovative in thinking through changing spatial patterns.[61] However, not so many researchers have simultaneously addressed processes at the different levels, tending to remain fixed at some intra-Cornish level.

Turning to the case studies I chose, the argument that Mark Stoyle's groundbreaking interpretation of the years from 1497 to 1648 needs revising has not found wide acceptance. Stuart Dunmore picked up on the proposal that ethnic realities on the ground were not so straightforward and need combining with changing notions of place identity, in an excellent survey of the linguistic history of the period.[62] Such interpretations have to negotiate problems as they challenge simpler, but widely held, foundation myths of a unified and united Cornwall coping with English aggression in this period.

Chapter 6 below qualifies some of the assertions that I made about political organisation and class in early nineteenth-century Cornwall. There has been less work on the micro-social history of Cornwall in its industrial phase, possibly because such work more generally has gone out of fashion in the academy, partly because of the difficulties of accessing suitable data, given Cornwall's very early industrialisation. Detailed studies of Cornish communities in this period, informed by a sociological or social anthropological perspective, could still do much to shed light on the specifics of the uniquely early industrial society created in Cornwall. Perhaps the TV series *Poldark* will renew interest in this period of Cornwall's past. Meanwhile, articles such as Peter Tremewan's on the poor law in Cornwall remind us of a continuing east-west contrast in this period.[63]

---

61 For example Imogen Tompsett, 'Social Dynamics in South-West England AD350-1150: an exploration of maritime oriented identity in the Atlantic approaches and Western channel region' (unpublished doctoral thesis, University of Nottingham, 2012).

62 Stuart Dunmore, 'Language Decline and the "Theory of Cornish Distinctiveness": The Historiography of Language and Identity in Early Modern Cornwall', *Proceedings of the Harvard Celtic Colloquium* 31 (2011), 91-105.

63 Peter Tremewan, 'The relief of poverty in Cornwall, 1780-1881: From collateral support to respectability', in Philip Payton (ed.), *Cornish Studies Sixteen* (Exeter: University of Exeter Press, 2008), 78-103. The micro-geography of the mining industry is summarised in Bernard Deacon, 'Mining the data: What can a quantitative approach tell us about the micro-geography of

Finally, as we shall see in Chapter 4 below, there has been a considerable volume of work that deconstructs the stereotypes and assumptions of elite actors both in Cornwall and outside and traces their historical roots. Not much of this explicitly describes those stereotypes as colonialist, even though they could be so termed.[64] There has been less work on the consequences of Empire for Cornwall and the way native and settler ideologies of race and racism might cross-cut and interact. Given the clear preference of the Cornish electorate for Brexit in 2016 and its increasingly conservative complexion, attention to this aspect would seem to be well overdue.

---

nineteenth-century Cornish mining?', in Philip Payton (ed.), *Cornish Studies Eighteen* (Exeter: University of Exeter Press, 2010), 15-32.

64 For an exception see Richard Tresidder, 'What no pasties? Reading the Cornish Tourism Brochure', *Journal of Travel and Tourism Marketing* 27 (2010), 596-611.

Chapter Two

The New Cornish Studies: New discipline or rhetorically defined space?

(First version published in Philip Payton (ed.), *Cornish Studies Ten*, (Exeter: University of Exeter Press, 2002), 24-43.)

The decades around the turns of centuries (even more so in the case of millennia) are perfect breeding grounds for the cult of the 'new'. In the 1900s New Liberalism emerged, to be succeeded in the 1990s by its distantly related offspring 'New Labour'. Meanwhile, 'new turns' and 'new directions' proliferate in academic disciplines.[1] Amongst these progeny of fin-de-siecle anxieties and beginning of century clean slate enthusiasms, the last ten years have seen the emergence of the New Cornish Studies, together with its sub-genres of the 'new Cornish social science' and the 'new Cornish historiography'. These explicit labels made their simultaneous appearance in 1995, although they were prefigured as early as 1993 when it was claimed that Charles Thomas, the first Professor of Cornish Studies, had effectively been 'arguing for the development of a critical Cornish social science' back in 1972.[2] Since 1995 the twin descriptors of 'new Cornish social science' and 'new Cornish historiography' have been regularly invoked. It is, therefore, high time these concepts were subjected to some interrogation.

In relation to New Labour, Steven Lukes has proposed that the 'third way' is neither a concept nor an ideology; instead it is better viewed as a 'rhetorically defined space'.[3] This is a space that bounds a number of different, even contradictory, concepts and has expansive and shifting boundaries defined in terms of a set of broad values rather than rigid ideological traditions. The New Cornish Studies may not, as we shall see,

---

1 For example John Brannigan, *New historicism and cultural materialism* (Basingstoke: Macmillan, 1998): Roger Backhouse (ed), *New directions in economic methodology* (London: Routledge, 1994); Amitai Etzioni (ed), *New communitarian thinking: persons, virtues, institutions and communities* (Charlottesville, VA: University Press of Virginia, 1995).

2 Philip Payton, *ICS Associates Newsletter* 4, May 1995, p.5; Philip Payton, 'Introduction', in Philip Payton (ed.), *Cornish Studies Four* (Exeter: University of Exeter Press, 1996), p.1. Philip Payton, 'Introduction', in Philip Payton (ed.), *Cornish Studies One* (Exeter: University of Exeter Press, 1993), p.1.

3 Steven Lukes, 'The Last Word on the Third Way', *The Review*, March 1999, 3-4.

share the ambiguity produced by the capacious 'rhetorical space' of New Labour. Nevertheless, it retains a certain elusiveness and the analogy suggests one apposite line of criticism. This might revolve around perceived gaps between the rhetoric of claims and the substance of achievements. In this review I shall present an 'insider', yet nonetheless critical, reflection on the New Cornish Studies. I shall indeed argue that the New Cornish Studies does, in many respects, fit the description of a 'rhetorically defined space'. Moreover, I shall also suggest that surveying the actual corpus of work produced within Cornish Studies in the past decade leads to the conclusion that, rather than a sharp discontinuity between 'old and 'new' Cornish Studies, we might detect a continuum between them. The New Cornish Studies builds on, re-emphasises and develops some of the concerns of the 'old' Cornish Studies. However, the rhetoric of the New Cornish Studies also reflects and clarifies real shifts in the context of Cornish Studies over the past decade. In doing so it presents opportunities for a research agenda that, although currently only in the process of fulfilment, offers exciting pointers for the next decade of work in Cornish Studies.

According to Lukes, boundary formation is crucial to all kinds of rhetorically defined spaces, whether political projects or academic disciplines. Just as New Labour might be viewed as having porous and flexible boundaries, so the boundaries around Cornish Studies have not remained static. In this article I begin by defining some possible boundaries, briefly tracing the etymology of the New Cornish Studies and contrasting it with 'old Cornish Studies'. In the process I identify some reasons why Cornish Studies adopted certain new directions after the 1980s. I then move on to identify some tensions within the New Cornish Studies project before focusing more specifically on the 'new Cornish historiography'. This course is adopted not because the 'new Cornish historiography' is more important than the 'new Cornish social science' but rather as Malcolm Williams elsewhere reviews the 'new Cornish social science' and offers his own view of its 'foundational myths'.[4] The article concludes by pulling together some possible pointers for the future direction of Cornish Studies. These are necessarily speculative and should be approached as preliminary observations on the present and future state of Cornish Studies, in the hope of stimulating and energising further debate about its direction.

The roots of Cornish Studies

In their volume *New Directions in Celtic Studies* Amy Hale and Philip Payton ask the question 'what is Celtic Studies'? We need to turn this question back onto Cornish Studies itself. In asking what it is, we have first

---

4   Malcolm Williams, 'The New Cornish Social Science', in Philip Payton (ed.), *Cornish Studies Ten* (Exeter: University of Exeter Press, 2002), 44-66.

to establish what it was and what else it might have been. Those involved in academic Cornish Studies based in and around the Institute of Cornish Studies, part of the University of Exeter but situated in Cornwall and part-funded by Cornwall County Council, represent Cornish Studies in its institutionalised variant. But institutionalised Cornish Studies, although inevitably the focus of this review, has a relatively short history and, furthermore, only represents one possible strand among several. We might, for example, identify at least three models of Cornish Studies that are available to us: Cornish Studies as local studies, Cornish Studies as national(ist) studies and Cornish Studies as Celtic Studies. These variants provide possible boundaries for its rhetorically defined space.

Cornish Studies as local studies originated in the antiquarian moment of the eighteenth and nineteenth centuries, when gentlemanly amateurs began to reconstruct the historical traces of their parishes. This gradually evolved into the local history groups of the later twentieth and early twenty-first centuries. In contemporary Cornwall the model is perhaps most clearly seen in the Cornwall Association of Local Historians. But it has also informed the explicitly more 'Cornish' activities of the Old Cornwall societies. While local historians valorise the 'local', other academic disciplines employ the local within a spatial hierarchy which treats it as a quarry for the wider academic community, providing the empirical data that informs wider perspectives and contexts and tests generalizations, models and theories. The application of this model to Cornish Studies has had two implications. First, it tends to lead to an emphasis upon the single place, parish or community. In this way it bears out John Marshall's observation that places are often examined without a 'visible territorial framework'.[5] Moreover, places can sometimes be studied with no discernible comparative context whatsoever. Second, it tends to put Cornish Studies into a box labelled 'local' while the really important academic work goes on elsewhere. This attitude was implied by the remark of a former Principal of Cornwall College in 1990: 'we use Cornwall and its environment as a resource but we are also aware of wider concerns'.[6] Past or present Cornwall, from this perspective, only provides a series of case studies that might illuminate broader academic generalizations.[7] Seeing Cornish Studies in this way strips

---

5   J.D.Marshall, *The Tyranny of the Discrete* (Aldershot: Scolar Press, 1997), p.3.

6   Communication reported at Perranporth Conference, 1990.

7   For some examples see James Vernon, 'Border crossings: Cornwall and the English (imagi)nation', in Geoffrey Cubitt (ed), *Imagining Nations* (Manchester: Manchester University Press, 1998), 153-172; James Potter, 'External Manufacturing Investment in a Peripheral Rural Region: The Case of Devon and Cornwall', *Regional Studies* 27 (1993), 193-206.

away its 'Cornish' aspect and renders it as mere local studies, with a resultant lowly positioning within the academic hierarchy.

The second possible approach is that of Cornish Studies as national(ist) studies. At the time of the formation of the Institute of Cornish Studies in 1971, Charles Thomas's own connections with the Cornish Revival and the support of the revivalist movement in the Institute's establishment guaranteed that issues dear to the Revival's heart, most obviously the Cornish language, played a considerable part in the content of academic Cornish Studies.[8] During the 1990s a less culturally confined and more politically focused strand of Cornish Studies as nationalist studies began to emerge. This adopted a colonial framework for viewing Cornwall's history and for explaining the waning of the Cornish language.[9] But, while vigorously articulated, the polemical tone of this writing and its cavalier treatment of historical evidence put it outside the mainstream of academic Cornish Studies, although many of its concerns and some of its assumptions are, as we shall see later, shared by that Cornish Studies community.

Finally, there is Cornish Studies as Celtic Studies. This clearly overlapped in the 1970s with Cornish Studies as national studies, both having a common interest in the Cornish language and dialect. It also provided the early Institute with ready-made academic legitimacy. However, Celtic Studies has its own disciplinary centre, one that revolves around linguistics and medieval literature. Those Celtic languages that have a rich set of resources for study, like Irish and Welsh, lie at the core of the discipline. Languages such as Cornish, with a smaller literature and a much smaller medieval language community, are of more marginal interest. In addition, the role of Revived Cornish was looked at by Celtic scholars with great suspicion and even hostility.[10]

Because of these problems academic Cornish Studies was never situated in its entirety within the Celtic Studies canon of 'Celtic' linguistics and medieval literature. While two of its first three staff did work in those fields, the definition of Cornish Studies adopted by Charles Thomas was always much broader:

---

8   For Charles Thomas's links with the Revival see his 'An Dasserghyans Kernewek', *Old Cornwall* 6 (1963), 196-205.

9   John Angarrack, *Breaking the Chains: Propaganda, Censorship, Deception and the Manipulation of Public Opinion in Cornwall* (Camborne: Cornish Stannary Publications, 1999); Pol Hodge, *Cornwall's Secret War: The True Story of the Prayer Book Rebellion* (Truro: Kowethas an Yeth Kernewek, 1999), pp.14-15.

10 See Glanville Price, *The Languages of Britain* (London: Edward Arnold, 1984), pp.134-145.

the study of all aspects of man and his handiwork in the regional setting (Cornwall and Scilly), past, present and future. The development of society, industry and the landscape in our fast-changing world is as much of concern ... as the history of those vast topics in the recent and remote past.[11]

In theory this meant that Cornish Studies could encompass a huge range of disciplinary concerns across the humanities and social sciences. In practice Cornish Studies was a pragmatic amalgam of traditional Celtic studies, plus Charles Thomas's own specialism, archaeology, while combining this with local history, from the Cornish Studies as local studies paradigm.

The New Cornish Studies and its context
But what is the New Cornish Studies and how does it differ from the old? While, as we have seen, the descriptors 'new Cornish social science' and 'new Cornish historiography' were regularly applied by Philip Payton to Cornish Studies from 1995 onwards, there is no key text that sets out the basis of the New Cornish Studies. Nevertheless, its main elements can be identified from Philip Payton's writings. While his evolving stance on New Cornish Studies can be gleaned most easily from the Introductions to the series *Cornish Studies* from 1996 onwards, one of the most succinct statements appeared in a less accessible source, the Australian journal *Locality*, in 2000.[12] Here, focusing on the 'new Cornish historiography', Payton claims that it leaves behind the 'stifling bonds of antiquarianism' and turns from that 'inward looking and uncritical chronicling of events west of the River Tamar' to a more interdisciplinary and more contextual approach, giving a sense of both people and place and setting these firmly into their comparative background.

Interdisciplinarity, comparison and context are the three central concepts of the New Cornish Studies. Indeed, we can incorporate these aspects into an ideal model of the contrast between 'new' and 'old' Cornish Studies, at least as articulated in the writings of Philip Payton.

---

11 Charles Thomas, *Bulletin of the ICS* 1, June 1972.
12 See also Philip Payton, 'Cornwall in Context: The New Cornish Historiography', in Philip Payton (ed.), *Cornish Studies Five* (Exeter: University of Exeter Press, 1997), 9-20. Philip Payton, 'Local and Regional History: The View from Cornwall', *Locality* 11 (2000), 18-22.

Figure 1: The rhetorical spaces of 'Old' and 'new' Cornish Studies

	Old Cornish Studies	New Cornish Studies
Theory	Empiricist	Informed by social theory
Content	The past	The contemporary
	Cornish particularities	Cornish difference and identity
Methods	Insights of specialist disciplines	Multi- and inter-disciplinary
	Pure	Applied policy engagement

Perhaps the starkest contrast is in the attitude to social theory. The plea for a direct engagement with social theory indicates a vision of Cornish Studies as closer to the social sciences than to the humanities. In his own major synthesis of Cornwall's past, *The Making of Modern Cornwall*, published in 1992, Payton adopts an explicit centre-periphery model.[13] More recently, the preferred model has become that of the 'new British history', suggesting that academic frameworks can be adopted from history and the humanities as well as the more theory-orientated social sciences.[14]

On taking over as Director of the Institute of Cornish Studies in October 1991, Philip Payton alerted its Associates to his desire to move the focus of activity of Cornish Studies 'towards contemporary Cornwall', towards its socio-economic condition, issues of governance and politics, and the cultural state of its communities.[15] In history too, there is a shift from the concern with the very distant past, as expressed in archaeological studies, to that of the modern period.[16] Two issues have been prominent in the preferred content of the New Cornish Studies. At first the issue was

---

13 Philip Payton, *The Making of Modern Cornwall* (Redruth: Dyllansow Truran, 1992).

14 For work using the 'new British history' as a framework see Mark Stoyle, *West Britons* (Exeter: University of Exeter Press, 2002). For other examples of the use of theories and frameworks in Cornish Studies see Bernard Deacon, 'The reformulation of territorial identity: Cornwall in the late eighteenth and nineteenth centuries', (unpublished doctoral thesis, Open University, 2001) and Alan Kent, *The Literature of Cornwall: Continuity, Identity, Difference 1000-2000* (Bristol: Redcliffe Press, 2000).

15 Philip Payton, Letter to Associates of ICS, 6 January 1992. This trend can be seen in Amy Hale and Philip Payton (eds), *New Directions in Celtic Studies* (Exeter: University of Exeter Press, 2000). But it is best illustrated in the contributions to David C.Harvey, Rhys Jones, Neil McInroy and Christine Milligan (eds), *Celtic Geographies: Old culture, new times* (London: Routledge, 2002).

'difference'; 'when all is said and done it is this Cornish "difference" that is at root the raison d'être of Cornish Studies as an area of academic inquiry'.[17] Because sensitivity to 'difference' raises the question of 'identity', a second strand to the content of new Cornish Studies increasingly apparent from 1997 was that of 'identity formation'. By 1998 it was being asserted that 'elucidation and analysis of [the Cornish identity] is perhaps the prime task of Cornish Studies as an academic discipline'.[18] Methodologically, the call was for inter-disciplinarity and the 'genuine cross-disciplinary transfer' of methods.[19] The aim was to move beyond multi-disciplinary studies to a more deliberately integrative approach to understanding Cornwall. The purpose of this quest for integrated knowledge was 'to marshal, synthesize and explain hitherto disparate knowledge'. Together with its interdisciplinary emphasis, the 'new Cornish social science' was claimed to be both empirical and applied.[20]

Superficially, as the references so far indicate, the New Cornish Studies seems heavily dependent on one person. Academic Cornish Studies has always been a small field in terms of personnel. This means that, to explain its development, we have to give a prominent place to individuals. And none more so than the Directors of the Institute of Cornish Studies. As editors of *Cornish Studies* in both its (first series) guise as an in-house journal and in its (second series) existence as annual volumes, and as spokespersons for the Institute, they have occupied a strategic role in interpreting and advancing the form that Cornish Studies takes. But, inevitably, the limited resources of the Institute and the marginal place of Cornish Studies within the academy also require Directors of the Institute to adopt a rhetorical stance on the field, attempting to steer its potential future as well as articulate its achievements in the present.[21] This both reminds us of, and partly explains, the rhetorical aspect of the New Cornish Studies, as

---

16 See Garry Tregidga, *The Liberal Party in South-West Britain Since 1918* (Exeter: University of Exeter Press, 2000).

17 Payton, 'Introduction', 1993, pp.2-3.

18 Philip Payton, 'Introduction', *Cornish Studies* 6, 1998, p.1. Despite these calls to study identity formation Cornish Studies has yet to produce anything resembling Le Coadic's interdisciplinary study of the contemporary Breton identity (Ronan Le Coadic, *L'Identité bretonne* (Rennes: Presses Universitaires de Rennes, 1998)).

19 Payton, 'Introduction', 1993, p.1.

20 Payton, 'Introduction', 1996, p.1.

21 Resource factors can also constrain the desired outcomes. For instance, the series *Cornish Studies*, given the small size of the disciplinary field, is forced into an eclecticism, both in terms of subject and of contributors, which to some extent blurs the vision of the ideal rhetorically defined space of the New Cornish Studies.

a statement of a desired epistemological position rather than as a necessarily accurate description of current practice.

However, the rhetorical nature of the New Cornish Studies project should not prevent us recognising that a real shift in the focus of Cornish Studies has occurred over the past decade. This shift has been accomplished by a group of scholars working in a loose network, if not exactly bonded by the close contact and shared aims sometimes imagined or projected. The other contributions to *Cornish Studies Ten* go a long way to record the breadth of coverage and the number of people who have, directly or tangentially, worked in and around the field of Cornish Studies over the past decade. Moreover, there are good contextual reasons why we should expect Cornish Studies to have changed direction since the 1980s, reasons that exist over and above changes in personnel at the Institute of Cornish Studies. These intellectual and social shifts have altered the terrain within which Cornish Studies has to survive.

The first of these has been provoked by growing academic debates in the humanities and social sciences around the notion of postmodernism. Postmodernist theorists have made explicit a scepticism about those 'grand narratives', such as liberalism or Marxism, that formerly held sway within the social sciences and which attempted to construct over-arching theories of society. Instead of the generalizing thrust of 'grand narratives', it is argued that scholars should return to a concern with the unexpected and the contingent, the heterogeneous rather than the homogeneous. This shift has had a profound effect and one that goes far beyond the often inaccessible work that passes itself off as 'postmodernist'. In general terms it has helped to produce an uncertainty about the former taken-for-granted canons and procedures of various academic disciplines. More specifically, it opens up a space for studying areas formerly viewed as marginal or liminal.[22] In this respect, as a result of a changing intellectual climate, the highly specialised and rigidly compartmentalised disciplines of social science and historical studies are under pressure. Some observers see this change as leading to a growth of interest in 'regional and local approaches'.[23] The broad turn to the regional and local makes it easier for Cornish Studies to claim credibility and establish its legitimacy within an academic community that has

---

22 Academic journals are noticeably more willing to accept Cornish Studies related submissions. See Bernard Deacon, 'Imagining the fishing: Artists and fishermen in late nineteenth century Cornwall' *Rural History* 12 (2001), 159-178; Ella Westland, 'D.H.Lawrence's Cornwall: dwelling in a precarious age', *Cultural Geographies* 9 (2002), 266-285.

23 Pat Hudson, 'Regional and Local History: Globalisation, Postmodernism and the Future', *Journal of Regional and Local Studies* 20 (1999), 5-24.

sometimes tended to approach Cornwall and Cornish Studies with a certain amount of wariness.

Furthermore, the turn to the local and the regional is often accompanied by the adoption of concepts of fluidity and hybridity. It is this that has multiplied uncertainties about formerly cherished assumptions. Celtic Studies is a disciplinary field that has, arguably, been more affected by growing uncertainty than many others. The work of Malcolm Chapman and Simon James has, from their vantage points of anthropology and archaeology, raised fundamental objections about the category 'Celtic' as a historical reality in the early medieval and preceding periods.[24] Their critique rests on the claim that those groups we now define as 'Celtic' did not use the word 'Celtic' to describe themselves. Instead, they propose that the Celts are a modern 'invented tradition' rather than the past reality they are uncritically taken to be. Such questioning of the core definitions of the discipline has opened up room for alternative definitions and approaches. This is perhaps best illustrated by the volume of essays edited by David Harvey et al. as *Celtic Geographies*.[25] Here hybridity and contestation is the name of the game as former certainties about what and who are 'Celtic' are displaced by more fluid notions of 'Celticity'. Moreover, Cornish Studies played its full part in this shift towards ambiguity and complexity in Celtic Studies, hosting two conferences on the 'new Celtic Studies' and publishing a volume of the same name.[26] In addition, the 'Cornish' chapters by Amy Hale and Alan Kent in *Celtic Geographies* succeed in establishing a more hybrid recognition of 'the Celt' and by implication 'the Cornish', helping the reader to resist the temptation to resort to simplistic and essentialist concepts of the 'Cornish Celt' and alerting them to other perspectives.[27]

Perhaps because of the marginal position of Cornish Studies within traditional Celtic Studies, the New Cornish Studies was hitched to the movement of Irish Studies (from 1985) and Welsh Studies away from an exclusive concern with language and literature to that of history, sociology, anthropology and geography.[28] This movement reflects New Cornish

---

24 Malcolm Chapman, *The Celts: The construction of a myth* (London: Macmillan, 1992); Simon James, *The Atlantic Celts: Ancient People or Modern Invention? (*London: British Museum Press, 1999). See Patrick Sims-Williams, 'Celtomania or Celtoscepticism', *Cambrian Medieval Celtic Studies* 36 (1998), 1-35 for a response from within the field.

25 Harvey et al, *Celtic Geographies*, 2002.

26 Hale and Payton, *New Directions*, 2000.

27 Amy Hale, 'Whose Celtic Cornwall? The ethnic Cornish meet Cornish spirituality', and Alan Kent, 'Celtic Nirvanas: Constructions of Celtic in contemporary British youth culture' in Harvey et al, *Celtic Geographies*, 2002, 157-170 and 208-226.

28 *The Times Higher,* 1 February 2002, p.18.

Studies' concern with the contemporary, but also recognises a second major contextual shift - that of society more generally. In conditions of 'postmodernity' or 'late modernity', it has been suggested that issues of identity politics and identity formation become more central, as 'social identities, geographical locations, and national allegiances all tend to be out of sync, at least more so now than in the recent past'.[29] This has certainly been the case in the Celtic territories of western Europe. The establishment of devolved assemblies in Scotland and Wales and the formation of the British-Irish Council of the Isles were belated responses by an over-centralised British state to the re-assertion of identity in Scotland, Wales and Northern Ireland that gathered pace after the 1960s. In a similar way, a growing confidence in Cornishness during the 1980s and 1990s underpinned the challenges to the status quo and conventional wisdom that ultimately resulted in the granting of Objective 1 European funding and the impressive declaration of support for the idea of a devolved Cornish Assembly tapped by the Cornish Constitutional Convention's campaign in 2000/01. This background 'lent an urgency and relevance to the discipline [of Celtic Studies]'.[30]

The New Cornish Studies: some problems

A changing context produced the circumstances in which Cornish Studies launched itself in new directions. The resultant New Cornish Studies has sought to channel this movement into a particular path. However, there exist some rarely discussed tensions around this project. This section will briefly review a few such issues before moving on to look in a little more depth at the case study of the 'new Cornish historiography'. First, we ought to note the practical questions that face the New Cornish Studies project. Who do we write for? The popular view of Cornish Studies is still one dominated by language and history, looking to the past and sharing some ground with notions of 'heritage'. Is Cornish Studies, in moving towards a more theoretically engaged and contemporary stance, in danger of losing this non-specialist audience? And who exactly owns it? Is it the property of the Institute of Cornish Studies or is it something broader? If it is something broader, then what are the processes and the arenas whereby the field is developed further and its direction shaped? As noted above, the relative lack of Cornish Studies personnel has always meant that its output turns out to be narrower than its declared aims. Thus, despite Charles Thomas' wide definition of Cornish Studies in 1972, the actual academic work of the Institute was much more narrowly centred on archaeology and place name

---

29   Vicente L.Rafael, 'Regionalism, Area Studies and the Accidents of Agency', *American Historical Review* 104 (1999), 1208-1220.
30   Hale and Payton, *New Directions*, 2000, p.4.

research in the 1970s and 1980s, with other projects dependent on the vagaries of short-term grant funding. Similarly, the current output of the Institute appears more focused on historical studies than the broader social sciences favoured by the New Cornish Studies. Is this a problem? And if it is, what do we do about it?

I do not intend to attempt to answer these questions here. But it is worth noting that it is not only lack of resources that has set up tensions between the rhetoric of the new Cornish Studies project and its fulfilment. By way of illustration, we might here identify two contradictions that cohere around the New Cornish Studies. As we have seen above, Philip Payton claims an applied aspect for the 'new Cornish social science'; for 'such a process cannot fail to inform, influence and guide planners and policy makers at every level, should they care to listen'.[31] But do they? The vision of an applied Cornish Studies that informs policy makers in Cornwall and elsewhere may conflict with the preferred content of the New Cornish Studies and its links to social theory. Some of the latter will no doubt be critical of the assumptions that lie behind policy-making in local government, or critical of the centralized framework within which this occurs. In many respects an open coalescence between policy actors in Cornwall and work inspired by critical social theory is an unlikely scenario. This is particularly so when we consider the context of Cornish policy-making over the past half-century. Cornwall has lacked that critical civil society within which transparent debate over policy can routinely take place. The absence of a genuinely investigative media, the missing university, the more general institutional vacuum, and the want of public space within which strategic debate can take place have combined to stifle real discussion about policy. In such a context 'applied Cornish Studies' can easily be reduced to the production of empirical data to reinforce and legitimate policy decisions rather than the insertion of academically grounded policy options that might inform the local process of governance and challenge the taken for granted assumptions of policy actors. On a broader, more philosophical, note we might also identify a contradiction between renewed intellectual uncertainties and the reassertion of identity politics that provides the context for possible political change in Cornwall and in other 'Celtic' peripheries. In challenging popular narratives of Cornishness and Celticity, academics tread a perilous tightrope between being alert to heterogeneity and deconstructing claims that may underlie the struggles of disempowered and voiceless groups. Bridging this potential gap will be a delicate task for the New Cornish Studies over the coming decades.

---

31 Payton, 'Introduction', 1996, p.1.

Luke Gibbons has written that 'a culture has not found its own voice until it has expressed itself in a body of critical as well as creative work'.[32] In cognate fashion, it can be suggested that an academic discipline has not come of age until it contains a critical edge, both about its own 'foundational myths' and about the concepts and theories it utilises.[33] In relation to this latter, the New Cornish Studies has been insufficiently critical hitherto of the various frameworks it employs. For example, the idea of centre and periphery might not allow for the situation where there is more than one centre or core, as was arguably the case in eighteenth-century industrializing Britain.[34] Similarly, the 'new Cornish historiography' might be insufficiently critical of the 'new' British history. This latter perspective, despite its apparent openness to diversity, often gives Cornwall little more space than did 'old' English histories.[35] More fundamentally, Pittock has pointed out how 'four nations' new British history is unconsciously subject to the status quo, for example overplaying Ireland's colonial past at the same time as it downplays that of Scotland and Wales. For Pittock, the 'new' British history is 'camouflaged anglocentrism', a point echoed by Nicholas Canny who adds a methodological dimension to his critique of the new British history, which he sees as widening the gulf between political and social/economic history and emphasising similarity at the expense of difference.[36] The 'new Cornish historiography' could engage with these criticisms, lending its voice to support or to qualify them. Even the turn to identity may be problematic. For example, Richard Handler has suggested that identity is a 'reified concept' that is imposed on past places and times even though it is actually 'peculiar to the modern western world'.[37]

---

32 Luke Gibbons, *Transformations in Irish Culture* (Cork: Cork University Press, 1996, p.xi.

33 See Malcolm Williams, 'The New Cornish Social Science', 2002.

34 See Bernard Deacon, 'Proto-regionalisation: The case of Cornwall, *Journal of Regional and Local Studies* 18 (1998), 27-41.

35 John Morrill, 'The British Problem, c1534-1707', in Brendan Bradshaw and John Morrill (eds), *The British Problem, c1534-1707: State Formation in the British Archipelago* (Basingstoke: Macmillan, 1996). See pages 1 and 6. Cornwall also gets little mention in Glenn Burgess (ed), *The New British History: Founding a Modern State* (London: I.B.Tauris, 1999).

36 Murray Pittock, *Celtic identity and the British Image* (Manchester: Manchester University Press, 1999), pp.98-100; Nicholas Canny, 'Irish, Scottish and Welsh responses to centralisation, c.1530-c.1640: A comparative perspective', in Alexander Grant and Keith Stringer (eds), *Uniting the Kingdom? The Making of British History* (London: Routledge, 1995), pp.147-148.

37 Nicholas Handler, 'Is "Identity" a Useful Cross-Cultural Concept?', in John R.Gillis (ed), *Commemorations: The Politics of National Identity* (Princeton, NJ: Princeton University Press, 1994), 27-40.

Handler's suspicion of identity echoes Colin Kidd's doubt about ethnic identities in the pre-modern British Isles. He proposes instead that ethnic identity was of 'second order' importance while the 'very notion of "identity" ... might itself be anachronistic' when applied to the period before 1700.[38] The rhetorical aspect of the new Cornish Studies should not mean that the project cannot assimilate such criticisms of the concepts and models that it employs.

Furthermore, the rhetorical space of New Cornish Studies contains an inbuilt tendency to draw clear contrasts between the 'old' and the 'new'. While a necessary rhetorical device, this results in practice in overdrawing distinctions and erasing continuities. We can pursue this aspect more easily in relation to the specific case of the 'new Cornish historiography'. This will also allow us to investigate that possible gap between the rhetoric of the 'new Cornish historiography' and its substance. More importantly, it also reveals an important but often understated basis of the New Cornish Studies.

The New Cornish historiography

The description 'new Cornish historiography' begs a number of questions; namely, in what way is it 'new', how is it 'Cornish', and why 'historiography'? This section deals with these three questions, although not quite in this order.

In what ways is the 'new Cornish historiography' new? Colin H. Williams has pointed out in relation to Celtic Studies that 'new approaches' do not always deliver what they claim.[39] The claims for the 'new Cornish historiography' are similar to those for the generic New Cornish Studies -- it has to engage with and contribute to 'new discourses ... such engagement should be our over-arching research strategy for the future'. And it should set developments in Cornwall 'firmly in a comparative context'.[40] Perhaps the most successful example of this is Mark Stoyle's volume *West Britons*.[41] But is the broad historical work that appears in *Cornish Studies* so clearly 'new'? Does it contrast markedly and unambiguously with the published work in, say, the *Journal of the Royal Institution of Cornwall*, with its roots in antiquarianism and local studies? For example Volume 3 of New Series 2

---

38 Colin Kidd, *British Identities before Nationalism: Ethnicity and Nationhood in the Atlantic World, 1600-1880* (Cambridge: Cambridge University Press, 1999), p.291.
39 Colin Williams, 'New Directions in Celtic Studies: An Essay in Social Criticism', in Hale and Payton, 'New Directions', 2000, p.202.
40 Payton, 'Cornwall in context', 1997, p.12.
41 Stoyle, *West Britons*, 2002. See also Philip Payton, *Cornwall* (Fowey: Alexander Associates, 1996).

of the *Journal of the RIC* contained several articles with a historical theme.[42] These allow us to draw a picture of the 'old' Cornish history. The articles are based for the most part on a detailed close reading of primary sources, tend towards the descriptive, are heavily empirical and focus on the agency of individuals rather than structural processes. In adopting this approach, they reproduce 'evocative tableaux rather than explanatory accounts of historical processes and structures'.[43] But many of the articles in *Cornish Studies*, while more likely to contain comparative academic and spatial references, are not that different in style. As has been noted of Celtic Studies in general, they give us detailed case studies rather than engage in theory construction.[44] Occasionally, indeed, the same authors publish in both places, the *Journal of the RIC* and *Cornish Studies*.[45] Consequently, on this evidence the boundary between the 'new Cornish historiography' as represented by Cornish Studies and the 'old Cornish history' of the *Journal of the RIC* is often more difficult to discern in practice than in theory.

As the claim to 'newness' rests on methodology, this aspect overlaps considerably with that of 'historiography'. The choice of this word suggests methodological novelty, with its implicit contrast between the new methodologically alert 'historiography' and the old unreflective 'history'. But historical writing in both *Cornish Studies* and the *Journal of the RIC* adopts recognisably 'historical' methods of source-critical interpretation and reconstruction through inferential or deductive reasoning within a narrative account.[46] Of course, it is possible to detect some differences. Contributions to *Cornish Studies* may be more marked by interpretation (by narrational emplotment) than reportage (by the what, where, when or who disclosed by the evidence). Articles in *Cornish Studies* are also more likely to adopt an explicit academic framework, grounding themselves in a wider academic

---

42 *Journal of the Royal Institution of Cornwall* 3.3-4 (2000). These ranged from studies of the medieval period to nineteenth-century political history.

43 Joseph M.Bryant, 'On sources and narratives in historical social science: a realist critique of positivist and postmodernist epistemologies', *British Journal of Sociology* 51 (2000), p.511.

44 Williams, 'New directions', 2000, p.205.

45 For example see Joanna Mattingly, 'The Helston Shoemakers' Gild and a Possible Connection with the 1549 Rebellion', in Philip Payton (ed.), *Cornish Studies Six* (Exeter: University of Exeter Press, 1998), 23-45 and 'Stories in the Glass – Reconstructing the St.Neot Pre-Reformation Glazing Scheme', *Journal of the Royal Institution of Cornwall* 3.3-4 (2000), 9-55 or Ronald Perry, 'The Changing Face of Celtic Tourism in Cornwall, 1875-1975', in Philip Payton (ed.), *Cornish Studies Seven* (Exeter: University of Exeter Press, 1999), 94-106 and 'Silvanus Trevail and the Development of Modern Tourism in Cornwall', *Journal of the Royal Institution of Cornwall* 3.2 (1999), 33-43.

46 cf. Bryant, 'On sources', 2000.

literature, although this is not exactly absent from many contributions to the *Journal of the RIC*. In any case, this is more academic 'good practice' than methodological innovation, a marginal stylistic as opposed to a major methodological contrast. Thus it would appear that there remains considerable overlap between the 'old' and the 'new'.

Furthermore, if the old is 'old' in that it is untouched by some of the debates rippling through the academy, so the new appears not so 'new', or only intermittently new, in its engagement with these debates. Nowhere is this more striking than in the way both 'old Cornish history' and 'new Cornish historiography' appear to avoid the historiographical debates triggered off by postmodernist critiques of 'objectivist' history as merely a fabricatory product of the present.[47] Even the local historians have tinkered, albeit rather gingerly, with this debate.[48] By way of concluding this comparison, and adopting Munslow's classification of historical perspectives, both 'old Cornish history' and 'new Cornish historiography' would appear to be broadly 'reconstructionist' in tenor ('seeking the most probably truthful ... interpretation inherent in the documents of the past') as opposed to 'deconstructionist' (interrogating discourses both of the past and of historians).[49]

If the epistemological radicalism of the 'new Cornish historiography' is more subtle than the rhetorical definition may lead us to expect, we find a greater distance between it and older variants in its ontological stance, in its underlying assumptions. Indeed, it is when seeking to establish how the 'new Cornish historiography' is precisely 'Cornish' that I contend that we meet the real 'newness' of the project. This lies not in its methodology but in its explicit normative assumptions. Philip Payton, in the Introduction to *Cornwall*, sums this up directly: 'until recently, our history has been so often the history of Cornwall without the Cornish people, and it is high time that we offered a corrective'.[50] There are echoes here of the work of the late Gwyn Alf Williams in Wales or the feminist position that asserts 'the right to name ourselves, to act as subjects rather than objects of history'.[51] Just as

---

47 For an introduction to this debate see Keith Jenkins (ed), *The Postmodern History Reader* (London: Routledge, 1997); Richard Evans, *In Defence of* History (London: Granta, 1997); Arthur Marwick, *The New Nature of History: knowledge, evidence, language* (Basingstoke: Palgrave, 2001).

48 See George Sheeran and Yanina Sheeran, 'Reconstructing Local History', *The Local Historian* 29 (1999), 256-262 and the responses in *The Local Historian* 31 (2001), 47-50.

49 Alan Munslow, *The Routledge Companion to Historical Studies* (London: Routledge, 2000).

50 Payton, *Cornwall*, 1996, p.vi.

51 Geraint H.Jenkins, *The People's Historian: Professor Gwyn A.Williams (1925-1995)* (Aberystwyth: University of Wales Centre for Advanced Welsh and

some feminists would argue that women have a privileged knowledge that enables them to write about women's history with an insight unavailable to men, however sympathetic, there is more than a hint here that the 'new Cornish historiography' offers a privileged, though nonetheless rigorous, vantage point on the Cornish past.

In claiming this, the 'new Cornish historiography' clearly parts company with 'old Cornish history', which is heavily influenced by local history. The latter, while clinging to a naïve empiricism, is strangely coy about its own assumptions. Lacking critical reflection on these, it ends up taking a conservative and/or romantic definition of Cornwall and its territoriality for granted, rarely admitting its origins in a deferential English local historical tradition that stresses order, stability and rurality. By way of contrast, the 'new Cornish historiography', looking as much perhaps for inspiration to the emigrant communities and the more open societies of the Cornish diaspora as to the class-bound hierarchies of rural nineteenth-century Britain, is less deferential and more critical.

The future of Cornish Studies

My argument therefore is that the New Cornish Studies is as much an ontological as an epistemological project, as much concerned with values and visions as with novel methodological approaches. In view of this, how might the field develop over the next decade? Here I will briefly sketch out four potential shifts for the New Cornish Studies. These are, first, from British history to microhistory; second, from Celtic Studies to cultural studies; third, from comparative work to extraversion and, fourth, from Cornwall to Cornwalls.

While the new British history has provided a springboard for some of the most exciting work of the 'new Cornish historiography' during the 1990s and early 2000s, we need to build on this and engage with other frameworks in order to develop our understanding of historical periods and themes beyond the early modern period. One such approach is that of microhistory. Microhistory is a new, more analytical, more theory-sensitive type of historical study, one that proposes 'to say a great deal about the wider world but from a less abstract perspective rooted in vernacular expression and experience'.[52] Microhistory recognises that 'big problems exist in small spaces' and aims to unite the general social processes and the local uniqueness that arise from them.[53] It studies the totality of people's lives,

---

Celtic Studies, 1996), p.7; Nancy Hartstock, 'Rethinking modernism: minority vs majority theories', *Cultural Critique* 7 (1987), 187-206.

52 Hudson, 'Regional and local history', 1999, p.15.

53 Neil Evans, 'Writing the social history of modern Wales: approaches, achievements and problems', *Social History* 17 (1992), p.492.

rather than privileging either the public sphere over the private or the economic over the cultural or vice versa. Done well, as in the work of Barry Reay,[54] microhistory achieves in doing precisely what the 'new Cornish historiography' sets out to do – influence wider generalizations and theories about the social world. There is a clear overlap here with anthropology and with the work currently growing up around the Cornish Audio Visual Archive Project, with its emphasis on oral history and the vernacular.[55] But microhistory is not confined to the twentieth century; it can be applied to any period.[56]

My second shift is from Celtic Studies to cultural studies. However, to advocate this is not to propose the wholesale jettisoning of the 'Celtic'. It is merely to admit that the New Cornish Studies has already broken the always tenuous link between Cornish Studies and the 'canon' of Celtic Studies. The 'Celtic' will remain one strand in Cornwall and in Cornish life. But what the New Cornish Studies might fruitfully do now is explicitly to engage with aspects of cultural studies. The concern of the latter with the diversity of cultures within the British Isles and with the limitations of the concept 'British' are obvious points of connection.[57] In many ways the 'new Celtic Studies' is a bridge between Cornish Studies and cultural studies. The three issues that Harvey et al claim that a concern with 'Celticity' can illuminate - the politics and economics of exclusion and division, the promotion of 'difference' in political, cultural and economic terms, and the search for identity in a consumerist society - are broad cultural issues and ones that are equally important in studies of contemporary Cornwall. For example, the commodification of Cornishness is an area that desperately requires more inter-disciplinary attention.

Third, Cornish Studies must progress beyond being comparative to being actively outward-looking. To engage fully with new discourses means breaking out of self-imposed ghettos, publishing in wider arenas and reaching larger audiences. One possible development would be to begin to apply Cornish Studies perspectives to 'mainstream' aspects, to deconstruct the assumptions and discourses of majority claims and imaginations.[58]

---

54 Barry Reay, *Micro-histories: Demography, Society and Culture in Rural England 1800-1930* (Cambridge: Cambridge University Press, 1996).

55 The academic outcomes of the CAVA project are still unclear. But it promises to be a major potential growth area of Cornish Studies.

56 See Keith Wrightson and David Levine, *Poverty and Piety in an English Village* (Oxford: Clarendon, 1979).

57 Susan Basnett (ed), *Studying British Cultures: An introduction* (London: Routledge, 1997).

58 For an example see Bernard Deacon, *Building the region: Culture and Territory in the South West of England* (Milton Keynes: Open University, 2002).

Finally, the New Cornish Studies will have to embrace the more fragmentary, fluid and heterogeneous accounts of society that have become fashionable in many academic circles. These offer the opportunity to re-think the very ways we imagine Cornwall and, by implication, ourselves.[59] Because, as the practitioners of Cornish Studies, through helping to construct differences and identities, we are inevitably 'forced to confront the construction of ourselves'.[60] To adopt this more reflective approach is to accept that the New Cornish Studies may be place-based, but it is not place-bounded. Like newer, broader definitions of Celticity, studies of Cornwall and Cornishness can also 'provide an opportunity through which more inclusive, multifacted, multi-ethnic, non-territorially bounded expressions of social cohesion can operate'.[61] I have argued in an earlier contribution to *Cornish Studies* that, in the next phase of Cornish Studies we might move from the spatial scale of Cornwall to both spatial and cultural 'Cornwalls', becoming increasingly alert to the multiple representations of Cornwall that exist both now and in the past.[62] For instance, while Harvey et al identify two spatial realms of Celticity, we might claim three spatial realms of Cornishness. There is the roots and tradition-seeking Cornishness of the diaspora, the romantic and wistful Cornishness of metropolitan England and the Cornishness of Cornwall. And while the last of these includes the familiar, nostalgic view of Cornwall and its heritage that tends to be moulded by a sense of loss and *'hireth'*, there is another under-theorised aspect of the Cornishness of Cornwall. This is a more civic, open and inclusive Cornishness, one that looks to democratic institutions and to aspects of the European project for a re-forged and progressive sense of regional identity. All these Cornwalls are potential points of analysis for the New Cornish Studies.[63]

Conclusion
I have pointed to some potential directions the New Cornish Studies might take. In this way, this review article is ultimately located squarely within the New Cornish Studies approach. For, in foregrounding the potential of Cornish Studies, based on its underlying values, which stress that Cornwall,

---

59 See Kent, 'Celtic nirvanas', 2002.
60 Peter Jackson and Jan Penrose (eds), *Constructions of Race, Place and Nation* (London: UCL Press, 1993), p.209.
61 Harvey et al, *Celtic Geographies*, 2002, p.12.
62 Bernard Deacon, 'In Search of the Missing "Turn": The Spatial Dimension and Cornish Studies', in Philip Payton (ed.), *Cornish Studies Eight* (Exeter: University of Exeter Press, 2000), 213-230.
63 See, for example, Chapter 8 in Philip Payton, *A Vision of Cornwall* (Fowey: Alexander Associates, 2002).

its communities, its past and its present are suitable subjects to study, we return to the heart of the Cornish Studies project. I have suggested in this article that New Cornish Studies is, indeed, as much a rhetorically defined space as a set of discrete, methodologically novel academic productions. Nevertheless, its rhetorical character should not disguise the fact that it both informs and reflects real shifts in the field of Cornish Studies since the 1980s. Some of those shifts, which to an extent mirror wider intellectual and social change, may have occurred independently, without the rhetorical space of the New Cornish Studies. Yet the importance of the latter is that it has imposed some overall sense of direction and purpose upon them and provided an aspiration or vision for Cornish Studies practitioners to aim at.

Moreover, those working within the New Cornish Studies field see that, by setting out to deconstruct certain powerful paradigms of Cornwall, they will also open up new possibilities for local actors. In short, the New Cornish Studies accepts that Cornish Studies is, inevitably, part of a struggle for place, part of an ongoing re-creation and conservation of that place we call Cornwall.[64] It recognises that Cornwall is neither essential nor unchanging but it also sets out to assert the right of the Cornish themselves to be involved in that process of change. It is a part of a discourse that states that the Cornish no longer wish to be marginalized, casually misrepresented or appropriated for other agenda. They are not just passive constructions of outside discourses. They are agents who made, within obvious constraints, their own history. The task of the New Cornish Studies is to recover that sense of agency, put it into a comparative context, open up our knowledge of the past and, ultimately, to empower people in Cornwall so that they are in a better position to make choices about their own future. The contrast with the 'old Cornish history' should be apparent. But 'old Cornish history' is not the same as 'old' Cornish Studies. Old Cornish Studies shared the same ontological assumptions about Cornwall as does the New, viewing it as a fit object of study in its own right. What New Cornish Studies does is to make this more explicit.

Postscript
In this second part of my triptych on Cornish Studies, I set out to evaluate the 'new Cornish Studies'. My rather sceptical view at the time concluded that, while there had been a shift in topic and content, there was nevertheless a detectable continuum between 'new' and 'old' Cornish Studies. The article wove its way along a narrow path, struggling to balance its conclusion that 'new Cornish Studies' was more of a rhetorical space than a novel methodology and yet contained something distinctly new. It did

---

64 cf. Michael Keith and Steve Pile (eds), *Place and the Politics of Identity* (London: Routledge, 1993), p.6.

not wholly succeed in avoiding the contradictions of such a position. Instead of methodology, my position was that Cornish Studies contained a distinctive world view, one that put Cornwall and the empowerment of its people at the centre, extending the first phase of the project. Given that the boundaries of Cornish Studies were ontological rather than methodological, other approaches could be incorporated into Cornish Studies. At the time, these approaches included microhistory (see Chapter 5 below), cultural studies, the deconstruction of dominant claims and the application of a Cornish perspective to 'mainstream' topics, and an awareness of hybridity, building on the call for more sensitivity to geographical scale in the first intervention.

I also asked questions about the Cornish Studies project, its ownership, its audience and direction. These were left unanswered in the original essay but remain pertinent today. They could also be linked to a second point made in this critique of 'new Cornish Studies' - the role and influence of individuals in an under-populated academic field. We now have a third Director of the ICS in Garry Tregidga. It may be significant that Garry, in his introduction to the third series of *Cornish Studies*, linked this phase of Cornish Studies to 'multidisciplinary perspectives', a subtle yet significant shift away from the explicit interdisciplinarity called for in the second phase.[65] Garry's own background in creating the Cornish Audio Visual Archive (CAVA) and the outreach project of 'Cornish Story' suggests a new emphasis on 'community engagement and democratic scholarship', this comprising a 'unique combination'.[66] While the second phase of Cornish Studies struggled to transcend the inherent contradiction between applied research and critical perspectives, it remains to be seen whether this laudable attempt to return Cornish Studies to the people can overcome potential dissonances between popular appeal and academic credibility.

---

65 Garry Tregidga, 'Studhyansow Kernewek: An introduction to Cornish Studies', in Garry Tregidga (ed.), *Cornish Studies One* (Penryn: Institute of Cornish Studies, 2015), 1-13.

66 For CAVA and the Cornish Story see http://cornishstory.com/archiving-cornwall-c-a-v-a/ and https://www.webarchive.org.uk/ukwa/target/65208889/collection/65208410/source/collection (accessed 21 July 2017)

Chapter Three

From Cornish Studies to Critical Cornish Studies: reflections on methodology

(First version published in Philip Payton (ed.), *Cornish Studies Twelve*, (Exeter: University of Exeter Press, 2004), 13-29.)

In reviewing the 'new Cornish social science' Malcolm Williams sums up part of the goal of 'a relevant Cornish social science' as the ability 'to describe what contemporary Cornwall is like and to understand what people in Cornwall think'.[1] By extending this to past times this could equally be an aim for Cornish historical studies – to describe what Cornwall was like and understand what people in Cornwall thought. And yet such a deceptively simple goal begs a number of questions. First, how precisely do we 'describe' Cornwall, either in the twenty-first or the eleventh century? If we wish to avoid the empiricist fallacy that claims that the 'truth' will emerge unproblematically from the 'facts', any researcher has to pose questions, select facts, choose methods, in short adopt a framework for their study.

Claims for a 'new' Cornish Studies are regularly accompanied by the idea, more often implicit than explicit, that it is, or should be, informed by social theory. This supposed role of theory marks it off from an 'old' Cornish Studies. However, claims for a theoretically informed Cornish Studies are more difficult to substantiate in its practice. Some contributors to Cornish Studies adopt theoretical frameworks; others do not. And if we review the whole field of Cornish Studies, what is striking is its eclectic pick and mix approach to theory. Theories are chosen for their utility in studying discrete issues within Cornish Studies, depending on the disciplinary origin of the researcher and the topic being investigated. Theoretical choice is not, in contrast, a function of Cornish Studies as a field of study.

What I wish to do in this article is to explore one particular branch of social theory in a little more detail, making a plea that it might be seen as particularly suited to the task of developing a critical Cornish Studies. In doing this I want to move on from questions of aims and content to those of methodology. In *Cornish Studies Eight* I proposed that studies of Cornwall should be sensitive to processes operating at multi-level scales, from the

---

1   Malcolm Williams, 'The new Cornish social science', in Philip Payton (ed.), *Cornish Studies Ten* (Exeter: University of Exeter Press, 2002), p.61.

global to the local.[2] An awareness of the issue of scale moves us from focusing on Cornwall to unravelling Cornwalls. Building on this, in *Cornish Studies Ten*, when deconstructing the rhetorically defined space that comprises 'New Cornish Studies', I called for an explicit recognition of its underlying normative stance.[3] Within this I laid out an agenda of micro-history, cultural studies and 'extraversion', as well as an openness to the heterogeneity of Cornwall and Cornishness.[4] The present contribution can therefore be read as the third part of an ongoing reflection on the disciplinary field of Cornish Studies. It is by no means the final word but rather a further effort to tie together some of the issues raised in the two earlier contributions, as we grope towards a more self-critical Cornish Studies project.

In both previous reflections I used the word 'discourse'. But it was employed loosely and descriptively. In doing this I echoed the seepage of the term into the social sciences since the 1980s, 'discourse' becoming a fashionable concept that had 'infected social theory'.[5] It is time to pin down this concept. Here, I try to do that, taking the reader on a brief tour around the idea of discourse, resting heavily on Laclau and Mouffe's model.[6] However, rejecting those analysts' over-reliance on discourse, I then propose that Cornish Studies could benefit from engaging with discourse in the guise of critical discourse analysis, which offers a way of combining social theory with a normative ontology (underpinning assumptions that are strongly committed to a particular view of the world). In adopting this approach critical discourse analysis offers intriguing signposts, pointing the way towards a critical Cornish Studies.

What is discourse?
This article began with Malcolm William's plea to 'understand what people in Cornwall think'. This, indeed, is a perfectly respectable aim as we are surprisingly ignorant about what people think, about Cornwall, about their localities, about their everyday lives.[7] Nonetheless, identifying what people think cannot stop there. In revealing the contents of their thoughts we will

2   Bernard Deacon, 'In search of the missing 'turn': the spatial dimension and Cornish Studies', in Philip Payton (ed.), *Cornish Studies Eight* (Exeter: University of Exeter Press, 2000), 213-30.

3   Bernard Deacon, 'The new Cornish Studies: new discipline or rhetorically defined space?', in Payton (ed.), *Cornish Studies: Ten*, 2002), 24-43.

4   This turn from Cornwall to Cornwalls is being reflected in the work of the CAVA and Cornish Communities research programmes at the ICS.

5   Norman Fairclough, Bob Jessop and Andrew Sayer, 'Critical realism and semiosis', *Journal of Critical Realism* 5 (2002), 2-10.

6   Ernesto Laclau and Chantal Mouffe, *Hegemony and socialist strategy: towards a radical democratic politics* (London: Verso, 1985).

inevitably then enquire into questions such as how do they think, where do the things they think come from, what institutions help to transmit the elements with which they think and how do they negotiate these, or what constraints are there to the thoughts they think. To do this, we have to go beyond Cornwall, to investigate the way people in other places and in external institutions think about Cornwall. Conceptually too, we have to go beyond the thoughts of the individual, to the system of thought, or more realistically, systems of thought, within which they do their thinking.

This is where discourses enter the arena. A discourse is a way of understanding and talking about the world that can be distinguished from other ways of understanding the world.[8] The analyst can categorise ways of understanding into several, sometimes conflicting, 'discourses'. Thus there is a 'Cornish nationalist' discourse that 'sees' Cornwall as having been oppressed and exploited by the English for over a thousand years. In contrast there is a 'Cornwall as English county' discourse that views Cornwall as an integral component of England. These are clearly competing discourses and there is not much overlap between them. Each makes up a network of meaning, similar to the structuralist description of language as *langue*, or a structure. Within such a network or structure words get their meaning from what they are not. In the 'Cornish nationalist' discourse Cornwall is not England; in the 'English county' discourse Cornwall is not Devon.

Discourses also clearly do more than just reflect the world, they actively constitute the world they describe. There is only one Cornwall, in the sense of its tangible and physical settlements, fields, roads, moors, cliffs and the like. Yet there are several, sometimes complementary and overlapping, discourses of Cornwall. By ascribing meaning, a discourse helps to construct the social world. And it does more; it makes certain actions relevant or 'practical', while ruling out others. If we take it for granted that Cornwall is an English county then other conclusions follow. If Cornwall is a county then how can it have a nationalist movement? If Cornwall is a county then how can it possibly claim regional status? Counties surely have local identities and not national identities and county councils rather than regional assemblies. Despite the contrast between the glaringly obvious

---

7   Here, research in Cornwall lags well behind that in other places, such as Brittany. See Ronan Le Coadic, *L'identité bretonne* (Rennes: Presses Universitaires de Rennes, 1998) for an in-depth ethnographic study of attitudes of Bretons to their culture and identity.

8   The following account draws heavily on Marianne Jørgensen and Louise Phillips, *Discourse analysis as theory and method* (London: Sage, 2002), an excellent introduction to what can often seem an impenetrable and jargon-laden area of study.

empirical absence of anything resembling a nationalist movement in any English county and the continuous existence of, albeit low level, political nationalist activity in Cornwall for over a half a century,[9] the existence of Cornish nationalism can still be routinely questioned, ignored or denied. Claims for a Cornish assembly are also dismissed with invocations of a feared domino effect as Devon, Dorset and Rutland all follow suit. The power of the 'Cornwall as English county' discourse thus has major implications for what are seen as practical policy options and poses considerable difficulties for those who think outside its assumptions.

This alerts us to two more aspects of discourses. First, they are engaged in a struggle for meanings. If the meaning of Cornwall can be fixed as an 'English county' then the process of loss of decision-making eastwards and the re-centralisation that accompanies south-west regionalization becomes easier to accept. Second, discourses possess different power resources. Bourdieu has called discourses such as that of 'flexibility' an example of a 'strong discourse', a discourse backed by the strength of banks, multinational companies, politicians and other discourses such as neo-liberalism.[10] In similar fashion, 'Cornwall as English county' is a 'strong discourse', backed by media, the education system, government and by everyday processes such as counterurbanisation and population change.

All this does not mean, of course, that society is 'just' about discourse. One of the criticisms of post-structuralist approaches is precisely that, that 'reality' is denied and everything is reduced to language, or discourse. The implication is that if we say or write something, the world can become the thing we write or say. If we wake up one morning and believe we are Chinese, Basque or Cornish we will be Chinese, Basque or Cornish. Obviously things are not so simple. Even poststructuralists usually accept that there is such a thing as reality and that language cannot on its own easily change that reality. But equally, they also make the point that we can only access reality through language. It is only by the use of words that we know, or are told, that we are, or are not, Chinese or Basque or Cornish. While some hermeneutic approaches might deny this role of language, substituting experience for feeling, for a social scientist language is clearly unavoidable when describing and explaining 'reality'. Discourse analysts differ among themselves concerning the role they give to this linguistic structuring of 'reality'. For some, such as Laclau and Mouffe, discourse is stretched to encompass all material practices. Thus the economy is analysed

---

9   See Bernard Deacon, Dick Cole and Garry Tregidga, *Mebyon Kernow and Cornish Nationalism* (Cardiff: Welsh Academic Press, 2003).

10   Pierre Bourdieu, 'L'essence du neo-liberalisme', *Le Monde Diplomatique*, March 1998.

as a set of discursive practices, an economy of signs and symbols.[11] However, as we shall see, not all discourse analysis denies a distinction between discourse/language on the one hand and material processes and practices on the other.

So far, I have written of linguistic 'structures' and of discourses as competing or complementary structures. This may lead to an over-determinist view of discourses. For, while making up a structure at any given point in time, discourses are also temporary and contingent; they comprise possible networks of meaning but never necessary networks and are always potentially open to change. Possibly the most valuable insight of post-structuralism is that meanings are never permanent but always potentially unstable. A brief backwards glance at Cornish history might illustrate this. In the early nineteenth century the Cornish were described as a dynamic, innovative and industrious people at the forefront of technological change.[12] But this structure of meaning, while fixed for a period in the nineteenth century, changed so that, by the late twentieth century, the Cornish were being viewed as undynamic, besotted with the 'dreckly' syndrome and contrasted, explicitly or implicitly, with 'dynamic' incomers.[13] Discourses of the Cornish have clearly changed considerably over the past 200 years, former meanings have been destabilized and new meanings attached, only perhaps to be discarded in turn.

This potential instability is produced in practice through *parole*, the actual process of language use. While we, as agents, make use of language that comes to us as a structure, with pre-given rules and constraints that we cannot entirely ignore, we also have some opportunity to use that structure in different ways, to re-negotiate existing meanings and to attach new ones. Discourses are, in other words, always to some extent malleable. I say to some extent because our ability as agents to change the meanings of discourses, particularly 'strong' discourses, is clearly limited by a variety of social positioning, such as our status and class, institutional location, educational background, gender, ethnicity or place of residence.

---

11 For a non-poststructuralist text that seems to make similar assumptions see Scott Lash and John Urry, *Economies of signs and space* (London: Sage, 1994).

12 For an example see J.D.Tuckett, *A History of the Past and Present State of the Labouring Population, volume 2* (London: Longman, Brown, Green and Longmans, 1846), pp.536-37.

13 And for an example of this see Cornwall County Council's contribution to the *European Development Fund, County of Cornwall: A National Programme of Community Interest 1988-1991* (Brussels: European Commission, 1987), para 1.2.8.

How do discourses work?

We have seen that discourses are aspects of the linguistic construction of the world, doors of perception through which we access and construct reality. But how does discourse work? Laclau and Mouffe provide various concepts with which we can model discourse in practice.

Language is composed of signs – words or groups of words. But these signs are empty until contrasted with other signs. For example the word *kye* in the Cornish language is meaningless until we know that it equates to dog in English. But what is a dog? Dog takes on its meaning through contrast with cat or horse. Similarly *kye* gains meaning in relation to *cath* or *marth*. For Laclau and Mouffe particular meanings emerge when signs are linked to other signs within discourses, and then they become 'moments'. These moments articulate with each other. Thus within the 'tourist' discourse of Cornwall, the sign 'Celtic' becomes a moment attached to 'romance', 'tradition', 'King Arthur', 'standing stones', 'jewellery' and so on. But within a discourse of Cornish nationalism, 'Celtic' may resonate rather differently, articulating with 'rebellion', 'internationalism' and 'language', amongst other moments. The nodal point of a discourse is that privileged sign around which others crystallise. In the 'neo-liberal' discourse, 'market' is the privileged sign; in a 'Cornish nationalist' discourse, the 'Cornish nation' becomes the privileged sign.

Discourses attempt to transform signs that are outside their boundaries into the moments of a discourse, articulating them with other signs and achieving a degree of closure, putting a temporary stop to the fluctuating meanings of signs. Thus, in a 'tourist' discourse of Cornwall, the sign 'romantic' is linked to 'Cornwall' in order to achieve 'romantic Cornwall', a moment that then articulates with other moments such as standing stones, cliffs, deserted engine houses, Tintagel and so forth, so that this relationship begins to appear naturalised, to be taken for granted. The signifier Cornwall then becomes inevitably and invariably associated with romance. However, this signifier remains a floating one, subject to different meanings in different discourses and at the core of a struggle between discourses to establish meaning. The way that different discourses define the same signs in differing ways can therefore become a subject of investigation. We might thus identify a 'south west regional' discourse, which positions 'Cornwall' differently, accepting some moments, such as 'rural' or 'romance', but excluding others such as 'nation'.

To sum up, discourses are systems with which we represent the world. They can be analysed semiotically (how their language is articulated and how meanings are made). Furthermore, this semiosis 'has real effects on social practice, social institutions and the social order more generally'.[14] It is

---

14 Fairclough et al., 'Critical realism', 2002.

thus 'performative'; people and groups act out the consequences of discourses in real life, taking actions on the basis of the discourse they use to understand the world. For example, if one summer a number of accidents at strategic points on the A30 produced a major gridlock on Cornwall's main roads this could be explained by means of a number of discourses. It could be seen as an act of God, or as the result of the lack of sufficient road space, or as the effect of population growth and tourism, or as the result of longer-term changes in transport and the growth of car ownership and mobility. Each discourse carries its own policy implications. For the first, there might be little to do but pray; for the second the answer would be to build more roads; the third implies policies that result in more sustainable development and an alternative to tourism and the final discourse might look to be broader policies necessary to change life-styles and make us less dependent on road travel.

There remains the question of how far discourses can be bracketed off, or separated, from those 'social practices, social institutions and the social order more generally'. For some discourse analysts, such as Laclau and Mouffe, everything is a discursive practice and everything is mediated by language. Cornwall's roads may be jammed with traffic but we can only understand that congestion through using one discourse or another. Others demur. For them distinctions can be made between the semiotic order of discourse and other social practices that cannot just be analysed discursively. Laclau and Mouffe's approach to discourse, for these analysts, remains linguistically reductionist and underplays the non-discursive constraints on discourse.

What is critical discourse analysis?
The brand of discourse analysis that retains an opening towards broader social theory is critical discourse analysis (CDA), especially that of Norman Fairclough, and this is the social theory that might offer particular methodological appeal for those seeking a critical Cornish Studies.[15]

For Fairclough, discourses do help to constitute the social world but they are also themselves constituted by wider social practices. There is therefore a dialectical relationship between discourse and society. In adopting this approach CDA steers a course between those who claim that discourses arise from the material world and are, to a varying extent, unproblematical representations of that social world, and those who claim that everything is

---

15 Norman Fairclough, *Language and Power* (London: Longman, 1989); *Critical Discourse Analysis: the critical study of language* (London: Longman, 1995); Lilie Chouliaraki and Norman Fairclough, *Discourse in late modernity: rethinking critical discourse analysis* (Edinburgh: Edinburgh University Press, 1999).

discursive, including material practices. Instead discourse can only be analysed within its broader, though not determining, social context.

CDA also offers a model for analysing discourses. Discourse has three dimensions. First, there is a communicative event, for example a written text, interview, speech, visual image, newspaper article, during which the discourse is actively reproduced and sometimes transformed at the micro-level. Second, we find an order of discourse. The latter comprises the semiotic order, defined as the network of social practices within which the text is located. There is for example an order of discourse of the academy, or an order of discourse of the media.[16] Orders of discourse contribute to social relations, reproduce systems of knowledge and help to construct social identities. For Fairclough this means that discourse has a relational function, an ideational function and an identity function. An order of discourse can be conceptualised in turn as containing particular discourses, genres and styles. We have seen that discourses are the ways we represent the world. Genres are ways of acting and interacting with other people by speech or writing or other communication. For example, the interview is a characteristic genre of the order of discourse of the media. Styles or voices are the ways of identifying or constructing the self, both individually and as part of social or institutional identities. Thus there appears to be a particular style of Cornish patriotism that entails bedecking oneself with symbols: tartan ties and caps, St Piran's flags, black and gold articles of clothing and so on. Finally, discourse is never just text, but is also context; there is a broader aspect of social structuration within which or together with which we can place the orders of discourse.

Practically, this all means that communicative events have three levels of analysis – the text, the discursive practice and the social practice. Analysis might proceed along all three levels. For example, in 2004 Cornwall Arts Marketing (partly funded by Objective One money) collaborated with the *Guardian* newspaper to produce a special supplement on 'Cornwall's creative scene', actually its artistic sector. This put forward a discourse of artistic culture in Cornwall, attempting to promote this culture as a dynamic aspect; 'artists have the potential to be an economic engine of Cornwall's future'.[17] The supplement – the communicative event – might be analysed in a number of ways.

First, we could focus on the way it uses language, the grammar and metaphors it employs, the sentences it constructs. At the level of the text we could, for example, investigate transitivity, how events are connected. Does

---

16 Norman Fairclough, Simon Pardoe and Bronislaw Szerszynski, 'Critical discourse analysis and citizenship', in A. Bora and H. Hausendorf (eds) *Constructing Citizenship* (Amsterdam: John Benjamins, 2003).

17 *The Guardian*, 'Living on the Edge', June 12 2004, p.13.

the document use passive or active forms of sentences, does it mask agency? Thus it is stated that artists are 'struggling to work in a county with soaring property prices'.[18] Soaring property prices appear to be a natural event with no obvious cause, a bit like the weather. By nominalising the phrase 'soaring property prices', no agent is directly implicated in the process. Yet rising prices are separated textually from mention of the 'increasingly affluent visitors who now see Cornwall as a fashionable holiday destination'.[19] The agency of those visitors who then decide to use their greater economic resources to buy property in Cornwall is thus masked and the indirect role of cultural tourism in generating higher property prices also rendered indistinct and unavailable for discussion.[20] Or we could probe its modality; the degree of affiliation there is to statements made. Are claims made as if they are expressions of the truth or is there some hedging? Discussing surfing culture a gallery owner in Newquay claims 'it really is laid back down here'.[21] This is a statement made in the form of a truth claim, asserting the laid-backness of Cornwall, rather than expressing this more tentatively, as by saying 'sometimes we can begin to believe it's really laid back down here'.

Second, we could focus on its discursive practice, on the origins of the assumptions and ideas in it, on the processes of its production and consumption, on its links to other discourses, such as the discourse of 'neo-liberalism' or 'Cornwall as English county'. The 'down here' phrase used by the gallery owner betrays a naturalised and taken-for-granted view of Cornwall as periphery, as somewhere 'on the edge', as does the very title of the supplement. Other discourses interact and inform the 'artistic culture' discourse. For example, the Principal of Falmouth College of Art is quoted as saying 'the current debate requires institutions to connect with this really strong tradition of cultural activity'.[22] This statement would seem to bring the artistic discourse close to the demands of the campaigners for a Cornish Assembly. However, the same interviewee is also quoted elsewhere as saying 'the south-west region has more arts practitioners per head than any other part of Britain apart from London, and within that region Cornwall is the hotspot'.[23] The 'Cornwall as English county' discourse here combines

---

18 *Guardian*, 2004, p.13.
19 *Guardian*, 2004, p.11.
20 Imagine the different meaning produced if the sentence were constructed actively; 'increasingly affluent visitors now see Cornwall as a fashionable holiday destination and those who buy second homes help make property prices soar'.
21 *Guardian*, 2004, p.14.
22 *Guardian*, 2004, p.11.
23 *Guardian*, 2004, p.10.

with the discourse of 'English regionalization' to put implied constraints on the sort of institutions that Cornwall might require.

In probing the assumptions of the text, gaps could also be identified. The director of Tate St Ives is reported as seeing 'a natural difference between the approach of artists who are drawn to live in the rural south-west of England and that of the ultra-hip art crowd in London'.[24] As well as being replete with discursive modalities – is the London art crowd really 'ultra-hip' – and dominant discourses, for example of 'deep rurality' and 'English regionalization', this phrase also constructs two groups, those who come to live in Cornwall and those who stay in London. In doing so, it ignores a third group, those who were born and/or grew up in Cornwall and choose to stay (or come back to) Cornwall. This is even more striking as in its earlier pages the supplement makes great play of the role of a 'revitalised sense of Cornish identity and pride' and of native-born artists.[25]

Finally, we might identify the social practice to which the artistic discourse belongs, using wider social theory, for example relating to cultural governance or, more generally, to cultural studies theories, that would allow us to relate it to other practices and to other fields. Here, we might be drawn to sociological theories about sub-cultures, or to economic approaches to regeneration and theoretical takes on the relationship between economics and culture, or perhaps political models such as network analysis, that would direct our attention towards the networks of individuals, groups, institutions, quangos and government departments that sustain the arts sector in Cornwall and in the south west of England.

For the critical discourse analyst all texts draw on particular social and institutional practices as different discourses and genres are articulated together. This interdiscursivity, a form of intertextuality (of relying on and being influenced by a chain of already existing texts) provides the space in which change occurs. Discursive transformations happen when combinations of discourses are used creatively and when discourses are articulated in new ways. For example, the South West Regional Development Agency (SWRDA) and the South West Regional Assembly (SWRA) have spent thousands of pounds on a South West England Brand Centre.[26] This body is engaged in discursive work, creating a logo, images, narrative, even a 'tone of voice' for businesses in the 'south west' of England to 'talk the same language and begin a conversation with people

---

24 *Guardian*, 2004, p.13.

25 *Guardian*, 2004, p.3.

26 South West England Brand Centre, 'Welcome to the South West England Brand Centre'; available at http://www.southwestbrand.info. Accessed 23 December 2003.

about the story of the South West England'.[27] In doing so discourses are being knitted together to try to create something new. Thus a 'neo-liberal' discourse of global competitiveness is articulated with a traditional 'tourist industry' discourse and a discourse of regionalization. And other discourses are in turn stitched onto these. For example, the South West England Brand Centre's website informs us sagely that the preferred 'tone of voice' for talking about the south west should be 'plain speech with attitude ... we use (polite) slang expressions like "party on"'.[28] This somewhat desperate effort to combine neo-liberalism with a version of retro-1980s Californian surfer dude discourse also indicates that it is one thing to combine discourses, another thing altogether for the new meanings to become successfully fixed. It is at this point that we would need to turn to social theory to assess the constraints and opportunities for such a newly configured discourse.

In what sense critical?
In the previous example I came close to the 'critical' aspect of CDA. Broadly, CDA has been described as taking up social questions, exploring how changes take place at a micro-level and 'how discourse figures in relation to other social elements in processes of social or institutional change'.[29] It is in what questions are taken up and why that the critical element of CDA enters into things. For CDA aims 'to uncover the role of discursive practice in the maintenance of unequal power relations, with the overall goal of harnessing the results of critical discourse analysis to the struggle for radical social change'.[30] It focuses on those representations and constructions of social groups which have detrimental consequences for those groups, on how these representations are constructed and the role they play in furthering the interests of other groups.[31] In common with other deconstructionist social analysis 'an important discourse analytical aim is to unmask and delineate taken-for-granted, common-sense understandings, transforming them into potential objects for discussion and criticism and, thus, open to change'.[32] Returning to my earlier example, if Cornwall is seen unproblematically as an English county, then this will have consequences for demands for constitutional change and for devolution of

---

27 South West England Brand Centre, 'Tone of Voice Guidelines'; available at http://www.southwestbrand.info/guidelines/tone-of-voice/index. Accessed 23 December 2003.
28 South West England Brand Centre, 'Tone of Voice Guidelines'.
29 Fairclough et al, 'Critical discourse analysis', 2003.
30 Jørgensen and Phillips, *Discourse analysis*, 2002, p.64.
31 Norman Fairclough, 'Global capitalism and critical awareness of language', *Language Awareness* 8 (1999), 71-83.
32 Jørgensen and Phillips, *Discourse analysis*, 2002, p.178.

decision-making to a Cornish level. But if that representation is deconstructed and revealed as a historical construct then it is potentially opened up for discussion and debate.

It is in this sense that CDA is not 'neutral' but is committed to social change through opening up possibilities. Fairclough argues that people have a right to know what insights discourses give them, what insights they are cut off from, whose discourse it is, what they gain (or lose) from its use, what other discourses are available and how dominant discourses have become so dominant.[33] This knowledge makes it easier to manage change, endowing individuals with the potential for greater agency and empowering them as citizens.

However, in taking this stance CDA at times skirts close to the argument that insists that there is a 'truth' out there; thus we are informed that CDA is concerned with 'truth, truthfulness and appropriateness of texts, their production, and their interpretation'.[34] At other times the word 'misrepresentations' is used. At first glance, this does not look to be too far away from approaches such as the ideology critique favoured by Marxist-influenced social theorists of the 1970s. Ideology critique sees language as masking reality. The reality is then revealed by the social researcher, armed with expert knowledge (marxist theory) unavailable to the ordinary person. Social constructionists have heavily criticised this position. According to discourse theory, the elevated observer can only exchange one discourse for another, as the inevitably discursive construction of 'reality' makes the latter unattainable. Adopting this social constructionist stance, it is difficult to see how one construction can be 'truer' than another because there is no point outside discourse from which to evaluate or critique individual discourses. Critics of discourse analysis regularly point to this peril of 'relativism', where there is no single truth, but where all statements are the result of historical and social positioning.

Perhaps a search for the 'truth' is too ambitious an aim. Embracing a degree of relativism, CDA has nevertheless been described as adopting a modified ideology critique, one where discourses are more or less ideological, depending on how far they contribute to relations of domination and give distorted representations of reality.[35] However, access to the truth is not viewed as a (social) scientific privilege. The aim is rather more modest than the definition of truth; as we have seen it is instead to 'denaturalise ... taken-for-granted understandings of reality' and in doing so to expose new

---

33 Fairclough, 'Global capitalism', 1999.
34 Fairclough et al., 'Critical review', 2002.
35 Jørgensen and Phillips, *Discourse analysis*, 2002, p.181.

areas to political debate, one in which any citizen has the right to be involved and to be heard and not just the researcher.[36]

But which discourses and what understandings of reality are we to deconstruct? Taken-for-granted or naturalised discourses, the ones most urgently in need of deconstruction, are exactly those discourses the researcher may not think of as problems. CDA in itself gives little guidance on which discourses are the best candidates for deconstruction, other than those that maintain unequal power relations, which leaves the potential field of research fairly wide open. However, while CDA of itself might not direct us, Cornish Studies can. Concerned with Cornwall and its people, a critical Cornish Studies could, without much difficulty, identify a number of discourses for deconstruction, some of which have already been mentioned here, such as those of 'regionalization', of 'romantic Cornwall', of 'Cornwall as English county'. Other taken-for-granted discourses, such as 'Celtic Cornwall', could also be candidates for deconstruction. Cornish Studies also provides the standpoint from which to critique these discourses. This is unmistakeably a critique from the periphery.

It is feminist research that here comes tantalisingly close to Cornish Studies research. Some feminists have argued that, as women are an overlooked group, their peripheral position viz-a-viz an androcentric centre means that their research is bound to be normative, criticising that which oppresses women. This has led to the emergence of feminist standpoint theory.[37] From this perspective women's experiences, to a degree outside or peripheral to that society, provide the standpoint from which to research a patriarchal society. In parallel, it has been proposed that 'ethnic minorities' can also 'on the basis of experience, deliver standpoints from which the dominant understandings can be identified and criticised'.[38]

This sounds familiar to those of us working in the Cornish Studies field, where otherwise naturalised discourses, such as those of 'English regionalization' or 'English nationalism', automatically present themselves as problems. However, Jørgensen and Phillips point out that standpoint theory comes with its own health warnings.[39] One is that it constructs the world in terms of an us and them, in the process homogenising the oppressed group and underplaying differences among that group. This is exactly the aspect of Cornish Studies that I have already indicated we need consciously to move away from, from an over-determined 'Cornwall' to a

---

36 Jørgensen and Phillips, *Discourse analysis*, 2002, p.185.
37 Dorothy Smith, *The everyday world as problematic: a feminist sociology* (Toronto: University of Toronto Press, 1987).
38 Jørgensen and Phillips, *Discourse analysis*, 2002, p.192.
39 Jørgensen and Phillips, *Discourse analysis*, 2002, pp.192-93.

sensitivity towards differing 'Cornwalls'.[40] The distinction between a them and an us also requires resisting as it can reproduce the naturalised distinctions of the centre and other simplistic categories of dominant discourses (categorization clearly evident in the occasional Cornish versus English bunfights that break out in the letters pages of the local press – exhilarating in their way but doing little to move debate beyond stereotyped ethnic battle lines).[41]

Standpoint theory, research from a situated position to some extent outside structures of domination, provides the Cornish Studies researcher with a position from which to view the world critically. But this healthy scepticism towards the taken-for-granted discourses of the metropolitan centre needs to be coupled with a strong reflexivity, an awareness of our own cultural and social location. Furthermore, it should not prevent us trying to work across difference. For instance, research on the discourse of Englishness and its consequences in constructing Cornishness should not be confined to the external. It would have to embrace the Englishness within Cornishness and the Englishness within all of us (to some degree). For a discourse of Cornishness has clearly overlapped, sometimes considerably, with a discourse of Englishness, an under-stressed, yet central, aspect of the Cornish identity in terms of understanding its difference from other British identities. CDA, however, can allow us to isolate the role of discursive practice, denaturalise the moments and articulations of that discourse, uncover the processes that determine its meaning and as a result empower individuals by yielding knowledge which opens up the space for discussion. In Cornwall such space often appears especially constricted and stifled as a result of the lack of a critical public domain and the institutional vacuum that allows taken-for-granted discourses to thrive in unquestioned luxury.

CDA method and its problems
Moving from the level of principle to that of practice, how do we actually go about CDA? The challenge of CDA research is to 'analyse empirically the many ways in which [a discourse] is constituted, reproduced and modified within the very process of communication'.[42] Through an iterative

---

40 Deacon, 'New Cornish Studies', 2002. For an example of work within the Cornish Studies field that shows this sensitivity see Amy Hale Amy Hale, 'Whose Celtic Cornwall? The ethnic Cornish meet Celtic spirituality', and Alan Kent, 'Celtic nirvanas: constructions of Celtic in contemporary British youth culture' in David Harvey, Rhys Jones, Neil McInroy and Christine Milligan, *Celtic geographies: old culture, new times* (London: Routledge, 2002), 157-70 and 208-26.

41 See for example *West Briton,* 13 May, 20 May, 27 May 2004.

42 Fairclough et.al., 'Critical discourse analysis', 2003.

analysis, moving between linguistic analysis and wider social theory, the aim is to 'find out how the world (or aspects of it) is ascribed meaning discursively and what social consequences this has'.[43]

To do this CDA imports a method of explanatory critique from critical realism.[44] This posits four stages. The first is to identify a problem, for example this could be the process of top-down regionalization that defines the space open to Cornish decision-making. The second stage is to identify the network of social practices that gives rise to this. This would involve isolating the peak regional institutions (such as Government Office South West, SWRDA and the SWRA) and identifying the discourse of regionalization and of Cornwall that is reproduced within those institutions.[45] Third, we can consider whether the problem sustains the system and in what ways. Who gains from the process of regionalization? Finally, the researcher identifies the possibilities of overcoming the problem. In traversing these four stages the researcher moves between linguistic analysis of texts, their production and reception, social theory relevant to their context and the institutional practices that give rise to them.

There are, of course, weaknesses associated with CDA, just as there are with any form of social theory, areas under-conceptualised, gaps unaddressed. For example, the distinction between discursive and non-discursive practices, the way they connect and the way we differentiate between them remains somewhat unclear in practice. CDA also stands accused of a weak understanding of group formation and agency.[46] In relation to this, although CDA directs attention to research on both the production and consumption of texts, the weight of research has in fact tended to be placed on the production of texts, rather than their consumption. And yet, in consuming texts, agents always have the possibility of re-negotiating, to a degree, the meanings of discourses. An analysis that avoids this potential re-negotiation remains in danger of adopting an over-structural approach to discourse.

Conclusion

Fairclough has claimed that everyday life has become more textually mediated and that people's lives are increasingly shaped by representations

---

43 Jørgensen and Phillips, *Discourse analysis*, 2002, p.145.

44 For critical realism see Andrew Collier, *Critical Realism: An Introduction to Roy Bhaskar's Philosophy*, (London: Verso, 1994).

45 For a preliminary analysis of the role of the peak institutions of the new regionalization see Bernard Deacon, 'Under construction: culture and regional formation in south-west England', *European Urban and Regional Studies* 11 (2004), 213-25.

46 Jørgensen and Phillips, *Discourse analysis*, 2002, p.90.

produced elsewhere, affecting 'even who they are and how they [should] see themselves'.[47] While now generalised, this is a familiar process for Cornwall and its people. From the rebellious periphery of the sixteenth century through the super-loyal royalism of the later seventeenth century, the West Barbary of the eighteenth, the representations of the Newlyn School of the late nineteenth and the tourist business-induced imagery and romantic novelists of the twentieth century, Cornwall has been awash with metaphors and buffeted by a veritable storm of signifiers. Both Cornwall and the Cornish people have been and are being discursively constructed in a number of often conflicting ways. The result is a confusing kaleidoscope through which 'real' Cornwalls can be glimpsed only hazily and intermittently.

However, this storm of discursive constructions makes Cornwall particularly suitable for the application of CDA, which could be employed both to deconstruct historical representations and narratives and contemporary discourses of Cornwall. It could also generate reflection on some of our own foundational myths, opening up the space for discussion of alternatives. Moreover, in terms of the content of a Cornish Studies research agenda, its implications are profound. For, if discourses are produced elsewhere then that 'elsewhere' has also to enter the frame of analysis. This demands that researchers raise their sights beyond Cornwall while, at the same time remain sensitive to differences within it. Furthermore, in its call for a dialectic between detailed textual analysis and social theory, CDA would appear to meet the multidisciplinary or multiperspectival aims of the 'new' Cornish Studies, as well as those I have previously offered in *Cornish Studies Ten*. CDA could thus act as a unifying approach for a critical Cornish Studies, bringing the rhetoric of the 'new' Cornish Studies together with a critical practice and providing a methodology to match its preferred content.

Postscript

Two years on from my assessment of the 'New Cornish Studies', I was clearly becoming frustrated and disenchanted by the pick and mix practice of Cornish Studies and on the lookout for an overarching methodology that could provide a core for Cornish Studies. Influenced, perhaps over-influenced, at the time by post-structuralist approaches and the fashionable issue of postmodernity and its discontents, I stumbled across critical discourse analysis. This method looked attractive for two reasons. First, it adopted a transparently critical approach to power relationships and a commitment to deconstruct the taken-for-granted assumptions that underpin those relationships, thus opening them up to potential transformation.

47 Fairclough, 'Global capitalism', 1999.

Second, its combination of linguistic and social analysis seemed to provide a balance between those approaches. Taken together, this appeared to offer an opportunity to uncover the discursive chains that bound the Cornish people and linked them to structures of subjugation, a necessary first step before their unshackling.

Unusually, there was an almost immediate critical response to the appearance of this essay in the following issue of *Cornish Studies*. Malcolm Williams made a robust case there for realism and for a methodological pluralism, resisting my attempt to straitjacket Cornish Studies within a specific method.[48] Although Malcolm perhaps overdrew our differences, which on reflection look more like differences of emphasis rather than substance, this was a very fair criticism. With hindsight I was leaning too far in a social constructivist direction.

At another level the call for an explicitly critical Cornish Studies was probably hopelessly unrealistic and a step too far, coming up against entrenched institutions and structural (as well as discursive) constraints. It was unlikely to sit that easily within an institutionalised Cornish Studies funded by an external agency and (decreasingly so) by Cornwall Council. Moreover, it would have have proved far too threatening to various elite actors both inside Cornwall and further afield, already deeply suspicious of a Cornish Studies informed by social theory. A wide-ranging network of elites whose careers and livelihoods were invested in the retention and extension of taken-for-granted discourses of Cornwall and, one might add, its ongoing de-facto colonial status, would hardly have welcomed a critical Cornish Studies with open arms.

Although critical discourse analysis has not been explicitly deployed as a central method of Cornish Studies, mentions of discourse have become two a penny since the above article was penned in 2004. As we shall discover in the next chapter, the various deconstructions of stereotypes that have appeared over the past decade and more have done much to open up dominant stereotypes to discussion. Although much has been done however, to echo a favourite phrase of our political class, much still needs to be done.

---

48 Malcolm Williams, 'Discourse and social science in Cornish Studies – a reply to Bernard Deacon', in Philip Payton (ed.), *Cornish Studies Thirteen* (Exeter: University of Exeter Press, 2005), 14-22.

Chapter 4

Cornish Studies and Cornish studies: the state of the field

The New Cornish Studies project was born out of a desire to study Cornwall via interdisciplinary, comparative and applied approaches. In its early guise, in the 1990s, the focus was on Cornwall's difference and its distinct identity. To this was added a concern for spatiality and hybridity in the 2000s.[1] These overlapping phases were soldered together in a normative project that asserted the importance of studying Cornwall and the Cornish in their own right rather than as case studies for other academic questions. Of course, working out from a Cornish standpoint might itself end up illuminating wider issues and problems just as much as working in from those problems. In that sense Cornish Studies with a capital S finds itself blurring into Cornish studies with a lower case s. Indeed, is it still fruitful to distinguish between studies of Cornwall that adopt the place as a case study (lower case Cornish studies) from studies of Cornwall that start with the aim of better understanding Cornwall, its society, its past and its people (upper case Cornish Studies)?

In the early to mid 2000s there was a move by those of us at the core of the Cornish Studies project to develop an overarching Cornish Studies methodology. A diffuse drive for a Cornish Studies unified theory lay behind the three articles generated in the early 2000s and reproduced above. Calls for sensitivity to scale and hybridity, the study of representations via discourse analysis and a combination of reconstructive and deconstructive techniques were part of an inchoate wish to carve out a new and distinct methodology for the field. This would finally escape a traditional Celtic Studies paradigm that, like British Studies, had little space for a Cornwall limited to its margins. Methodology, rather than content, would establish Cornish Studies as distinct from, although sharing the concerns of, cognate area studies such as Welsh or Irish Studies. The brief flirtation with New Celtic Studies at the turn of the millennium was a more ambitious version of this, but failed to develop after an initial flurry of interest.[2] Peppering the

---

1   For the evolving project see Philip Payton, Introductions to *Cornish Studies*, second series (Exeter: University of Exeter Press, 1993-2013).

2   Amy Hale and Philip Payton (eds), *New Directions in Celtic Studies* (Exeter, University of Exeter Press, 2000); *Celtic Geographies: Old Culture, New Times*, ed. by David C. Harvey, Rhys Jones, Neil McInroy and Christine Milligan (London: Routledge, 2002). For a partial revival of this project from

early 2000s, these methodological speculations, in themselves a somewhat novel departure in the context of Cornish Studies, should however be seen more as provocations designed to stimulate a debate about the form and the future of the academic field described as Cornish Studies. Predictably, criticisms of this tentative quest to underpin Cornish Studies with a more explicit and distinct methodology were not slow to appear.

First, there were those who favoured methodological pluralism and bridled at the implication that one methodology should be prioritised. Malcolm Williams put forward a strong case for a pluralist but 'objective' scientific methodology. This rests on a realist ontology that accepts that research can produce partial truths. For him, to be relevant, Cornish Studies had to be able 'to describe what contemporary Cornwall is like and to understand what people in Cornwall think'.[3] Description could involve the reconstruction of the structures within which social actors operate. Understanding might introduce a deconstruction of the discourses with which those actors make sense of the world.

The second reaction was more radical. Alan Kent proposed that Cornish Studies needed to go further than cutting and pasting assorted methods from wider academic fields. Instead, it should establish 'new methodologies' better fitting Cornish experience than those offered by traditional Anglocentric scholarship.[4] This agenda would in turn be viewed as wildly impractical by a third, diametrically opposed line of criticism that saw even the more modest provocations appearing in the *Cornish Studies* series as over-ambitious. Colin Williams argued that the agenda of Cornish Studies, a normative or ideological project 'searching for group recognition and collective self-realization' was over-ambitious and unattainable. He was uneasy at desires 'to redress past injustices, to expose historical discrimination, the slighted "national" character of the Cornish and the

---

a different perspective see Marion Gibson, Shelley Trower and Garry Tregidga (eds), *Mysticism, Myth and Celtic Identity* (Abingdon: Routledge, 2013).

3   Malcolm Williams, 'The New Cornish Social Science', in Philip Payton (ed.), *Cornish Studies Ten* (Exeter, University of Exeter Press, 2002), 44-66 (p.61) and 'Discourse and Social Science in Cornish Studies – A reply to Bernard Deacon', in Philip Payton (ed.), *Cornish Studies Thirteen* (Exeter: University of Exeter Press, 2005), 14-22.

4   Alan M. Kent, 'Scatting it t'lerrups: Provisional notes towards alternative methodologies in language and literary studies in Cornwall', in Philip Payton (ed.), *Cornish Studies Thirteen* (Exeter, University of Exeter Press, 2005), 23-52. For an example see Alan M. Kent, *Towards a Cornish Philosophy: Values, Thought and Language for the West Britons in the Twenty-First Century* (Cathair na Mart: Evertype, 2013).

unfulfilled potential of a co-equal Celtic nation' that he detected lying behind the efforts of Cornish Studies practitioners.[5]

In Colin Williams' opinion, this agenda was difficult, if not impossible, to combine with the 'evidence-based scholarship' that was essential to deepen links to civil society and government or appeal to funders in (unstated) narrow, neo-liberal policy-making contexts. He had a point. Potential contradictions between the normative commitment of the Cornish Studies project and the claimed 'objectivity' of academic research bedevilled the stated aim of the New Cornish Studies to be more applied and fed the suspicions of political and economic elites in Cornwall.

Nevertheless, for most of those researching aspects of Cornwall's society or history, such concerns were irrelevant. Measured by the number of doctorates and articles in academic journals, the output of what might broadly be described as studies of Cornwall has surged over the past decade and a half. Almost 50 doctoral theses have focused on aspects of Cornwall since 2002, the majority of these appearing in the past eight years. Around two thirds to three quarters of them make reference of the work of Cornish Studies scholars, and around ten of them might be described as explicit works of Cornish Studies.

Similar reference to the core body of Cornish Studies work is less prevalent in the journal literature. However, even here over 40% of the 60 or so articles on Cornwall published in the humanities and social sciences since 2003 have made explicit reference to Cornish Studies work. More tellingly, this proportion rose from 30% in the six years from 2003 to 2009 to 50% in the seven years from 2010 to 2016. Cornish Studies is certainly far from being ignored by the 'mainstream' academy, although some disciplines and sub-disciplines are noticeably more likely to acknowledge its output than others.

But how far does the corpus of new work on Cornwall reflect those methodological provocations of the early 2000s? The remainder of this article takes us on a journey through the recent journal and thesis literature, providing a critical review of the state of Cornish Studies and studies. (The focus is here on the less accessible doctorates and articles in academic journals rather than the core output of the *Cornish Studies* series edited by Philip Payton). At the conclusion I'll return to the question of a discrete Cornish Studies methodology and briefly reflect on what lessons, if any, the recent literature might hold for the direction of Cornish Studies as a distinct academic field.

---

5   Colin H. Williams, 'On ideology, identity and integrity', in Payton (ed.), *Cornish Studies Ten*, 2002), 67-79 (p.67). Malcolm Williams also described Cornish Studies as a 'politicized discipline' in 'New Cornish Social Science', 2002, p. 48.

Landscapes of Cornwall

Landscape is a concept that attracted increasing attention in cultural geography in the 1990s before spreading to the other social sciences, history and literary studies.[6] It also has the advantage of resonating with everyday life with, in the Cornish context, a particularly salient place in the tourist gaze. The growing pull of the concept may be seen for example in the renewed interest in the life and work of Peter Lanyon, the Cornish artist.[7] Lanyon's work, breaking down notions of the solid and the fluid, with an emphasis on lived experience and the connections between embodiment and landscape, prefigured a more fluid and hybrid approach to Cornwall that has now become the norm. Connections between visions and experience, between material culture and representations of it, between insiders and outsiders, weave their inescapable threads through this consensus approach. For example, Ella Westland echoes them in her study of D.H.Lawrence's fraught time in Cornwall from 1915 to 1917. Lawrence struggled to reconcile his 'Celticized vision' woven from the ideological web of Edwardian constructions of Cornwall, with his experience, one that Westland argues actually had more in common with the locals than we might expect.[8]

The difficulties Lawrence encountered when setting his image of Cornwall against the more mundane realities of everyday life and the identity of its inhabitants alert us to a critical distinction that underlies the cultural landscapes of Cornwall. On the one hand we have a regional image, a set of representations of Cornwall (and its people) mainly produced and reproduced outside Cornwall. On the other there is a regional, Cornish identity, reproduced in the main inside Cornwall. It is essential to distinguish between these, although both combine to produce an identity of Cornwall (as opposed to a Cornish identity).[9]

Some research projects tend to conflate and confuse these two facets. In the 2000s the interest in cultural landscapes and the relationships between

---

6   Stephen Daniels, *Fields of Vision: Landscape Imagery and National Identity in England and the United States* (Cambridge: Polity, 1993); Simon Schama, *Landscape and Memory* (London: HarperCollins, 1995).

7   M. E. Parish, 'Peter Lanyon: A Life Geographic' (unpublished doctoral thesis, University of Plymouth, 2011); Anthony Wallersteiner, 'A Cornish palimpsest: Peter Lanyon and the construction of a new landscape, 1938-1964' (unpublished doctoral thesis, University of Kent, 2000).

8   Ella Westland, 'D.H.Lawrence's Cornwall: dwelling in a precarious age', *Cultural Geographies* 9 (2002), 266-285.

9   For this distinction I am indebted to the work of Anssi Paasi. See in particular his 'The institutionalization of regions: a theoretical framework for understanding the emergence of regions and the constitution of regional identity', *Fennia* 164 (1986), 105-146.

place and community was recognised when the Arts and Humanities Research Council funded a major research enquiry into 'Mysticism, myth and Celtic identity: a case study of Cornwall'. Concentrating on 'literary and performative work' since the eighteenth century, the project turned its eye towards the Cornish landscape and its relationship to 'nationalism'. However, this particular academic gaze was beset by a number of contradictions, not the least of which was a failure to differentiate clearly between the image of Cornwall and the identity of its people. Moreover, building on that post-millennial turn to hybridity, the researchers were exercised by, or perhaps I should put this more forcefully, fascinated with or even obsessed by, notions of liminality, uncertainty, contestation, malleability, fluidity, gaps and absences. Instead of power geometries or structures of institutional inertia, it saw mystical and mythic discourses. In such an ambiguous context, generalisations are of necessity few and far between. Those working on the project claimed that words such as 'Cornish' or 'English' were 'signifiers without clear signified, names without self-evident tribes, let alone nations'.[10]

Things are rarely so clear cut as they might appear. Yet, however carefully qualified, adopting 'mysticism' as a central concept brings with it an unavoidable air of spiritual intangibility. 'Spectral topographies' may well help produce cultural objects, but those objects seem insubstantial when set in a context of concern for the mystical. Furthermore, the contributors and editors of the collected essays in *Mysticism, Myth and Celtic Identity* straddled an uncomfortable gap of their own – that between deconstructing the temporally specific and culturally produced myths that underpin identities on the one hand and on the other diminishing and, by implication, demeaning the beliefs and self-identities of those who are committed to the 'myths' being examined. Pointing out the 'fictive' character of Celtic nationalism runs the risk of looking like an attack on the confidence it might give rise to or the hopes and dreams its proponents hold. Trembling under such an academic gaze, those being gazed at could be forgiven for thinking everything solid has melted into air, or assuming their identities have been erased, leaving ... what?

While allowed, even encouraged, to question popular assumptions about Celticity, these and similar academic gazes on Cornwall usually stop decidedly short of analysing their own representations. The myths subscribed to by the media, politicians, bureaucrats, developers, fellow-academics and others are tellingly rarely discussed under the umbrella category of 'mysticism'. Yet a commitment to traditional stereotypes of Cornwall or a boundless faith in the tenets of neo-liberalism could be seen as just as spiritual as beliefs in Celtic Cornwall. While deconstruction of

---

10   Gibson et al., *Mysticism*, 2013, p. 16.

potential ideologies of resistance or emancipation can proceed, ideologies of dominance or exploitation remain taken-for-granted. This is of course the classic sign of a successful ideology, unrecognised as ideological. So this particular academic genre is not speaking truth to power, which in any case doesn't particularly want to hear it, but to the powerless.

Linking Cornwall to concepts such as mysticism or myth, then bracketing these with Celtic nationalism, serves two convenient functions. First, it renders Celtic (and Cornish) identities relatively harmless, relegated to a second-order, spiritual, other-worldly realm. Second, it mystifies a project that elites both inside and outside Cornwall have been vigorously pursuing, either wittingly or unwittingly, since the 1990s. Let me explain. The mystical Cornwall paradigm enjoys its frisson of excitement by dabbling with ideas of ghosts and haunting, which are claimed to have a special place in Cornish life. Others might point out that, if textual haunting means 'an unsettling presence which is often marginal, off the page, or under erasure',[11] then Cornwall is more obviously haunted by another unsettling presence. This is the transformation of its material and cultural landscapes since the 1960s. Transformation is perhaps too neutral a term. It removes agency from the equation, feeding a perspective that views this transition, involving a rupture with 'traditional' Cornwall, as natural, even benign, certainly something we are powerless to resist, an inevitable part of the progress to 'modernity'. It might be more appropriately called re-engineering, which has the advantage of re-inserting agency into the process. The project, one we might term Lifestyle Cornwall, serves the purposes of various socio-economic groups. It involves the growing commodification of Cornwall and its culture, major demographic change, a preferred economic phantasm that privileges catering for visitors and the continued imposition of a narrow set of old stereotypical representations of place and people.

The driving forces and the precise reproductive mechanisms of this particular haunting seem invisible to the metropolitan academic gaze, one that adopts a 'prospect' vantage point, overlooking Cornwall from a distance. Yet they have begun to receive attention from Cornish Studies scholars who have been chipping away at the edifice of the Lifestyle Cornwall project. As we shall see below, some over the past decade have stepped beyond the narrow limits of prevailing paradigms to deconstruct the myths and stereotypes of 'opinion-formers' and decision-makers and contrast them with the presence of alternative insider discourses of place.

Even studies of Cornwall undertaken from other disciplinary perspectives can hardly fail to avoid a fissure running through Cornish

---

11   Jo Esra, 'Cornish Crusaders and Barbary captives: returns and transformations',
      in Gibson et al., *Mysticism*, 2013, 155-170 (p. 156).

society, hardly visible at some times, gaping widely at others. For example, Jane Bailey and Iain Briggs used 'deep mapping', an arts-orientated action research method, to investigate older adults' perceptions and connections to landscape on the north-eastern edge of Bodmin Moor at St Breward and Blisland. The 'first theme' they encountered was the 'differentiation and degree of tension between "locals" and "incomers"' which was an issue of 'particular potency'.[12] More centrally concerned with collective discourses of regional identity and the way they influence spatial narratives is Joni Vainikka's case study of civic organisations in Cornwall and Devon, comparing them with similar voluntary sector organisations in Finland. Vainikka discovers a difference between Cornwall - constructed as an 'absorbed region' - and Devon, an 'archetypal region'. But he also notes a 'radical difference ... between the Cornish by origin and incomers'. The latter were more cautious about claiming a regional identity, not feeling entitled to do so, thus weakening the sense of an inclusive regional community in Cornwall.[13]

Jasper Knight and Stephan Harrison, on the other hand, gloss over any such tensions in arguing for a strong relationship between geomorphology and cultural heritage, again using Bodmin Moor (along with West Penwith) as examples.[14] While adopting a somewhat superficial definition of heritage, they suggest that over time in Cornwall there has been a 'conscious or deliberate move towards the memorialization of iconic landscapes' as heritage. Echoing the conclusion of Cornish Studies practitioners, they suggest an 'ongoing narrative' of 'reinvention, rediscovery and reimagining' has made Cornwall and its people distinct. But this discursive change had a material context in the economic role of Cornwall's geology, which produced its former industries of mining and quarrying.

Shelley Trower approaches the relationship between geology and people from a literary perspective. In her book *Rocks of Nation*, she argues that the geology of Cornwall affected ideas of Cornwall as a nation. It did this in two ways, through producing the material basis for an economy that encouraged a 'proto-nationalism' in the nineteenth century with an emphasis on Cornish 'difference' and, metaphorically, by linking ideas of 'primitive' rocks to a 'primitive' race. She goes on to claim that literary

---

12 Jane Bailey and Iain Briggs, '"Either side of Delphy Bridge": A deep mapping project evoking and engaging the lives of older adults in rural North Cornwall', *Journal of Rural Studies* 28 (2012), 318-328.

13 Joni T.Vainikka, 'Reflexive identity narratives and regional legacies', *Tijdschrift voor Economische en Sociale Geografie* 106 (2015), 521-535.

14 Jasper Knight and Stephan Harrison, '"A land history of men": The intersection of geomorphology, culture and heritage in Cornwall, southwest England', *Applied Geography* 42 (2013), 186-194.

representations of Cornwall have contributed to a spiritual connection between Cornwall's rocks and feelings of belonging to a 'motherland'. Cornish identity, literally grounded in this way, is however, for Trower, at bottom an example of irrational, blood and soil (or rocks) nationalism. For her, this is a worrying thing. It produces a 'history of racial nationalism' and 'exclusive ethnicity', as well as ideas of difference that lead inevitably to separation, division and exclusiveness as 'the ghostly presence of rocks themselves appear to be actively hostile to non-Celtic strangers'.[15]

Trower's work, and the broader 'mystical' turn it arises from, stems from that modernist suspicion of nationalism that we can trace back to the post-war period in the middle of the twentieth century. She admits that 'derogatory' representations of the Cornish are as unacceptable as ethnic exclusiveness and that all nationalisms have their irrational core. Which they do. But the over-wrought concern with exclusive ethnicity and racial imaginings in Cornwall smothers the possibility that some peripheral nationalisms could be emancipatory. Instead, wittingly or unwittingly, it veers towards effectively undermining all nationalist imaginations. From the 'mystical academic gaze' these are at worst transformed into 'racial' imaginations or at best deconstructed to the point of anodyne harmlessness. While the work of the mystical school has tended to elide nationalism and place identity, from within a Cornish Studies perspective, these are normally treated separately.

Garry Tregidga and Kayleigh Milden for example delve further into contrasts within what Bailey and Briggs described as 'native' identities in their account of the construction of ancestral memories within Cornish families.[16] They suggest a 'vibrant oral tradition' can still be encountered in Cornwall linked to place. But, like Knight and Harrison, they submit this has a material underpinning. A 'plethora of images and competing narratives', with a 'central role [for] buildings, monuments and landscapes in the act of remembering events and personalities' are transmitted within the family. However this chain of 'ancestral memory' is broken and

---

15   Shelley Trower, *Rocks of Nation: The Imagination of Celtic Cornwall* (Manchester: Manchester University Press, 2015), pp. 251, 5 and 228. Academics associated with the University of Exeter seem to have an unfortunate tendency to be over-hasty in impugning the motives of Celtic nationalists. In 2015 Nick Groom wrote that 'disgracefully, the Welsh Nationalists went so far as to send an official delegation to Berlin in 1940'. As Richard Wyn Jones points out this claim is 'wholly baseless' and involves a 'scandalous lack of respect for basic scholarly standards' (Richard Wyn Jones, *The Fascist Party in Wales? Plaid Cymru and the Accusation of Fascism* (Cardiff: University of Wales Press, 2014, p.x)).

16   Garry Tregidga and Kayleigh Milden, '"Before my time": Recreating Cornwall's past through ancestral memory', *Oral History* 36 (2008), 23-32.

fragmented by the impact of migration, which removes families from the mnemonic role of place. They suggest that this break did not just occur as the result of the global Cornish diaspora but can be caused even by short-distance migration.

Tregidga's edited collection, *Memory, Place and Identity: The cultural landscapes of Cornwall* brings together a number of explorations of the significance of cultural memory and its transmission in relation to place.[17] This volume sought explicitly to extend Cornish Studies by engaging with community-based research and includes contributions that range from the Tamar Valley and the Rame peninsula, via Newquay, Truro and the Lizard, down to Mousehole. It provides a more bottom-up, microhistorical and grounded approach to place identities, a corrective to the 'prospect', overarching vantage point adopted by the mystical gaze.

The promise of an oral history approach in potentially responding to Malcolm Williams' call for a greater understanding of what people in Cornwall think has however been slow to appear. The best example appears in Anna Green and Tim Cooper's account of memories of the Torrey Canyon oil spill of 1967. Explicitly noting that hitherto a Cornish Studies perspective has ignored what that incident can reveal about community identity and relations, Green and Cooper investigate its long-term impact and everyday meaning. Their description traces the memories of tensions between centre and periphery in the post-wreck clear-up. During that phase, local hierarchies of knowledge were displaced and devalued by an elite group of external agents. Green and Cooper tease out the way those in coastal communities resisted their subaltern status through the processes of remembering, trickster tale-telling (reminiscent of nineteenth century dialect tales) and black humour. In a richly textured account the authors speculate on the degree to which this incident contributed to the growth of community solidarity and Cornish identity and offer some tantalising insights.[18]

Cultural memory or the 'collective consciousness' was also at the heart of Michael Ireland and Lucy Ellis's study of the role of old black and white photographs in the production of collective meanings in Sennen Cove. They drew a sharp contrast between the value of such photos for second-home owners and the tourist industry and their function in stimulating a sense of place among indigenous 'Covers'. For the latter, the commodification of photos felt like the 'expropriation of once sacred images' which could

---

17   Garry Tregidga (ed.), *Memory, Place and Identity: The Cultural Landscapes of Cornwall* (London: Francis Boutle, 2012).

18   Anna Green and Timothy Cooper, 'Community and exclusion: the Torrey Canyon disaster of 1967', *Journal of Social History* 48 (2015), 892-909.

conversely serve to 'strengthen cultural identity in the face of an acquisitive and consuming phenomenon, which is tourism'.[19]

Landscapes of Cornishness
Whether mystical, microhistorical, metaphorical or material, approaches to Cornwall tend to tiptoe around the issue of the quantity and quality of the Cornish identity in conditions of rapid socio-economic change, as experienced over the past two generations. However, there have been attempts to both quantify the Cornish identity and (more frequently) to describe it. Kerryn Husk undertook a detailed examination of various ethnicity datasets in order to calculate the proportion of those who prefer to adopt a subjective Cornish identification.[20] He concluded that the 6.7% explicitly expressing a Cornish identity in the 2001 Census, via a convoluted and counter-intuitive process of writing in their identity, were the tip of the iceberg and only comprised a minority of this consciously Cornish group. Other datasets routinely pointed to a proportion somewhere around a quarter or more. Unfortunately, the timing of Husk's research precluded an account of the results of the 2011 Census which, even though a Cornish tick-box was still denied, suggested that the proportion of those prepared to claim an explicit Cornish identity in this way had more than doubled over the first decade of the twentieth century. While this might just be a result of the method, more encouragement being given to the write-in option in 2011, a growing number of people expressing a Cornish identity is also strongly suggested by the annual Pupil Level School Census in Cornwall. This reports that the proportion of children self-identifying as Cornish rose steadily from 24% in 2006 to reach 49.5% in 2015.

Although Husk concluded that there was 'not a strong case' for a census tick-box for the Cornish, he proposed a need for continued analysis of the under-researched issue of the socio-economic exclusion of the Cornish in Cornwall relative to the non-Cornish.[21] The current bi-modal distribution of Cornish identifiers he posits from the 2001 Census – clustering around manual workers and those with poorer health on the one hand and a

---

19   Michael Ireland and Lucy Ellis, 'Is the conscience collective black and white?', *Visual Anthropology* 18 (2005), 373-387.

20   Kerryn Husk, 'Ethnic group affiliation and social exclusion in Cornwall; analysis, adjustment and extension of the 2001 England and Wales Census data' (unpublished doctoral thesis, University of Plymouth, 2012).

21   See also Kerryn Husk, 'Ethnicity and Social Exclusion: Research and Policy Implications in a Cornish Case Study', *Social and Public Policy Review* 5 (2011), 7-25 and Kerryn Husk and Alison Green, 'Cornish ethnicity and undercounting: utilising the 2001 England and Wales census to develop an accurate measurement methodology', *Methodological Innovations* 7 (2012), 1-12.

property-owning intelligentsia on the other – could surely be clarified with more explicit census data that might allow for sophisticated cross-tabulation. This could in turn enable more research into the process of gentrification by an in-migratory professional middle class elite.

Empirical work by Stuart Burley demonstrates how, while much in-migration to Cornwall displays 'low levels of economic dynamism', the proportion of in-migrants in the top socio-economic occupations is also 'far higher' than that of non-migrants. His valuable research into the character of the large counter-urban migration streams that have been ongoing since the 1960s is reinforced by Katarzyna Kowalczuk.[22] She suggests late career migrants to Cornwall are part of a 'retirement transition' or 'lifestyle migration', in the process supporting the common-sense assumption that tourism is a key factor in environmental migration to Cornwall. In-migrant flows have been greatest to rural areas, where in 2001 half the residents had moved to Cornwall since 1966.[23] As half of those migrants in turn were in the highest, professional/managerial social class bracket, this has, she argues, resulted in 'growing inequalities' and a 'social polarisation' since the 1960s.

In an important paper linked to his quantitative research Husk joins with Malcolm Williams to note the role of external elites in the legitimation (or lack of it) of the Cornish identity.[24] They identify that familiar dichotomy between the internal identity and external representations. The former has strengthened over the recent past, driven by the activities of cultural entrepreneurs and material factors of industrial decline and economic disadvantage. In combination these produced a merging of formerly separate Celtic and industrial discourses of identity after a crisis of identity that they argue occurred in the 1970s and 1980s. However, while the 'ethno-cultural-political movement' of Cornishness has enjoyed greater internal legitimacy and visibility, popular media representations continue to be 'clichéd and self-deprecating', presenting an idealistic image of a 'romantic environmental beauty and bucolic backwardness'. Such an image, it might be added, is increasingly at odds with the reality of a Cornwall that since the

---

22 Stuart Burley, 'Migration and economy in Cornwall' (unpublished doctoral thesis, University of Plymouth, 2007); Katarzyna Kowalczuk, 'Population growth in a high amenity area: Migration and socio-economic change in Cornwall' (unpublished doctoral thesis, University of Plymouth, 2010). These studies of Cornwall's in-migrants extend the pioneering research of Ronald Perry in the 1980s in Ronald Perry, Ken Dean and Bryan Brown, *Counterurbanisation: International Case studies of Socio-Economic Change in Rural Areas* (Norwich: Geo Books, 1986).
23 Kowalczuk, 'Population growth', 2010, p. 269.
24 Kerryn Husk and Malcolm Williams, 'The Legitimation of Ethnicity: The Case of the Cornish', *Studies in Ethnicity and Nationalism* 12 (2012), 249-267.

1960s has been growing, in terms of population and built environment, at a rate two to three times faster than most other parts of the UK.

While the outcome of the struggle between an imposed categorization and a resistant categorization rests on issues of inter-group power, Husk and Williams come up with a further, under-played insight. This concerns the character of the internal Cornish identity. They note that, among the young, Cornish identity is increasingly symbolic, stripped of its familiar material contours by the process of economic change. Husk and Williams' observation adds the issue of quality to that of quantity in descriptions and analysis of the Cornish identity.[25] External commentators are apt to miss a phenomenon that appears unmissable to an older generation of insiders. The decline of some older cultural practices associated with Cornishness - traditional industries, chapel-going and the like - can produce the unnerving sense of being part of a last generation, belying claims for a vigorous and revived cultural identity, instead stimulating an end-of-Cornwall rhetoric.

Overall, recent years have witnessed a growing literature on the nature of identity in Cornwall. This has subjected both subaltern identities of Cornishness and elite imageries of Cornwall to critical analysis and greatly advanced the early work of the New Cornish Studies on the Cornish identity, going beyond simple contrasts to investigate slippages and fractures within identity discourses.

In an important intervention that fizzes with ideas, Neil Kennedy brings an insider perspective to the identity shift of recent years.[26] He addresses the possibility of discovering 'usable cultures', ones that can be relevant to a beleaguered sense of residual Cornishness, devalued and more usually ignored in academic analyses of the Cornish identity. Kennedy offers a sophisticated and nuanced understanding, borrowing Bourdieu's concept of habitus, in which he includes a constellation of dispositions, shared knowledges and tacit understandings. These, he submits, make up a 'Proper

---

25   Robert Dickinson's empirically based and qualitative comparison of the contemporary Cornish identity in east and west Cornwall makes a valuable contribution to Cornish Studies scholarship on this issue - see Robert Dickinson, 'Meanings of Cornishness: A study of contemporary Cornish identity', in Philip Payton (ed.), *Cornish Studies Eighteen* (Exeter: University of Exeter Press, 2010), 70-100. See also Garry Tregidga and Lucy Ellis, 'Talking identity: understanding Cornwall's oral culture through group dialogue', in Philip Payton (ed.), *Cornish Studies Twelve* (Exeter: University of Exeter Press, 2010), 88-105 and Garry Tregidga (ed.), *Narratives of the Family: Kinship and Identity in Cornwall* (Redruth: Cornwall Centre, 2009).

26   Neil Kennedy, 'Employing Cornish Cultures for Community Resilience' (doctoral thesis, University of Exeter, 2013). This is published as *Cornish Solidarity: Using Culture to Strengthen Communities* (Portlaoise: Evertype, 2016).

Cornish' habitus. In this the traditional emphasis on cultural practice and symbols is attenuated, becoming less important than personnel, attitudes, emotions and feelings induced by context.

Kennedy qualifies simple notions of an undynamic traditional or residual Cornishness, as well as that unproblematic blending or merging of popular or working class Cornish culture with revivalist culture proposed by Husk and Williams.[27] He dates a period of 'classic Cornishness' to the nineteenth century and first half of the twentieth. Challenging concepts of fossilisation or paralysis that gained influence in the 1990s, Kennedy suggests that classic Cornishness retained a level of dynamism, while reproducing democratic manners and tastes with some resemblance to working class communities in the industrial English north and Welsh south. This reassessment of classic Cornishness is supported by Susan Skinner's work on male voice choirs.[28] She discovers a post World War One 'revitalisation' of cultural life and identity and then another burst of creativity following World War Two in the 1950s, which decade was a 'golden age' for male voice choirs in Cornwall. The rather rapid atrophying of the choral tradition took place from the 1970s and by the 1990s Cornish male voice choirs had become 'neither working class nor middle class, but a retired class'. Although even here in this aspect of traditional Cornishness, she detects a renaissance in the 2000s.

Male voice choirs were not shaping a new, more confident sense of Cornish identity. But other components of classic Cornishness can, and did. Sport, in the form of rugby union for example, bridged the period between the classic Cornishness of modernity and Kennedy's 'Proper Cornishness' of postmodernity. Dilwyn Porter contrasts the role of rugby in the late twentieth century with the distinct pre-industrial sports of hurling and wrestling. While the latter were reduced to limited performances of Cornishness, in effect becoming heritage sports, rugby, he argues, had a capacity to project Cornish identity onto a wider stage in the 1980s and 1990s. However, by the turn of the century, this capacity was beginning to fade as the result of changes in English rugby, notably professionalization and commercialism. He also reminds us of the paradoxical relationship with

---

27   The idea of a mix of Celtic and industrial cultures became a staple of the Cornish Studies literature at the end of the last century. See Bernard Deacon and Philip Payton, 'Re-inventing Cornwall: Culture change on the European periphery', in Philip Payton (ed.), *Cornish Studies One*, (Exeter: University of Exeter Press, 1993), 62-79; Amy Hale, 'Representing the Cornish: contesting heritage interpretation in Cornwall', *Tourist Studies* 1 (2001), 185-196.

28   Susan Skinner, 'A history of the Cornish male voice choir: the relationship between music, place and culture' (unpublished doctoral thesis, University of Plymouth, 2013).

England that persisted even at the high point of rugby fever, ultimately containing Cornwall within a 'county' championship framework.[29]

With the exception of rugby, since the 1950s, as its material props were removed, classic Cornishness became a residual set of practices confined to a shrinking elderly demographic. This accompanied growing themes of loss and narratives of historic victimhood, together with an everyday sense of 'marginalization, exclusion and embattlement'. Yet, what Kennedy terms 'Proper Cornishness' is in stasis rather than paralysed by the prospect of inevitable and imminent extinction. While the practices of classic Cornishness have ceased to be transmitted, attitudes and sentiments have not. These reproduce a 'common Cornish habitus', a set of dispositions, shared knowledge and tacit understandings that reproduce Cornishness even as its traditional markers evaporate.

Kennedy seeks ways to re-valorise this common Cornish habitus to add to its self-esteem, thus inserting that missing element of Cornish resilience, when compared with other Atlantic margins in Brittany and Galicia. This could provide an 'aspirational vision of a society rooted in community narratives'. Nonetheless, 'usable culture' has to overcome two problems. The first is the Cornish revivalist project itself. As others have pointed out, this offers a 'discursive and symbolic' route to defend and enhance Cornish cultures. Less rooted in declining social formations and discarded cultural practices than traditional Cornishness, observers have tended, somewhat uncritically, to view it as a means to cultural regeneration.[30]

In contrast, Kennedy argues this possibility is compromised by the 'wrong turns' of Cornish revivalism. The first wrong turn occurred in the 1920s when revivalists embraced cultural hygienes, re-imagining a myth of 'Celtic' cultural purity unsullied by English interference. In so doing, they dismissed 'non-folkloric, Cornu-English and industrial scripts'. Now, according to Kennedy, the revival is on the verge of taking a second wrong turn. This re-symbolizes Cornish culture, packaging it as part of an 'alternative', counter-urban, leisure-orientated sub-culture, appealing to the picturesque expectations of tourism. This strategy offers little opposition to, and indeed veers dangerously close to complicity with, a 'Lifestyle Cornwall' commodification, becoming a superficial leisure pursuit rather than an ethno-cultural element of social capital that could enhance Proper

---

29   Dilwyn Porter, 'Sport and the Cornish: difference and identity on the English periphery in the twentieth century', *National Identities* 16 (2014), 311-326.
30   Bernard Deacon, *Cornwall; A Concise History* (Cardiff: University of Wales Press, 2007), p. 229; Philip Payton, *Cornwall: A History* (Fowey: Cornwall Editions, 2004), pp. 284-285; Andrew Donaldson, 'Performing regions: territorial development and cultural politics in a Europe of the regions', *Environment and Planning A* 38 (2006), 2075-2092.

Cornishness. In short, the 'revamped Revivalist package risks becoming part of the upgraded lifestyle offer', helping to create a Cornish pastiche or Kernowland simulacrum.[31]

If a growing discordance between traditional Cornish identity constructions and revivalist cultural hygienes poses the first problem for a forward-looking Proper Cornishness, then the latter is rendered doubly illegitimate by a second constraint. 'Empowered institutional decision-makers' have 'little or no interaction or exposure to grass roots counter-discourses or identity narratives'.[32] Indeed, Kennedy notes that such narratives are treated with deep suspicion or even disdain by local elites while the much-touted 'knowledge economy' turns out in practice to merely complement counter-urban lifestyles and tourism.

This lack of sympathy can be gleaned, for example, from some of the interviews Kerryn Husk reported with 'knowledgeable individuals' working in charities and community organisations.[33] A number of 'the respondents reported that [the Cornish] were lazy', while they claimed the income divide between natives and incomers was exacerbated by 'insularity' which contributed to a lack of self-esteem. Yet there was an 'attitude of expectance' and a belief that the Cornish had special entitlements based on their ethnicity and connection to their land. Clearly, some of the professionals interviewed by Husk had little sympathy for such feelings.

Representational landscapes
The attitudes of incoming 'career-transients' returns us to the issue of the regional image. The myths that circulate within the project class are usually taken for granted as they are embedded within a dominant ideological framework. But work from within Cornish Studies has begun to chip away at those myths and stereotypes and chart their consequences, both intended and more usually unwitting. For instance, in 2004 I showed how the elites embedded in regional institutions in the 'South West' shared an old, romantic everyday discourse of Cornwall that predisposed them to path-dependent views of regeneration resting on tourism and inward investment.[34]

One of the most prolific scholars currently working in the field of Cornish Studies is Joanie Willett, who has elaborated on that preliminary investigation into elite stereotypes. As she notes, elite texts on Cornwall and

31 Kennedy, 'Employing Cornish cultures', 2013, pp. 158, 163 and 263ff.
32 Kennedy, 'Employing Cornish cultures', 2013, p. 255.
33 Husk, 'Ethnic group affiliation', 2012, pp. 197-203.
34 Bernard Deacon, 'Under Construction: Culture and Regional Formation in South-west England', *European Urban and Regional Studies* 11 (2004), 213-225. For the concept of the 'project class' see Deacon, *Cornwall*, 2007, p. 226.

its identity will shy away from ideas of nationalism or measures to protect the ethnic Cornish as a group. Yet, in an article in *Studies in Ethnicity and Nationalism* Willett problematizes the simplistic contrast often made between ethnic nationalism as exclusive or 'bad' and civic nationalism as inclusive and 'good'. Her argument is that ethnic nationalism can promote the liberal democratic ambition to protect the rights of minority groups and can be inclusive as long as it avoids an ethnic essentialism. Civic nationalism on the other hand is now aligned with neo-liberalism. In this, regions are just brands that enhance competition in the global market place. Furthermore, instead of pursuing the good of universal humanity, neo-liberal civic nationalism prioritises 'self-regarding personal fulfilment and happiness'. In other words, its priority is a self-absorbed lifestyle economy or, more bluntly, greed. In pursuing that agenda, the gradual removal of ethnic values from project class documents in Cornwall now reduces distinctiveness to 'desirability as a place to consume'. This is the context for the rise of Lifestyle Cornwall, a cool pleasure periphery created for consumption. The Lifestyle Cornwall version of regional branding excludes those without the economic wherewithal to participate, in contrast to ethnic nationalism, which can potentially embrace all residents, irrespective of economic worth. She identifies as an intrinsic 'part of the problem' in Cornwall that same regional development elite that formerly signed up to the south west regional discourse. Their 'perception of Cornish ethnicity, and their subsequent dismissal of it', is ultimately more harmful than helpful to Cornish regeneration discourses.[35]

In a further article Willett and John Tredinnick-Rowe pursue the relationship between regional identity and regional development, arguing that in Cornwall economic regionalism has provided a space for the articulation of national identity. In this article the authors claim to find a correlation between confidence in the Cornish identity and regional development practices, leading to the willingness of 'mainstream' political parties to adopt core identity issues such as boundary maintenance and support for a Cornish Assembly or the Cornish language.[36] However, aspects of this study, one which employs discourse as a central concept, are

---

35 Joanie Willett, 'Liberal Ethnic Nationalism, Universality, and Cornish Identity', *Studies in Ethnicity and Nationalism* 13 (2013), 201-217. Elsewhere Willett pursues the role of a phenomenological ethnic Cornish identity in the acquisition of EU regional structural funding in 1999, concluding that such identities can be 'emancipatory and enabling' for governance (Joanie Willett, 'National identity and regional development: Cornwall and the campaign for Objective 1 funding', *National Identities* 15 (2013), 297-311).

36 Joanie Willett and John Tredinnick-Rowe, 'The fragmentation of the nation state? Regional development, distinctiveness and the growth of nationalism in Cornish politics', *Nations and Nationalism* 22 (2016), 768-785.

open to question. First, their claim that the percolation of political demands traditionally associated solely with MK has happened 'relatively recently' is arguable. The Liberal Party in Cornwall's embrace of devolution in the 1960s and the adoption (or at least acceptance) of the demand for EU regional status (and funding) by Labour in the late 1990s implies that mainstream parties have a longer record of intermittently accepting regionalist demands. Moreover, the lack of movement on the Assembly and indeed the curtailment of central government funding for the Cornish language might suggest the salience of 'regionalist identity politics' is less obvious than they claim. Second, in this contribution regional identity appears as a rather homogenous and undifferentiated discourse. In short, those distinctions that Willett earlier identified between ethnic distinctiveness and lifestyle consumption versions of identity are skated over.

This is surprising as Joanie Willett published a very incisive account of exactly that difference in 2014.[37] This analysed regional economic development as a site of exclusion, inequality and power relationships, focusing on its narrative and proposing that successful regional narratives are those that 'open up spaces of possibility for future action and facilitate adaptation'. This is precisely what a 'quality of life' narrative, absorbing what Willett terms a creative industries assemblage into a visitor assemblage, fails to do. Cornwall, she explains, becomes a place to consume leisure pursuits, a site of hedonism, constructed as the opposite of modernity. Echoing the work of Ronald Perry in the 1980s, Willett argues this narrative is anything but 'dynamic'. The innovative aspect of her contribution is the way she weaves attitudes to time into the analysis. The quality of life imagery of Cornwall offers 'little real becoming' but, 'forever returning to an imagined past', deepens path-dependent structures that lock Cornwall into its status as a place of consumption, not action, closing off opportunities to become part of the contemporary knowledge economy. Contrasting the dominant narrative of empty futureless consumption with a more insider narrative grounded on territory and continuity, Willett concludes that it is 'unhelpful' and hinders potentially more fruitful efforts to explore, foster and advertise Cornwall's existing strengths.

Willett's work from a social science perspective is complemented by Rachel Moseley's media studies approach to representations of Cornwall. She has analysed the production of the 'place-image' of Cornwall, showing how, for example, the first TV series of *Poldark*, broadcast in the 1970s, drew on and constructed a specific image of Cornwall, involving the typical aspects of 'over-simplification, stereotyping and labelling'. However, this

---

37   Joanie Willett, 'The production of place: perception, reality and the politics of becoming', *Political Studies* (2014), 1-16.

was not a straightforwardly Romantic image, as it contained within it the 'potential for disruption', harking back to the 'grey Cornwall' of Walter Langley rather than the 'sunny Cornwall' of Laura Knight and the Great Western Railway (GWR).[38] Furthermore, the 1970s *Poldark* was a product of its time, an escape from the uncertainties of that transitional decade between Keynesian social democracy and neo-liberalism. It would be interesting to speculate on the role of the more recent *Poldark* series, coinciding with a time of equal political and cultural uncertainty in the UK.

In a second article, Moseley deconstructs the visual trope of the woman on the cliff (think Demelza in *Poldark* series 2), one that has been linked to Cornwall since before World War One. Cornwall, a contested territory, with an identity that Moseley claims is 'uncertain, anxious, perpetually in process', representationally liminal, is a perfect location for television and film representations of 'personal and national crisis'. However, this is not a Cornish national crisis, but a crisis of British (or English) national culture. This is why the woman on the cliff is a particularly common motif in times of war and crisis, when Cornwall becomes the 'space to speak about unsettling questions around gender, sexuality and disruption of national discourses'. Is it destined to play this essentially passive role in post-Brexit times of uncertainty too? The problem, as Moseley spells out, is that a place-image mobilising ideas of 'beauty, mysticism, danger, sexuality and uncertainty' within a 'discourse of romantic, Celtic difference and bucolic ruralism' leads to 'difficulty in perceiving the region in other ways'.[39] We might also add that it relegates and ignores the existence of a parallel Cornish (as opposed to British) national crisis.

The traditional stereotypes and myths held by members of the project class have a venerable genealogy. They can be traced back to the nineteenth and twentieth centuries, as work on the 'Cornish Gothic' has uncovered. Somewhat tangential to this is Christopher Pittard's article on Daphne du Maurier. By reading *Castle Dor* as a psychogeographical text, he challenges the idea of du Maurier as a nostalgic genre writer, but reconstructs her as the inaugurator of postmodern Cornish fiction, prefiguring D.M.Thomas's *Birthstone* or Alan Kent's *Clay*. In du Maurier's writing, binary oppositions, as between Cornwall and England, are destabilised and Cornwall

---

38 Rachel Moseley, '"It's a wild country. Wild … passionate … strange": Poldark and the place-image of Cornwall', *Visual Culture in Britain* 14 (2013), 218-237.

39 Rachel Moseley, 'Women at the edge: encounters with the Cornish coast in British film and television', *Continuum: Journal of Media and Cultural Studies* 27 (2013), 644-662. We await with interest her forthcoming book *Picturing Cornwall* (Exeter: University of Exeter Press, 2017/18).

constructed as an 'anachronistic space'.[40] The same outcome is uncovered in studies of late Victorian/Edwardian literature. Shelley Trower also notes how the Cornish cliffs became an ambiguous space, a locus for instability, both the destination and a point of infiltration for the late Victorian tourist/explorer. The Cornish Gothic emerged in the works of writers such as Bram Stoker and Arthur Conan Doyle as the domestic counterpoint to Empire Gothic.[41] Here were the seeds of that familiar exotic-domestic trope that in the twentieth century became the core of tourism marketing campaigns such as those of the GWR.

Half a century before novelists were exciting themselves by playing with the Cornish Gothic, Wilkie Collins was constructing it, according to Paul Young.[42] Collins, in his *Rambles beyond Railways*, published in 1850, understood Cornwall as a Gothic location, compromising the rational, Enlightenment project by harbouring 'unreasonable, uncivilised and unprogressive customs or tendencies'. 'Beyond' the reach of the train, mid-nineteenth century Cornwall was structured by Collins as also beyond metropolitan modernity, 'fathomless, wild, at times grotesque', its 'landscape and people defying rational comprehension'. Young notes how Collins' positioning of Cornwall on the 'edge of modern life' challenged (and began the process of obscuring) Cornwall's significance for globalised modernity, or its early industrialization and its role in the development of the steam engine, the visible symbol of Victorian industry.

Collins had to ignore the fact that railways were hardly unknown in Cornwall, having appeared in the 1830s, while mineral tramways can be dated back to 1809. At the peak of Cornwall's mining industry over 200 working engine houses would have been visible and mines were commonplace across Cornwall, directly employing a third of its workforce. Nonetheless, Collins could, rather amazingly, get away with describing a Cornish mine as 'isolated, strained and uncanny'. However, Young also qualifies this by suggesting hostility to modernity could also be seen as inspiring resistance, something worth celebrating rather than fearing. It's notable how this aspect of the Cornish Gothic could also later feed into revivalist imaginations, revaluing the 'primitive and simple', yet also eclipsing Cornwall's central role in the transition to modernity.

---

40   Christopher Pittard, '"We are seeing the past through the wrong end of the telescope": Time, Space and Psychogeography in Castle Dor', *Women: A Cultural Review* 20 (2009), 57-73.

41   Shelley Trower, 'On the cliff edge of England: Tourism and Imperial Gothic in Cornwall', *Victorian Literature and Culture* 40 (2012), 199-214.

42   Paul Young, '*Rambles Beyond Railways*: Gothicised Place and Globalised Space in Victorian Cornwall' *Gothic Studies* 13 (2011), 55-74.

It comes as more of a shock to discover how far the Cornish Gothic is still deeply entrenched in twenty-first century representations of Cornwall. When looking for factors explaining the stubbornness of this representation it has long been assumed that the role of the tourist sector has been profound since the Edwardian period. Graham Busby notes the role of tourism in constructing a Cornish gaze while Sam Rayne also assumes the tourist sector was a key identity entrepreneur in Cornwall. Yet that role may have a wider and more pervasive effect than previously realised. Hilary Orange for instance has discovered that public perceptions even of industrial mining archaeology in Cornwall 'tends towards mythologising industrial culture through a romantic and/or demonic and/or heroic lens'.[43]

In pursuing the relationship between marketing and representations, Richard Tresidder has written what should be one of the key Cornish Studies texts of recent times, even though it has no explicit reference to the actual output of Cornish Studies.[44] He provides a social semiotic reading of a Visit Cornwall tourist brochure. This is done for supposedly functional reasons, to help tourism marketeers to develop strategies tailored to market segments. However, those tourist promoters will surely be most uncomfortable with his conclusions. While Wilkie Collins had falsely constructed Cornwall in 1850 as 'awful nature, emptied of human existence', we find Visit Cornwall's brochure, 160 years later, doing much the same. The brochure is peppered with photos of empty landscapes and couples on deserted beaches as it strains to construct Cornwall as a place of rural escape. Tresidder proceeds to deconstruct this tourism location of Cornwall as post-industrial, 'existing in the present, while being reproduced in the past'. For him, this is the product of an ideology that results from the power to construct Cornwall as 'timeless and spaceless' outside modernity, nothing less than a 'semiotic colonization'. Cornwall becomes an example of Lefebvre's notion of 'dominated and appropriated space'.

Furthermore, this appropriation and regulation of Cornish space is done in the interests of certain social institutions. Tresidder bluntly concludes that, 'conceptually, tourism development in Cornwall can be seen as just another form of cultural colonialism', part of discourses that 'marginalize

---

43   Graham Busby, 'The Cornish church heritage as a tourism attraction: the visitor experience' (unpublished doctoral thesis, University of Exeter, 2006); Samantha Rayne, 'Henry Jenner and the Celtic Revival in Cornwall' (unpublished doctoral thesis, University of Exeter, 2012); Hilary Orange, 'Cornish mining landscapes: Public perceptions of industrial archaeology in a post-industrial society' (unpublished doctoral thesis, University College London, 2012), p. 186.

44   Richard Tresidder, 'What no pasties? Reading the Cornish Tourism Brochure', *Journal of Travel and Tourism Marketing* 27 (2010), 596-611.

not only the landscapes of Cornwall, but also the history, heritage, culture and society of the destination', which is placed in a 'state of conscious and permanent invisibility'.[45] This startlingly forthright analysis of the practices and effects of the contemporary tourist industry is capped by the rather optimistic call for the 'industry to operate in an ethical and sustainable manner', with 'more objective empirical research' on tourism to 'inform practice and chart influences and the significance they have for host and guest'. If tourism is cultural colonialism then appealing to the colonisers to act more humanely seems a rather forlorn hope, given past examples of colonialism.

Gemma Goodman offers a fuller account of how representations were imposed on Cornwall historically. Her thesis, explicitly informed by Cornish Studies, shows how dominant and alternative versions of literary Cornwalls have been connected and internalized, but offer the possibilities of new understandings and multiple Cornwalls.[46] As we can see, analysis of representations of Cornwall in literature, the role of the tourist industry in reproducing them and their impact on governance has advanced immensely over the past decade. This is less the case however for studies of the Cornish language, which, while numerous, appear more mired in traditionalism.

Linguistic landscapes
The Cornish language began to be revived even before it died, although the efforts of eighteenth century revivalists failed to prevent the demise of the spoken, historic version of Cornish. What is now taken to be Cornish is the product of a conscious twentieth century revival. On the one hand the historic language continues to attract traditional analyses of its linguistic structure, lexicon and morphology.[47] On the other hand, uncritical narratives of the historic language are still plentiful.

---

45 See also Hale, Representing', 2001.
46 Gemma Goodman, 'Cornwall: An alternative construction of place' (unpublished doctoral thesis, University of Warwick, 2010). The story is brought up to date in Robert Dickinson, 'Changing landscapes of difference: Representations of Cornwall in travel writing, 1949-2007', in Philip Payton (ed.), *Cornish Studies Sixteen* (Exeter: University of Exeter Press, 2008), 167-182.
47 See particularly the work of Nicholas Williams in the *Cornish Studies* series and his *Geryow Gwir: the lexicon of Revived Cornish* (Cathair na Mart: Evertype, 2013). See also Talet Chaudhri, 'Studies in the consonantal system of Cornish' (unpublished doctoral thesis, University of Wales, Aberystwyth, 2007) and Jon Mills, 'Computer assisted lemmatisation of a Cornish text corpus for lexicographical purposes' (unpublished doctoral thesis, University of Exeter, 2002).

These combine a story of linguistic oppression with the repetition of old myths that give an exaggerated account of the state of early sixteenth century Cornish.[48] For example, we are told that 'most of the population' were still speaking 'only their native Cornish' at the time of the Reformation in the 1540s, while Cornish had only just begun to weaken in the east. The hammer blow then came courtesy of the suppression of the 1549 rising, when half the Cornish speaking male adult population are claimed to have been slaughtered. (The numerical relationship between these two claims is rarely explored). Nonetheless, resistance to anglicization is simultaneously re-asserted. For example, the *Ordinalia*, normally dated to the later fourteenth century, was apparently written after 1497 as its reference to 'Joseph, the smith' is to the blacksmith in St Keverne rather than the blacksmith of Nazareth.[49] Such accounts are strongly influenced by the wishful thinking school of Cornish revivalist history. Others are more sceptical. Gillian Brennan paints a less traumatic picture of language change in the sixteenth century, while Remco Knooihuizen's suggestion that the standard-likeness of west Cornish English was due to dialect contact rather the vertical imposition of a standard, also hints at a calmer process of language shift.[50]

Recycled traditional historical narratives have now been joined by more studies of the neo-Cornish revival. That revival can still be regarded as central to the reproduction of modern Cornish identity, along with the tourist sector, which commandeered images of Celtic Cornwall created by early revivalists. This position is argued by Sam Rayne.[51] Her largely positive, indeed hagiographic, assessment of Henry Jenner accompanies a set of other, more critical re-assessments of the Cornish revival and its relationship with a romanticised, dominant set of representations of Cornwall.

---

48 For a recent example see Siarl Ferdinand, 'A brief history of the Cornish language, its revival and its current status', *E-Keltoi Journal of Inter-disciplinary Celtic Studies*, 2 (2013), 199-227.

49 Jon Mills, 'Genocide and ethnicide: The suppression of the Cornish language', in John Partridge (ed.), *Interfaces in Language* (Newcastle: Cambridge Scholars, 2010), 189-206 and 'The depiction of tyranny in the Cornish miracle plays', in Liam MacAmhlaigh and Brian O Curnáin (eds), *Ilteangach, Ilseiftivil: A festschrift in honour of Nicholas Williams* (Arlen House: Dublin, 2012), 139-157.

50 Gillian Brennan, 'Language and nationality: the role of policy towards Celtic languages in the consolidation of Tudor power" *Nations and Nationalism* 7 (2001), 317-338; Remco Knooihuizen, 'Language shift and apparent standardisation in early modern English', *Journal of Historical Sociolinguistics* 1 (2015), 189-211.

51 Rayne, 'Henry Jenner', 2012.

The best analysis of the revival's context appears in Carl Phillips' study of the mystical geographies of Cornwall.[52] He places the revival's origins in the decades after the 1870s as a version of mystical Cornwall attached to Anglican Christianity. Anglo-Catholicism was extended in the inter-war period in the more populist institutional context of the Old Cornwall societies to incorporate other Christian denominations, Arthurianism and Paganism, a combination seen most dramatically in the Gorseth. However, after the 1960s the revival was marked by a 'loss of control' as other understandings of mystical Cornwall emerged around prehistoric mysticism, megalithic 'science' and 'alternative archaeology'. Although Phillips does not specifically mention them, the orthography wars that ripped through the language revival in the 1980s and 1990s can also be seen in this context of a loss of control and a more disordered approach to the Cornish linguistic landscape.

As we have seen, Neil Kennedy has argued that Cornish revivalists, having taken a first wrong turn in the 1920s back to an impossibly high-Celticism and purity alien to everyday life, are stumbling into a second. They are now in danger of opening up Cornish culture to the commodified, lifestyle Cornwall that is penetrating Cornish society, dissolving and re-making it in the process. Casting another critical eye over the Cornish revival, Jesse Harasta has made a spirited defence of Modern Cornish based on the last vernacular form of the language, while attempting to link attitudes to the language to class structure. More convincingly, he notes that the standardization of Cornish orthography since 2006 has led to the re-assertion of the medievalist values central to the *Kernewek Kemmyn* project (the largest pre-standardization group) and to a shrinking pluralism within the language movement.[53]

In contrast, in his doctoral thesis, Dave Sayers adopted a less critical stance on orthographic standardization. He viewed it as overriding 'the loyalties of any particular faction and an agreement on a totally new version of Cornish'. His more recent work revises this assessment however. In 2012 he discussed the standardization of neo-Cornish orthography in the context of the pressures for measurable outcomes and performance targets introduced by the New Public Management. This usefully assesses the role of state bureaucracies in contemporary neo-Cornish and suggests that standardization was not imposed but emerged during the language planning process. His conclusion was still that 'no side gained primacy'. But a later

---

52 Carl Phillips, 'Mystical Geographies of Cornwall' (unpublished doctoral thesis, University of Nottingham, 2006).

53 Jesse Harasta, 'In search of a single voice: the politics of form, use and belief in the Kernewek language' (unpublished doctoral dissertation, Syracuse University, 2013).

publication concludes that there has in practice been a 'gradual, diffuse, largely unplanned drift towards an orthography that looks like *kemmyn*', as the original aim of two *equal* main variants has been conveniently lost. The most recent bureaucratization phase of this 're-invented (re-invented)' language has thus had the unintended consequence of adding tacit state legitimation to the wrong turns of revivalism and its purist hygienes.[54]

While Sayers provides a comprehensive and valuable record of the process of standardization and bureaucratization since the mid-2000s, studies of the language revival are too often marked by gullibility as they tend to repeat uncritically the central claims of Cornish linguistic revivalism. They also rely on an outdated secondary literature for their historical context. For instance, Zsuzsanna Renkó-Michelsén uses Halliday's work, written in the early 1950s. Applying Fishman's Graded International Disruption Scale, a measurement of the level of endangerment of languages, to Cornish, she claims to finds examples of intergenerational transmission, although the source was a language activist living in London. Sayers and Renkó-Michelsén apply another linguistic model, Haugen's four steps of language revitalization, to Cornish. This includes a useful institutional history of MAGA (the Cornish Language Partnership) and provides some insights into the language, for example that reconstructed Cornish has an 'inescapably constrained and circuitous relationship to the ashes of the historically spoken vernacular' and 'is a new minority language just as much as an old one'.[55]

The application of various theoretical frameworks from linguistics seems to share a common and basic misunderstanding. Cornish is not an endangered language equivalent to Gaelic, Welsh or Breton; in many respects it's a new language. Academic approaches struggle to get beyond the myths of revivalism and become trapped by its conceits. Anina Carkeek offers a partial corrective in her study of attitudes to the language. She detects a reawakened emotional attachment to Cornish emerging since the late 1990s, this being strongest among those self-identifying as Cornish, brought up in Cornwall or with a Cornish family history. While the revivalists' dream of a vernacular revival is a 'hopeless task', she suggests

---

54 Dave Sayers, 'Reversing babel: declining linguistic diversity and the flawed attempts to protect it' (unpublished doctoral thesis, University of Essex, 2009); Dave Sayers, 'Standardising Cornish: the politics of a new minority language', *Language problems & Language Planning* 36 (2012), 99-119; Dave Sayers and Zsuzsanna Renkó-Michelsén, 'Phoenix from the ashes: Reconstructed Cornish in relation to Einar Haugen's four-step model of language standardisation', *Sociolinguistica* 29 (2015), 17-38.

55 Zsuzsanna Renkó-Michelsén, 'Language death and revival: Cornish as a minority language in UK', *Journal of Estonian & Finno-Ugric Linguistics* 4 (2013), 179-197; Sayers and Renkó-Michelsén, 'Phoenix', 2015.

that Cornish could be a usable group core value as a 'heritage language', fulfilling an emotionally symbolic function.[56]

Indeed, Cornish is probably better viewed as a post-vernacular language, one which has entirely ceased to be the language of any community. In such languages the symbolic use becomes more important than the communicative. Attempts at language planning imported from still living language communities therefore miss the point. Instead of trying to ape those, the central focus has to be on the best way to utilise revived Cornish as a symbol, linking it to living Cornish identities more broadly, in order to enhance and revalue them, rather than create a pool of speakers. Research needs to be directed towards how the revived language symbolically relates to identity and to project class representations and what its effects might be on different forms of Cornishness. Again, Neil Kennedy offers introductory insights into this process, noting the complex relationships between Cornish revivalism and the commodified Lifestyle Cornwall brand, with revivalists torn between colluding with it and bewailing its effects.[57]

At present, the ongoing linguistic hygienes of revived Cornish contain clear dangers. They can erect barriers between the language and traditional Cornish identity constructions, rendering the latter 'doubly illegitimate'.[58] This is perhaps best seen in the way revivalism has tended to disparage Cornu-English dialect, despite the efforts in the earlier inter-war Nancean synthesis to combine living dialect and former language, an attempt fatally compromised by Nance's own turn to medieval Cornish. Anina Carkeek concludes that the Cornu-English 'accent' is unable to fulfil a core symbolic role because of its perceived low status. Meanwhile, Alan Kent, in his academic interventions, novels and poetry, has been pursuing his project to revalue Cornu-English dialect.[59] Kent is not alone. The use of Cornish

---

56 Anina Carkeek, 'Cornish language revival: Attitudes, behaviour and the maintenance of an ethnic identity' (unpublished doctoral thesis, University of East Anglia, 2009), pp. 267-270. Merryn Davies-Deacon hints at the peculiar status of Cornish in her contrast between Cornish (a revived language) and Breton (a revitalised language) - 'Orthographies and ideologies in revived Cornish', (unpublished MA thesis, University of York, 2016).

57 Kennedy, 'Employing Cornish cultures', 2013, p. 269. Similar contradictions were exposed in revivalists' attitudes in 2012-15 to proposals for a Cornish sports stadium near Truro, paid for by an associated 1,500-2,000 housing development

58 Kennedy, 'Employing Cornish cultures', 2013, p. 172.

59 For examples see Alan M.Kent, *Proper Job, Charlie Curnow!* (Tiverton: Halsgrove, 2005); '"Bringin' the dunkey down from the Carn": Cornu-English in context, 1549-2005 – A provisional analysis', in Hildegaard L.C.Tristram (ed.), *The Celtic Englishes IV: The Interface between English and the Celtic Languages* (Potsdam: Potsdam University Press, 2006), 6-33; *Oogly es Sin:*

dialect in social media may be a tantalising and fruitful area for further research, as there are growing hints there of its revaluation amidst some novel uses.[60] Recently, the First Kernow bus group has introduced buses in west Cornwall with snippets of Cornu-English on the back, 'proper' or 'wozzon' for example. This revalorisation of the dialect is a welcome step.

Heritage landscapes

Work on the Cornish identity and language share a 'death and resurrection' approach. Apparently in terminal decline, residual proper Cornishness can be re-valorized by the adroit application of 'usable cultures'. Reviving the language as a spoken vernacular may be an impossible project but nonetheless offers key symbolic support for engendering pride in place and local communities. From outside the Cornish Studies bubble, similar prescriptions are offered. Tim Martindale notes that fishing communities are sites of 'loss, rupture and decay' but also salvage and regeneration. He proposes a 'critical nostalgia', a positive role for heritage beyond the museum, together with a policy focus on spatial regulation (such as marine protection zones) rather than quotas in order to negotiate the potential precariousness and insecurity of disenfranchised inshore fishermen.[61]

Martindale's focus on a positive role for heritage implies that it may serve as a strategic link between issues of representation and identity and the resources of the past/attitudes to the present. Heritage could also be an element in the formation of both Cornish and local identities, which Hilary Orange optimistically concludes can be produced through length of residence.[62] Can heritage help reproduce a focus on a past of dynamic innovation to counter those demeaning myths of Cornwall as a passive leisure periphery with an invisible or hopelessly romanticised ethnicity being peddled by Lifestyle Cornwall entrepreneurs? Bethan Coupland's comparison of Geevor and Big Pit in south Wales warns us that the process of heritagisation involves a 'cultural memory' located in a 'rather detached, somewhat romanticised narrative of mining frozen in the past'. This tends to

---

the Lamentable Ballad of Anthony Payne Cornish Giant (London: Francis Boutle, 2007); *The Hope of Place: Selected Poems in English 1990-2010* (London: Francis Boutle, 2010).

60　See Colin Leggo, *Satnav voiceover in a Cornish accent*, online video recording, YouTube, 27 May 2014 <https://youtu.be/Koxl4-t3i4M> [accessed 6 November 2015] and posts and comments at Kernow King's Facebook page.

61　Tim Martindale, 'Livelihoods, craft and heritage: Transmissions of knowledge in Cornish fishing villages' (unpublished doctoral thesis, Goldsmiths, University of London, 2012).

62　Hilary Orange, 'Industrial Archaeology: Its Place Within the Academic Discipline, the Public Realm and the Heritage Industry', *Industrial Archaeology Review* 30 (2008), 83-95.

bleach out and subsume the living memories of loss and trauma encountered in the local communities. Such a process thus endangers communities' ownership of their own pasts, erasing their lived experience of the recent past and replacing it by a remoter version of the more distant past.[63] A later article by Bethan and Nikolas Coupland qualifies this somewhat pessimistic conclusion. The centrality of mining to discourses of Cornishness is implied in their study of the promotional and interpretive discourses of mining heritage. Comparing Geevor with Big Pit, their study notes that both sites rely on claims to authenticity, but 'authenticity' arrives in different forms, some of which look to the past and some to the present. These blend to produce a complex mix of practices. As a result heritagisation is 'not inherently deauthenticating or somehow false but can legitimise material sites as monuments to place and place identities'.[64]

Patrick Laviolette's social anthropological studies of Cornwall offer a novel view of the phenomenon of loss but parallel regeneration. His article on surf culture provides a comprehensive coverage of that scene and offers thoughts on the changing ways in which water and sea relate to shifting identities in Cornwall. This is extended by an article published in the same year on maritime art.[65] This looks at how nautical relics in Cornwall have been transformed into works of art but expands on this as a metaphor for wider cultural distinction. The example of 'recyclia', recycling identities, histories and social relations, leads to insights about Cornishness, many expressions of which 'are a kind of statement about existing on a somewhat topographical edge'. Sometimes, Laviolette's style verges close to *Private Eye*'s Pseud's corner - 'such a coastal gaze is thus a material metaphor of hydro-geological proportion', for example. Nonetheless, there are real insights in his work about Cornwall's 'tenuous relationship with modernity', which also allows it, for some, to challenge marginality. This adds to the growing body of work that problematises a simple binary distinction between romantic external representations and lived internal identities.

---

63 Bethan Coupland, 'Heritage and Memory: Oral History and Mining Heritage in Wales and Cornwall' (unpublished doctoral thesis, University of Exeter, 2012).

64 Bethan Coupland and Nikolas Coupland, 'The authenticating discourses of mining heritage tourism in Cornwall and Wales', *Journal of Sociolinguistics* 18 (2014), 495-517.

65 Patrick Laviolette, 'Green and Extreme: Free-flowing through seascape and sewer', *Worldviews* 10 (2006), 178-204; 'Ships of Relations: Navigating through Local Cornish Maritime Art', *International Journal of Heritage Studies* 12 (2006), 69-92.

This is taken further in his earlier article on deathliness in Cornwall, which should be a key text of post-millennial Cornish Studies.[66] In this he argues that a diffuse sense of deathliness pervades Cornish culture. It does this in three ways. First, there is a particular role for death and ancestry in local folklore, influenced by the place of standing stones in Cornish life.[67] Second, there is a pride in dying forms of subsistence as traditional industries disappear, or are in the process of dying. Finally, there is the belief that the Cornish identity itself is about to expire. Laviolette recognises the end-of-Cornwall rhetoric, the belief that the land itself is slipping away, suffocated by excess infiltration which dilutes 'localness'.[68] Although pinpointing the widespread discourse that an 'entire society is on the route towards extinction', Laviolette throws in a lifeline. Deathliness in fact 'helps keep Cornwall alive'. It becomes more than nostalgia; it can feed regeneration. Death and resurgence in practice become ambiguous metaphors. Laviolette concludes that 'in short, … death is itself a meta-narrative about cultural survival'.

This intriguing and paradoxical notion of a Cornwall teetering on a 'post-Cornish moment' yet undergoing a cultural renaissance is echoed (but in a less ghoulish fashion) by Neil Kennedy in his work on culture and community resilience. Both Laviolette and Kennedy offer the possibility of resurgence while recognising the effects of socio-economic and demographic change. In doing so, they open new windows onto a richer, less superficial characterisation of Cornish identities. Kennedy's 'post-Cornish moment' summons up an elusive period just beyond living memory but after history.[69] It recalls a slightly earlier version of ourselves but one that is not yet (quite) history, while no longer that of everyday experience, a stubborn ghostly presence hovering at the margins of memory. This point perhaps provides a potential epicentre for Cornish cultural regeneration, one that blends an insider awareness of the ambiguities and subtleties of Cornish identity with a selective heritage appropriation and a sensitivity and respect for living memory. However, its elucidation and form have still to be worked through and developed.

In 2001 Amy Hale identified a growing focus on industrial heritage as mining became a central feature in the assertion of an alternative narrative

---

66 Patrick Laviolette, 'Landscaping Death: Resting Places for Cornish Identity', *Journal of Material Culture* 8 (2003), 215-240.

67 For the latest and possibly final word on this enduringly fascinating topic see Ann Preston-Jones and Elisabeth Okasha, *Early Cornish Sculpture* (Oxford: Oxford University Press, 2014).

68 This is echoed in my polemic: Bernard Deacon, *The land's end: the great sale of Cornwall* (Redruth: CoSERG, 2013).

69 Kennedy, 'Employing Cornish cultures', 2013, p. 82.

of Cornish 'difference'.[70] This has established itself as the concept of the 'industrial Celt', a blend of classic Cornishness and Celtic revivalism. Along with others in recent years, Kennedy repeats the possibility of making use of this mythology of the Cornish as industrial Celts to valorise and empower Cornish culture and communities and provide an alternative to Lifestyle Cornwall representations of remote, timeless rurality that 'confirm and reinforce constructions of inferiority'.[71] Work by historians on Cornwall's industrial period may provide some of the resources for this narrative.

Historic landscapes

The familiar staples of Cornwall's classic industrial period - Methodism, mining and migration – have continued to attract attention. Alessandro Nuvolari has described how west Cornwall in the period from the 1810s to 1840 became a 'collective invention setting', where firms shared technological knowledge. The efficiency of the steam engine was boosted by a series of innovations by working engineers once the block posed by Boulton and Watt's patent had expired. Native genius and a culture of empirical tinkering allowed Cornish engineers to place their region at the forefront of steam technology. In a later paper Nuvolari and Bart Verspagen revisited the 'precocious adaptation of the high pressure steam engine in Cornwall' in the first few decades of the nineteenth century. They ask why this adoption was delayed in the rest of Britain, concluding that the transferability of the 'remarkable' Cornish achievements was minimal, as this was a 'process of technological learning taking place in a very favourable context', driven by a wave of innovative investment and the rapid, open dissemination of technical knowledge in a tightly bounded industrial region. Such conditions were not in place elsewhere, where steam technology did not in any case offer similar advantages in productivity growth.[72]

If Cornish engineers were at the forefront of technological change in the early nineteenth century, then so apparently were Cornish financiers. Liam Brunt uses the example of Praed of Truro to show how this bank operated more like a venture capital firm than a country bank in the period from the 1770s to the 1830s. The firm was not risk averse, on the contrary lending to a network of mines that were bound together by relations of trust and

---

70   Hale, 'Representing', 2001.
71   Kennedy, 'Employing Cornish cultures', 2013, p. 254.
72   Alessandro Nuvolari, 'Collective invention during the British Industrial Revolution: the case of the Cornish pumping engine', *Cambridge Journal of Economics* 28 (2004), 347-363; Alessandro Nuvolari and Bart Verspagen, 'Technical choice, innovation, and British steam engineering, 1800-1850', *Economic History Review* 62 (2009), 685-710.

reciprocity enabled by close geographical proximity. John Dirring is more cautious in his comprehensive account of Cornish banking since 1771.[73]

Meanwhile, other studies of Cornwall's nineteenth century mining economy have usefully delineated the limits of exceptionalism. Roger Burt has investigated allegedly unique features of the Cornish context – labour relations and emigrant mining networks.[74] He concludes that there was no great gulf in the causes or chronology of strike action between metal mines in Cornwall and coal mines upcountry. In the early part of the century a proto-industrial workforce concentrated on defending traditional rights but after the 1850s adopted strike action.[75] The apparent slowness in unionization is easily explained by recourse to the difficult context for organising after the 1860s. The course of industrial relations showed 'no Cornish exceptionalism'. This same claim reinforces Roger Burt and Sandra Kippen's earlier conclusion that the decision by Cornish miners in the mid nineteenth century to become geographically mobile rather than occupationally mobile when the industry began to falter can be explained by cash rather than culture.[76] Because earnings in mining were relatively high, Cornish miners entered the mines even though they were aware the choice was likely to shorten their working lives. This behaviour was hardly unusual.

Catherine Mills has also addressed social aspects of Cornish mining, asking why risky behaviour was tolerated and perpetuated in Cornish mining from 1875 to 1914, when accidents ran at a relatively high level and

---

73   Liam Brunt, 'Rediscovering Risk: Country Banks as Venture Capital Firms in the First Industrial Revolution', *The Journal of Economic History* 66 (2006), 74-102; John Dirring, 'The organisation and practice of banking in Cornwall, 1771-1922: Motivations and objectives of Cornish bankers' (unpublished doctoral thesis, University of Exeter, 2015).

74   Roger Burt, 'Industrial relations in the British non-ferrous mining industry in the nineteenth century', *Labour History Review* 71 (2006), 57-79; 'Freemasonry and business networking during the Victorian period', *Economic History Review* 56 (2003), 657-688. The fortunes of Cornish mining in the critical period around the Napoleonic Wars is covered by Jim Lewis, 'Cornish copper mining 1795-1830: economy, structure and change', in Philip Payton (ed.), *Cornish Studies Fourteen* (Exeter: University of Exeter Press, 2006), 164-186.

75   See also Bernard Deacon, 'The reformulation of territorial identity: Cornwall in the late eighteenth and nineteenth centuries' (unpublished doctoral thesis, Open University, 2001), chapter 8.

76   Roger Burt and Sandra Kippen, 'Rational Choice and a Lifetime in Metal Mining: Employment Decisions by Nineteenth-Century Cornish Miners', *International Review of Social History* 46 (2001), 45-75.

were rising not falling, as they were elsewhere.[77] She concludes that unsafe practices were better explained by economic factors than the cultural milieu (by a subculture of machismo or self-images involving bravado). Instead, the individualised nature of risk and piecework in the Cornish mines plus the financial incentives for risky behaviour are all that are needed to construct a credible explanation. These might perhaps be coupled with cost-cutting, endemic in the investment-starved Cornish mines of the period.

Although these economic historians put a case for the Cornish miner as an economically rational actor, even for them culture enters the picture as a (minor) player. Burt posits a greater role for freemasonry than ethnicity in fusing together overseas mining networks, although admitting there were 'strong filial religious and cultural links' that underlay the role of the institutional setting.[78] While valuable correctives to any tendency towards cultural determinism, such 'rational choice' accounts of behaviour can themselves of course be situated in a wider cultural framework where neo-liberal ideological perspectives on 'economic man' tend to predominate. The timing of their appearance is no accident.

The 'classic' industrial society created by Cornwall's early industrialization is potentially illuminated further by work on Methodism. David Harvey et al. claim to take Methodism beyond the chapel, identifying how Sunday school tea treats and parades channelled and embedded both a Methodist religious culture and a community identity in the century after 1830. These public displays allowed performances of faith, recruited members and provided a spectacle or carnival for the less committed. Meanwhile, arising from the same research project, Adrian Bailey et al. use Cornwall to illustrate the micro-geography of nineteenth century practices in constructing childhood and attitudes to embodiment. In doing so, they provide a useful summary of the history of teetotalism in mid-nineteenth century Cornwall, an under-researched topic. Overall though, this work does little to expand on the social history of Methodism in Cornwall or explore its relationship with local society in depth. Historians had in fact already done much to place early Methodism in a wider social context.[79]

---

77 Catherine Mills, 'A hazardous bargain: Occupational risk in Cornish mining 1875-1914', *Labour History Review* 70 (2005), 53-71.

78 Burt, 'Freemasonry', 2003.

79 David C. Harvey, Catherine Brace and Adrian R. Bailey, 'Parading the Cornish subject: Methodist Sunday Schools in west Cornwall, c.1830-1930', *Journal of Historical Geography* 33 (2007), 24-44; Adrian R. Bailey, David C. Harvey and Catherine Brace, 'Disciplining Youthful Methodist Bodies in Nineteenth-Century Cornwall', *Annals of the Association of American Geographers* 97 (2007), 142-157. For the existing body of work see David Luker, 'Revivalism in Theory and Practice; The Case of Cornish Methodism', *Journal of Ecclesiastical History* 37 (1986), 603-619 and John Rule, *Cornish Cases:*

The work of the cultural geographers of the 2000s adds little to our understanding of the consequences of the denominational competition after the 1850s or the course of Cornwall's salvation industry in the later nineteenth and early twentieth centuries.

Other work on the social history of the nineteenth and early twentieth centuries adds detail to accounts of Cornish culture in these years. Mike Tripp, in a thesis firmly grounded in a Cornish Studies approach to 'difference', views Cornish wrestling as an 'icon of Cornishness' as it was transformed from a popular sport to a mid-twentieth century heritage sport. Meanwhile, in an idiosyncratic but nonetheless interesting piece, Guy Jaouen pinpoints the contrast in the fortunes of Cornish wrestling, at its peak in the nineteenth century but moribund nowadays, and Breton wrestling, which declined in the 1800s but is thriving now. Merv Davey's account of Cornwall's folk song and dance tradition delineates the history of this aspect of Cornish culture and also has a focus on Cornish difference. Arguing that Cornwall's folk tradition provides a 'medium well placed to express the Cornish identities of the future', here is one candidate for Kennedy's 'usable culture'. But Davey also addresses the competition between a Celto-Cornish folk movement and a folk revival rooted in English folk dance after the 1960s. This clash of 'speech communities' introduces the issue of power into the cultural arena of folk 'traditions'. Other work began to open up the question of sub-Cornwall difference. One example was Peter Tremewan's valuable study of an under-researched aspect of Cornish history, the patterns of poor relief in late eighteenth century and nineteenth century Cornwall.[80]

Essays in Eighteenth and Nineteenth Century Social History (Southampton: Clio Publishing, 2006), chapters 6 and 7. For some suggestions for further research see Bernard Deacon, 'Religion and Community: Frameworks and Issues', *Family & Community History* 5 (2002), 33-44.

80   Michael Tripp, 'Persistence of difference: A history of Cornish wrestling' (unpublished doctoral thesis, University of Exeter, 2009); Guy Jaouen, 'Transforming Cornish and Devon wrestling (Britain) and Gouren (Brittany-France) through sportification', *International Journal of the History of Sport*, 31 (2014), 474-491; Mervyn Davey, '"As is the manner and the custom": Folk tradition and identity in Cornwall' (unpublished doctoral thesis, University of Exeter, 2011); Peter Tremewan, 'The relief of poverty in Cornwall, 1780-1881: From collateral support to respectability', in Payton (ed.), *Cornish Studies Sixteen*, 2008, 78-103. The micro-geography of the mining industry within Cornwall is summarised in Bernard Deacon, 'Mining the data: What can a quantitative approach tell us about the micro-geography of nineteenth-century Cornish mining?', in Payton (ed.), *Cornish Studies Eighteen*, 2010, 15-32. For the original statistical data at an individual mine level see Roger Burt, with Raymond Burnley, Michael Gill and Alasdair Neill, *Mining in Cornwall &*

Following the Cornish miner (and others) overseas Sharron Schwartz applied the concept of transnationalism to Cornish communities but argued that the more sporadic connections of the Cornish diaspora better warranted a description of translocalism rather than transnationalism. In a further article, this idea of translocalism was fleshed out and applied in a scalar way, suggesting that global connections in the nineteenth century linked communities overseas with communities in Cornwall rather than Cornwall as such. The latter had to await the more nostalgic imaginings of the Cornish Associations of the late Victorian and Edwardian periods. Meanwhile Dean Mullen and Peter Birt suggest that archaeological evidence from the riverbank dwellers at Burra, in Australia, can tell us something about Cornish ethnicity. The greater number of ceramic bowls indicate the Cornish ate more stews, porridges and soups and for Mullen and Birt indicated a 'pride in their regional society' and a 'preference for tradition', as well as a disregard for notions of propriety. Meanwhile, Lesley Trotter offers a more convincing analysis of the often ignored topic of the women 'left behind' by emigrating miners, restoring to women an active role in Cornwall's emigration history.[81]

Simon Naylor has used several Cornish examples as illustrative material for his innovative work on the history of science. He cites the activities of the Penzance Natural History and Antiquarian Society, formed in 1839, to show how 'knowledge is locally produced and situated'. Expanding on this, his work on nineteenth century meteorology deconstructs the notion of homogeneous and placeless scientific endeavour. The set of emerging practices associated with British meteorology extended unevenly across the physical landscape and was constructed on the periphery as well as in the centre. Furthermore, Naylor shows how the geography of power was

---

Devon: Mines and Men (Exeter: University of Exeter Press, 2014).

81   Sharron Schwartz, 'Bridging "The Great Divide": The Evolution and Impact of Cornish Translocalism in Britain and the USA', Journal of American Ethnic History 25 (2006), 169-189; Bernard Deacon and Sharron Schwartz, 'Cornish identities and migration: a multi-scalar approach', Global Networks 7 (2007), 289-206; Dean Mullen and Peter J. Birt, 'Modernity and Tradition: Considerations of Cornish Identity in the Archaeological Record of a Burra Dugout', Australian Archaeology 69 (2009), 59-67; Lesley Trotter, 'Desperate? Destitute? Deserted? Questioning perceptions of miners' wives in Cornwall during the Great Emigration, 1851-1891', in Philip Payton (ed.), Cornish Studies Nineteen (Exeter: University of Exeter Press, 2011), 195-224, '"Husband abroad"; Quantifying spousal separation associated with emigration in nineteenth-century Cornwall', in Philip Payton (ed.), Cornish Studies Twenty (Exeter: University of Exeter Press, 2012), 180-198 and '19th century emigration from Cornwall as experienced by the wives "left behind"' (unpublished doctoral thesis, University of Exeter, 2015).

negotiated and relational, rather than predetermined, illustrating this by reference to the successful campaign to prevent the closure of Falmouth's observatory in 1883, a conclusion that may have relevance for twenty-first century Cornwall.[82]

Other articles add to our understanding of Cornwall's transition to modernity. Taking Cornwall as a case study, Graeme Kirkham sketches the way in which archaeological monuments - barrows, fort ramparts, earth banks and the like - were grubbed up and destroyed as farmers increasingly saw them as convenient resources for improving soil fertility.[83] Depredations grew in the eighteenth and nineteenth centuries as an expanding population, the enclosure of heaths and downs, the introduction of wheeled transport and a general 'improving' approach to agriculture increased the pressure on formerly respected landscape features. This paralleled shifts in popular perceptions as the superstitions surrounding and to some extent protecting monuments began to fade. There's not much evidence here for the celebration of ancient monuments claimed by Laviolette. Far from being the epitome of the timeless tradition of late nineteenth century novelists, folk in Cornwall were at the forefront of changing, more functional attitudes to landscapes, discarding the relevance of the 'ancient'. New attitudes, fostered by precociously early industrialization, had created a 'teeming and vibrant', innovative and questioning culture, particularly in the west.

Dafydd Moore suggests that Richard Polwhele's *History of Cornwall*, written at the turn of the nineteenth century, and long overlooked by 'serious' historians of Cornwall, is one of the best re-creations of a 'sense of immersion' in this culture. Moore comes close to re-defining Polwhele's collage, festooned with footnotes, 'unsystematic, unorganised, rambling and

---

82 Simon Naylor, 'The field, the museum and the lecture hall: the spaces of natural history in Victorian Cornwall', *Transactions of the Institute of British Geographers* 27 (2002), 494-513; 'Nationalizing provincial weather: meteorology in nineteenth-century Cornwall', *The British Journal for the History of Science* 39 (2006), 407-433. See also his 'Provincial Authorities and Botanical Provinces; Elizabeth Warren's "Hortus Siccus of the Indigenous Plants of Cornwall"', *Garden History* 35 (2007), 84-95 and *Regionalizing Science: Placing Knowledges in Victorian England* (London: Pickering & Chatto, 2010).

83 Graeme Kirkham, '"Rip it up, and spread it over the field": Post-Medieval Agriculture and the Destruction of Monuments, a Case Study from Cornwall', *Landscapes* 3 (2012), 1-20. Laviolette, 'Deathliness'. Cathryn Pearce contributes an equally thought-provoking corrective to romantic notions of the Cornish wrecker in her comprehensive study of the realities and myths surrounding this activity (Cathryn Pearce, *Cornish Wrecking 1700-1860: Reality and Popular Myth* (Woodbridge: Boydell, 2010).

at times unreadable', as prefiguring a postmodernist fascination with the mundane, everyday and trivial. He also uses Polwhele as an example of a regional Romanticism within a 'four [sic] nations' or 'archipelagic' approach to literary criticism. This de-centres notions of Britain and/or England and replaces monolithic metropolitan notions of English Romanticism with a 'more carefully nuanced set of cultural contexts'.[84]

This reference to the 'four nations' or 'New British History' approach brings us neatly to the seventeenth century. At one time, this was seen as an appropriate context for Cornish history more generally, although work on Cornwall from within this paradigm has been limited to Mark Stoyle's output on sixteenth and seventeenth century Cornwall. Recently, Stoyle has provided an interesting, forensic and very close-grained account of the course of the 1549 rising to re-assess its Cornish dimension.[85] On the basis of this, he challenges the consensus view that the Cornish rose before the men of Sampford Courtenay in Devon, dating the Cornish rising a month later. Instead he proposes that the Cornish force moved east to join an existing siege of Exeter before being defeated by the state's counter-attacks. While revising the timing of the rising, Stoyle re-affirms that the Devonian and Cornish risings were 'quite distinctive', with the Cornish being more assertive and aggressive, something he links to their sense of ethnic difference.

In an excellent historical geographical account of the relationship between the Cornish language and identity in the early modern period, Stuart Dunmore paints a more complex picture than Stoyle, who he suggests loses sight of a model of cultural heterogeneity between east and west Cornwall in his drive to construct the whole century from 1548 to 1648 as a linked and continuous process of defending ethnic identity. Instead Dunmore plumps for changing political behaviours from the sixteenth to the seventeenth centuries and multiple ethno-linguistic identities. While Cornish was the medium of community life in the west, it was already an 'iconised symbol of distinctiveness' among non-speakers in the east. (In other words it was already a post-vernacular language for many Cornish

---

84 Dafydd Moore, '"The Romance of Real Life": Richard Polwhele's Representation of the Literary Culture and Language of Cornwall', in Shelley Trower (ed.), *Place, Writing, and Voice in Oral History* (Basingstoke: Palgrave MacMillan, 2011), 41-58 and 'Devolving Romanticism: Nation, Region and the Case of Devon and Cornwall', *Literature Compass* 5 (2008), 949-963.

85 Mark Stoyle, '"Fullye bente to Fighte Oute the Matter": Reconsidering Cornwall's Role in the Western Rebellion of 1549', *English Historical Review*, 129 (2014), 549-577. Stoyle's output on early modern Cornwall has been brought together in *West Britons; Cornish Identities and the early Modern British State* (Exeter: University of Exeter Press, 2002).

people). In the seventeenth century this symbolic status could begin to feed into a newer, embryonic identity based on territory rather than culture.[86]

The question of how far this identity change was structured by a rupture of older and long-lasting links south across the sea to Brittany is still open. While the Breton-Cornish connection of the medieval period awaits its historian, John Allan's work on Breton immigrants in Cornwall in the early sixteenth century does much to quantify their presence. He suggests that most were young men in their late teens. While the majority were described as labourers there was a significant number of carvers and carpenters who played a key role in introducing Breton techniques to Devon and Cornwall.[87] While his detailed examples come from Devon, the role of Breton immigrants in mid and west Cornwall, where the heaviest concentrations were found, and their influence of identity maintenance in the first half of the sixteenth century is an intriguing one and surely worth further examination.

The fifteenth century is a less-researched period, partly owing to a paucity of sources, but it has been the subject of a few articles. Hannes Kleinike applies to Cornwall (and Devon) the idea of a 'representational revolution' in the fifteenth century when parliamentary representation shifted from local merchants to outsiders and landowners. She found that by the 1470s not one Cornish borough was conducting a free election, as they were unable to resist the power of the Crown and influential local magnates.[88]

Moving from parliamentary politics to the economy, Phillipp Schofield uses the Arundell estate papers to complement John Hatcher's account of the Cornish economy in the fifteenth century based on Duchy records.[89] The

---

86　Stuart Dunmore, "anguage Decline and the "Theory of Cornish Distinctiveness": The Historiography of Language and Identity in Early Modern Cornwall', *Proceedings of the Harvard Celtic Colloquium* 31 (2011), 91-105. See also Deacon, *Cornwall*, pp. 88-89. For an example of this symbolic use of the language see Matthew Spriggs, 'William Scawen (1600-1689) - a neglected Cornish patriot and father of the Cornish language revival', in Payton (ed.), *Cornish Studies Thirteen*, 2005, 98-125.

87　John Allan, 'Breton woodworkers in the immigrant communities of south-west England, 1500-1550', *Post-Medieval Archaeology* 48 (2014), 320-356.

88　Hannes Kleinike, 'The Widening Gap: The Practice of Parliamentary Borough Elections in Devon and Cornwall in the Fifteenth century', *Parliamentary History* 23 (2008), 122-135.

89　Phillipp Schofield, 'The Arundell estates and the regional economy of fifteenth-century Cornwall', in Mark Bailey and Stephen Rigby (eds), *Town and Countryside in the Age of the Black Death* (Turnhout: Brepols, 2012), 277-297. The classic account of Cornwall's fifteenth-century economy can be found in John Hatcher, *Rural Economy and Society in the Duchy of Cornwall*

results are ambiguous. He argues that the stability of the later fifteenth century was experienced on a local rather than regional Cornish scale. Moreover, he concludes that estate records and the manorial economy were perhaps relatively unimportant in Cornwall and in consequence cannot tell us much about the Cornish economy. One sector that was growing in the fifteenth century was commercial fishing. Maryanne Kowaleski describes and explains the rise of fish curing and the pilchard fisheries in the late fifteenth century with reference to expanding markets.[90] Overall however, the fifteenth century economy remains puzzling historical territory. The contradictions between evidence for a diversified and expanding Cornish economy, yet continuing demographic decline into the early sixteenth century have yet to be convincingly teased out.

As we might expect, work on medieval Cornwall before the fifteenth century shows little explicit engagement with a Cornish Studies perspective.[91] This is despite some interesting recent doctoral work in archaeology. For instance, new perspectives have been adopted by Kirsten Jarrett on identity in the Roman and post-Roman south west, by Imogen Wood on the 'fragmented micro-networks' and lack of 'centralised authority' in the seventh to ninth centuries and Imogen Tompsett, who proposes a maritime core and an inland periphery in early medieval Cornwall.[92] Wood's work links to David Harvey's conclusion that in later

---

1300-1500 (Cambridge: Cambridge University Press, 1970) while the Arundell estate documents have been published in Harold S.Fox and Oliver J.Padel (eds), *The Cornish Lands of the Arundells of Lanherne, Fourteenth to Sixteenth Centuries* (Exeter: Devon and Cornwall Record Society, 2000).

90 Maryanne Kowaleski, 'The expansion of the South-Western Fisheries in Late Medieval England', *Economic History Review*, 53 (2000), 429-454.

91 For an exception see Cara Sheldrake, 'The History of Belerion: An investigation into the discussions of Greeks and Romans in Cornwall' (unpublished doctoral thesis, University of Exeter, 2012).

92 Kirsten Jarrett, 'Cives and Saxones: the expression of Ethnicity in southwest Britain in the Early Middle Ages', in Lorna Bleach, Katariina Närä, Sian Prosser and Paola Scarpini (eds), *In Search of the Medieval Voice: Expressions of Identity in the Middle Ages* (Cambridge: Cambridge Scholars, 2009), 80-100; Imogen Wood, 'Changing the fabric of life in post-Roman and early medieval Cornwall: an investigation into social change through petrographic analysis' (unpublished doctoral thesis, University of Exeter, 2011); Imogen Tompsett, 'Social Dynamics in South-West England AD350-1150: an exploration of maritime oriented identity in the Atlantic approaches and Western channel region' (unpublished doctoral thesis, University of Nottingham, 2012). Tompsett echoes conclusions about Cornwall's place as an inside-out industrial and maritime region a millennium later in the late eighteenth century in Bernard Deacon, 'Cornwall: An Inside-out industrial region', in Philip Payton, Alston Kennerley and Helen Doe (eds), *The*

west Cornwall there was a communal identity independent of 'dynastic loyalty or spiritual superstition' that gave non-lordly people the capacity to exercise control over their own lives. These findings fed into my attempt to re-imagine a narrative for early medieval Cornwall that might be more directly influenced by a Cornish Studies perspective.[93]

Landscapes of power

Twentieth century Cornwall continues to attract much less attention from historians than the nineteenth. What work exists tends to focus on Cornish politics. Within that corpus, Liberalism still attracts the bulk of academic attention from Cornish Studies specialists. Garry Tregidga, for example, suggests that rural Liberalism in the late 1930s, far from being doomed, displayed hints of a resurgence. Moves towards an electoral pact with Labour, which withdrew from a by-election in North Cornwall in 1939, promised Liberal gains in the 1940 election that never took place due to the war.[94]

John Ault examines the post-1950s resurgence of Cornish Liberalism, asking whether culture, personalities (such as Bessell, Pardoe and Penhaligon), or campaigning best explain the growth in Liberal and then Liberal Democrat support to its high point in the 1997-2005 period.[95] Perhaps not surprisingly for the co-author of *The Liberal Democrat Campaign Manual* (2000), Ault concludes that community politics and campaigning (defined as the number of leaflets per constituency) were the keys to Liberal Democrat success. The historic strength of Liberalism in Cornwall prompts him to suggest that Cornwall 'might be the area most pre-disposed to maintaining this Liberal tradition'. Unfortunately for this

---

Maritime History of Cornwall (Exeter: University of Exeter Press, 2014), 276-283.

93 David C. Harvey, 'Territoriality, parochial development, and the place of "community" in later medieval Cornwall', *Journal of Historical Geography* 29 (2003), 151-165. Bernard Deacon, *Cornwall's First Golden Age: from the Romans to the Normans* (London: Francis Boutle, 2016), which includes a far fuller bibliography of work on early medieval Cornwall.

94 Garry Tregidga, 'Turning of the Tide? A Case Study of the Liberal Party in Provincial Britain in the Late 1930s', *History* 92 (2007), 347-366. See also Garry Tregidga, *Killerton, Camborne and Westminster: The Political Correspondence of Sir Francis and Lady Acland 1910-1929* (Exeter: Devon and Cornwall Record Society, 2006). (For the nineteenth century see Edwin Jaggard, *Cornwall Politics in the Age of Reform 1790-1885* (Woodbridge: Boydell, 1999).

95 John Ault, '"Culture, Character or Campaigns?" Assessing the electoral performance of the Liberals and Liberal Democrats in Cornwall 1945-2010' (unpublished doctoral thesis, University of Exeter, 2014).

argument, the 2015 election resulted in a drop of 19.2 percentage points in Lib Dem support in Cornwall, compared with 16.1 points in England. It remains to be seen whether Cornish Liberalism is in a terminal condition or whether this proves to be merely another temporary setback (like the early 1930s or the 1940s and early 1950s), from which, phoenix-like, it will rise again and the whole cycle repeat itself. The results of the 2017 general election, the first since the 1950s when Labour polled more votes in Cornwall than Liberals, might indicate that Liberalism in Cornwall is in danger of being replaced by Labourism.

There are perhaps lessons in the Popular Front movement of the 1930s that can be applied by those seeking to challenge the current Conservative Party hegemony in Cornwall in a context of a disproportional first past the post voting system. However, this hegemony is nothing particularly new and is well overdue for some research. While Ed Jaggard has provided a useful study of Edward Boscawen, Lord Falmouth's ultra-Toryism in 1826-32 and the run-up to the first Reform Act, similar work on the ideologies and constituencies of support for twentieth and twenty-first century Cornish Toryism is still wanting and would add to our understanding of Cornish politics.[96]

The ongoing campaign for devolution to Cornwall continues to attract attention. MK persists, but remains stuck at a low level and fails to break through, particularly at a parliamentary level, despite the claimed evidence for a strengthening identity.[97] Although some other institutions pay lip service to devolution, these are unconvincing, either confusing regional government with local government, masking institutional agendas for enhanced (or protected) budgets, or stymied by neo-liberal arguments about 'unaffordable' financial and informational costs. Nonetheless, a low level broader campaign for democratic (as opposed to institutional, top-down) regionalism spluttered erratically into life in demands for a Cornish Assembly, in the early 2000s and in ongoing, defensive campaigns against border-blurring. Since the 1970s the Duchy of Cornwall has also often been cited as a possible pole for devolution. However, John Kirkhope has deconstructed the historical constitutional claims of the Duchy, pointing out how many Duchy 'rights' were only claimed in modern times and were usually driven by short-term financial motives rather than long-term historic rights.[98]

---

96   Edwin Jaggard, 'Lord Falmouth and the Parallel Political Worlds of Ultra-Toryism, 1826-32', *Parliamentary History* 33 (2014), 300-320.

97   Bernard Deacon, Dick Cole and Garry Tregidga, *Mebyon Kernow & Cornish Nationalism* (Cardiff: Welsh Academic Press, 2003) and see below, Chapter 8.

98   John Kirkhope, 'The Duchy of Cornwall – a feudal remnant?: An examination of the origin, evolution and present status of the Duchy of Cornwall'

Wider studies have lessons for Cornwall. Echoing the distinction made above between the regional image and the regional identity, Martin Jones and Gordon Macleod differentiated the regional spaces imposed by the state, such as the former South West region, from spaces of regionalism, encouraging or forged by 'insurgent regionalism', as in Cornwall. Mark Sandford contrasted regionalism in the North East of England, elite-focused and technocratic, with the identity politics of Cornwall, ignored and dismissed by policy elites. In his view this was because campaigners failed to make the economic arguments that drove New Labour's regional policy. His work has been taken further by Joanie Willett and Arianna Giovaninni, who place more weight on the cultural and political reasons for this contrast between the top-down regionalism of the North East and the bottom-up version in Cornwall. The former concentrated on economic development and good governance and was led by an elite group with close links to the centre. The latter was a grassroots campaign in an area which did not fit the state's 'rational' boundaries, was politically insignificant for Labour and furthermore unpredictable and hard to control. In the event, it made no difference. The failure to exploit the North East's embryonic regional identity meant that centralised English regionalism fell at the first hurdle, with New Labour acting as the 'silent orchestrator of regional devolution's demise'.[99]

After the first Scottish independence referendum, there was a temporary spike of interest in devolution within the UK state. This may be confirmed and enhanced by the decision to exit the EU and the possible emergence of an inward-looking and even more xenophobic and nostalgic brand of English nationalism. In that context claims for more autonomy or even statehood from the other nations of the UK may gain ground. Technically, since their recognition as a national minority in 2014 the Cornish are now one of those nations. So far however, this appears to have made little impact on policy-makers both within and outwith Cornwall. Instead, Cornwall Council did manage to obtain one of the first of the Government's post-Scottish referendum 'devolution deals' in 2015. But Joanie Willett adopts a sceptical take in her assessment of this. It did very little to alter the

---

(unpublished doctoral thesis, University of Plymouth, 2013).

99 Martin Jones and Gordon Macleod, 'Regional Spaces, Spaces of Regionalism: Territory, Insurgent Politics and the English Question', *Transactions of the Institute of British Geographers* 29 (2004), 433-452; Mark Sandford, 'English Regionalism through the Looking Glass: Perspectives on the English Question from the North East and Cornwall', *National Identities* 8 (2006), 77-93; Joanie Willett and Arianna Giovannini, 'The Uneven Path of UK Devolution: Top-Down vs. Bottom-Up Regionalism in England – Cornwall and the North-East Compared', *Political Studies* 62 (2014), 343-360.

centralised aspects of English governance or create spaces for local actors to feed back into state policy. In short, it was the familiar top-down and hierarchical 'space of regionalism', more about devolving the implementation (and responsibilities) of central government policy than devolving democratic powers over policy-making itself.[100]

Any potential moves to devolve meaningful powers to Cornwall are of course hamstrung by that image of Cornwall that, as we have seen, many scholars from different perspectives – sociological, historical, literary – have done much to identify and deconstruct. From within political studies Joanie Willett and Thilo Lang have recently added to this corpus of work in an article that suggests previous analyses of core/periphery relationships and the construction of peripheral regions have given insufficient space to the role of agency. In their contribution, which repeats the argument made in Willett's 2014 piece in *Political Studies* (see above, note 37), they provide a useful summary of how regions are discursively produced. But they insist that people, businesses and politicians in peripheries are also 'active agents in shaping the spaces within which they live'. The very act of constructing a place as a periphery creates spaces of opportunity for resistance. This is backed empirically by an account of a small number of people in Cornwall who, it is claimed, may be disempowered in terms of political structures but not by discourse which they are able to subvert or resist. However, Willett and Lang then resort to relying on local elites to utilise 'topics, memes, meanings' to energise local communities. Despite recognising that power relationships are involved in the production of regions, their characterisation of those relationships is ultimately ambiguous, obscured and obscuring. Regions are free-floating, drifting in a discursive space, but unattached to material interests which drive specific regional agendas and projects.[101]

While Liberalism, devolution and the discursive production of 'Cornwall' are now relatively well covered in research on contemporary Cornwall, there are many areas that remain untouched. Social scientist Colin Williams called for the production of more data and evidence about contemporary Cornish socio-economic patterns. This was echoed by Malcolm Williams, who identified a number of gaps in Cornish Studies and its over-concentration on historical material.[102] Specifically, he noted there was little on the Cornish economy, second homes, recent politics and the

---

100 Joanie Willett, 'Cornwall's devolution deal: towards a more sustainable governance?', *Political Quarterly*, 87 (2016), 582-589.

101 Joanie Willett and Thilo Lang, 'Peripheralisation: A politics of place, affect, perception and representation', *Sociologia Ruralis*, 57 (2017).

102 Colin Williams, 'On ideology', 2002; Malcolm Williams, 'New Cornish Social Science', 2002.

endurance of nationalism, empirical accounts of the identity, the role of language revival in its formation and how stereotyped images feed into local perspectives. We might add to this list the economics of devolution, the dynamics and drivers of the Lifestyle Cornwall project and the impact of EU regeneration spending, all of which have received little or no attention.[103] However, as we have seen, since Williams made his list in 2002 there has been considerable work on identities in Cornwall and the Cornish identity in particular and the effect of stereotyped representations on the way people think. There has also been work on the campaigns for devolution.

However, gaps remain. Moreover, work on contemporary Cornwall tends to reflect the web of representations that surround and enmesh Cornwall, both old (the role of the maritime) and new (the rise of Lifestyle Cornwall). As we have seen, the heritage industry and its links to the commodification of Cornwall's past have been the subject of some attention. Patrick Laviolette and Kingsley Baird provide a preliminary, somewhat nebulous and postmodernist, account of the Heartlands project at Pool while Hilary Orange and Patrick Laviolette revisit the marketing of Tintagel and discover that a mixed message persists.[104] There is archaeological criticism of the Arthurian myth but collusion with that myth to sell stuff. The failure of English Heritage, who manage the site, to provide such archaeological evidence in a local context comes in for criticism but is hardly surprising given the fundamental contradiction of a body with this title managing such a site in the first place.

Moreover, there has been little research on the potential impact of World Heritage Site status or the contradictions and tensions involved in packaging an industrial past as part of a Lifestyle Cornwall marketing 'offer'. Tourism has been the subject of some work, but with a telling tendency to focus on the new lifestyle aspect of gastronomic tourism. Graham Busby et al. analyse the influence of TV chef Rick Stein on Padstow and suggest that he has created a complementary link in efforts to market the town, although not pursuing the longer term effects of those links. Sally Everett and Cara Aitchison interview a dozen restaurateurs and arrive at the 'exploratory'

---

103 Attitudes to the EU by some of the political elite in Cornwall make an appearance in a comparative case study by Frank Mols and S. Alexander Haslam, 'Understanding EU Attitudes in Multi-Level Governance Contexts: A Social Identity Perspective', *West European Politics* 31 (2008), 442-463.

104 Patrick Laviolette and Kingsley Baird, 'Lost Innocence and Land Matters: Community regeneration and memory mining', *European Journal of English Studies* 15 (2011), 57-71; Hilary Orange and Patrick Laviolette, 'A Disgruntled Tourist in King Arthur's Court: Archaeology and Identity at Tintagel, Cornwall', *Public Archaeology* 9 (2000), 85-107.

conclusion that food tourism enhances regional identity. This of course depends on how regional identity is defined and the authors of this article adopt a superficial view of place identity engineered from tourist representations, one comprising festivals, distinct local produce and educational visitor attractions, more a regional image in fact than a regional identity.[105]

Meanwhile, Andy Newing et al. completed a detailed analysis of the effect of visitor demand on seasonal grocery sales in Cornwall. Their conclusions reinforce common sense, that there is a spatial clustering of visitor demand as well as the more generally recognised temporal clustering. While making use of sources such as South West Tourism and even planning applications to reach some stereotyped assertions, for example that 'Cornwall is one of the most remote counties in the UK' and that it 'relies heavily on tourism', the detailed findings are of interest and provide a good snapshot of tourist spending. What is somewhat at odds with their assumptions is the finding that tourist spending has 'very little, if any, seasonal effect' on inland supermarkets while their estimate of the proportion of tourist spending at two coastal stores amounts to just 28% of the total. Even in August they discover that local residential demand amounts to 50-60% of spending in the coastal stores. What is required now is more critical exploration of the contradiction passed over in silence in Newing et al. - that tourism is 'one of Cornwall's most valuable industries' yet 'the dependence on low skilled, low paid and seasonal occupations in the tourist industry [has] resulted in widespread deprivation'.[106]

More challenging conclusions are arrived at in a brace of articles flowing from an EU-funded study of the inshore fishing industry in the UK. Julie Urquhart and Tim Acott note how fishing policy has favoured large scale, 'efficient', boats, even though industrial fishing has caused a global fisheries crisis. They argue that inshore fisheries need to be integrated more explicitly into rural development strategies, with shorter supply chains, more local value added, and improved processes of certification to

---

105 Graham Busby, Rong Huang and Rebecca Jarman, 'The Stein Effect: an Alternative Film-Induced Tourism Perspective" *International Journal of Tourism Research* 15 (2013), 570-582; Sally Everett and Cara Aitchison, 'The Role of Food Tourism in Sustaining Regional Identity: A Case Study of Cornwall, South West England', *Journal of Sustainable Tourism* 16 (2008), 150-167.

106 Andy Newing, Graham Clarke and Martin Clarke, 'Identifying seasonal variations in store-level visitor grocery demand', *International Journal of Retail & Distribution management* 41 (2013), 477-492 and 'Visitor expenditure estimation for grocery store location planning: a case study of Cornwall', *International Review of Retail, Distribution and Consumer Research* 23 (2013), 221-244.

guarantee authenticity and provenance. Matt Reed at al. build on Urquhart and Acott's observation that inshore fishing contributes to community cohesion and identity through maintaining a cultural heritage based on fishing. They pinpoint the role of fishing in place-making and the tensions between that role and the traffic of fish as a commodity. Noting how technocratic management creates resentment, they call for a 'slow food' approach and local branding, linking catches to locality. But significantly, to do this they also conclude that the reinsertion of local democratic control over the fishing industry is essential.[107] Although this work was not informed by Cornish Studies, its policy prescriptions clearly mesh with an approach that puts the re-valorisation of Cornish culture at the centre of economic strategies.

Conclusions

With the advantage of hindsight, we can see that the idea of a unified Cornish Studies theory looks to be dead in the water and awaiting a decent burial. There seems to be no emerging methodological preference among Cornish Studies practitioners. Those provocations of the early 2000s, calling for a distinctly Cornish Studies methodology beyond a normative commitment to Cornwall and its people would therefore appear to have been over-ambitious, or perhaps premature. The preference is for a pluralist approach, ranging from qualitative methods to quantitative, from discourse analysis through action research to empirical studies. Nonetheless, to survive as a respectable field of study Cornish Studies has to avoid reverting to the state of a 'fun subject', happy to trundle along with no discernible theoretical or methodological perspective. In fact, as this review has illustrated, work from a Cornish Studies perspective since the turn of the millennium has done much to advance our understanding on a number of fronts.

Unsurprisingly, given its underlying normative project to ensure Cornwall, its people and its past, remain fit objects of study in their own right, achievements have been most notable in the area of representations and identities. This has encompassed both externally reproduced identities and internal identities, with a refreshing willingness to challenge the foundational myths of the field itself, for example by rethinking revivalism, the forms it has taken and the consequences it had, in particular its largely unwitting complicity with Lifestyle Cornwall. More recent work, especially

---

107 Julie Urquhart and Tim G. Acott, 'Re-connecting and embedding food in place: Rural development and inshore fisheries in Cornwall, UK', *Journal of Rural Studies* 32 (2013), 357-364; Matt Reed, Paul Courtney, Julie Urquhart and Natalie Ross, 'Beyond fish as commodities: Understanding the socio-cultural role of inshore fisheries in England', *Marine Policy* 37 (2013), 62-68.

by writers such as Alan Kent and Neil Kennedy, has begun to re-valorise traditional Cornishness and rescue it from the condescensions of posterity. These twin processes - deconstructing and historicizing the dominant taken-for-granted ideological stereotypes and representations that underpin Lifestyle Cornwall, and re-examining the character of Proper Cornishness and Cornu-English culture - are themselves legitimated by a turn to hybridity and the notion of alternative, plural, heterogeneous Cornwalls. As Gemma Goodman neatly puts it 'awareness of multiple versions of place operating simultaneously is therefore the starting point for unlocking alternative Cornwalls'.[108] To build on this, heritage as an interface between contemporary and past Cornwalls and a connection of living and cultural memory may have an as yet largely unexplored role as a cultural regeneration resource, if locally directed and imbued with a strong dose of 'critical nostalgia'.

While the area of representations and identities has seen the biggest advances over the last decade or so, there has been solid, if patchy, progress in historical studies, literary studies and some social sciences. Nevertheless, a Cornish Studies perspective, recognising the existence of ethnic boundaries in Cornwall, could still in many cases potentially add a lot more value to existing work on Cornwall. For example, Simon Hill et al. found that suicide rates in Cornwall have risen steadily over recent decades and are now higher than the UK average.[109] This contrasts with the historic pattern before the 1960s when suicide rates were lower (and interestingly belies the image of a laid-back Lifestyle Cornwall). Although employing variables of age, class and gender to try to address this shift, Hill et al. failed to apply ethnic distinctions. It would be interesting to know if the increased suicides since the 1960s were among the native population, a possible reaction against the socio-demographic transformation which significantly set in during that decade, or among the incoming migratory population, disillusioned by the failure of reality to match up to myth. Or perhaps, as rural suicide rates have risen generally across the UK, other factors are at work here.

---

108 Goodman, 'Cornwall', 2010, p.289. Helen Cornish's work on Padstow folk festivals alerts us again to complex and overlapping spatial levels of analysis, with locals' defence of Padstow going beyond claims to Cornish distinctiveness ('Not all singing and dancing: Padstow, folk festivals and belonging', *Ethnos: Journal of Anthropology* 81 (2016), 631-647.)

109 Simon A. Hill, Colin Pritchard, Richard Laugharne and David Gunnell, 'Changing patterns of suicide in a poor, rural county over the 20th century: A comparison with national trends', *Social Psychiatry and Psychiatric Epidemiology* 40 (2005), 601-604.

More frustratingly, some of the gaps identified more than ten years ago remain. For instance, given its political centrality, critical work is urgently needed on the effects of EU funding and the consequences of its disappearance, while the interface between contemporary and historic cultural identity on the one hand and current socio-economic patterns on the other requires more work to draw these two, often parallel and non-communicative strands of enquiry, together. The aim might now be to provide more inter-disciplinary studies of the trajectories of twenty-first century Cornwall and its people, combining the various insights into its representations and identities with analysis of the emergent project of Lifestyle Cornwall and its location in more global material and ideological structures. To return to Malcolm Williams' aims for a 'relevant' New Cornish Studies we might conclude that we now better understand what people in Cornwall think; the focus can now turn to more sophisticated descriptions of what contemporary Cornwall is like and where it's likely to be heading.

Indeed Cornish Studies, like Cornwall itself, is and perhaps should be, Janus-faced, experimenting with different approaches, open to eclecticism and innovation, self-reflexive yet committed. It offers hope, a point again succinctly made by Goodman – 'the framework established by New Cornish Studies gives practitioners within the field greater confidence to counter hegemonic definitions of Cornwall and Cornwall's past, to question erroneous stereotypes or historicising from an English-centred perspective'.[110] This could be built on. Cornish Studies can provide the space for a counterweight to the less reflexive but more ideologically grounded work on Cornwall undertaken by commercial research organisations, operating usually on commission from business interests, the tourist lobby or local/central government. Cornish Studies offers a standpoint from which comparative data and understanding of structures and processes affecting contemporary Cornwall can be generated, critically seeking those objective partial truths that can then be triangulated with the claims, assertions and assumptions of neo-liberal, conservative and commercially-driven social research.

We have come full circle. The heterogeneous character of work on Cornwall in recent decades suggests that the fundamental base of Cornish Studies is not its methods, nor its purpose (research questions or issues), nor its outcomes or conclusions, all of which it can and does share with Cornish studies with a lower case s, but its attitude to Cornwall and its people.

---

110 Goodman, 'Cornwall', 2010, p.10.

Chapter 5

'Poor people cannot do all they could': Microhistory and mining families in 1841

The term microhistory is often used in a general sense to describe the intensive investigation of a small area or a single case study. Given the geographical focus of microhistory and its gradual move from the margins of cultural and social history into the mainstream since the 1970s, it's perhaps perplexing that it has played little explicit role in Cornish historical studies. Even though Cornish historians have eschewed using the term, a lot of their work would seem to fit the genre, in particular when the subject under investigation is being studied in its own right rather than being used to illustrate broader generalisations. The genealogy of microhistory is also intriguing, stretching as it does back to the social history of E.P.Thompson and by implication to the work of Cornwall's most accomplished social historian, John Rule, who wrote from within a firmly Thompsonian tradition.[1] What I intend to do here is to apply the microhistorical approach to Cornwall's mining communities in the year 1841, to see how far the details provided by just one source can open up a window into the everyday lives of members of that community and bring us closer to their lives and experiences.

But first, what do we mean by microhistory? Having come of age in the academy, microhistory has taken on a more specific meaning. Microhistorians are supposed to prefer the 'little facts' of history, the peculiarities of place, the particularities of the past rather than grand narratives. This would seem to increase its attraction for those toiling away in the Cornish archives. This more precise use of the term microhistory takes its inspiration from the Italian *microstoria*. Pat Hudson, who prefers the term historical microscopy to the more specific microhistory, identifies some central elements in the microhistorical approach. These include its point of view, its concern with everyday life and the space it provides for issues of agency.[2]

---

1 E.P.Thompson, *The Making of the English Working Class* (London: Gollancz, 1963); John Rule, *Cornish Cases: Essays in Eighteenth and Nineteenth Century Social History* (Southampton: Clio, 2006).

2 Pat Hudson, 'Closeness and distance: A response to Brewer'. *Cultural and Social History* 7 (2010), 375-385.

In terms of viewpoint, John Brewer identifies two types of historical writing – prospect history and refuge history.[3] When seen from the perspective of prospect history, the past is viewed from a single, superior point of view. Its actors take on the shape of an aggregated, undifferentiated mass. Refuge history is contrasted as a closer-up perspective, alert to the details of the past, able to look past structures and recover the experiences of agents, thus connecting the observer more intimately with the observed. While this dualism perhaps over-simplifies the contrast, Brewer's concern revolves around the location of the historian in relation to the past, his or her closeness or distance from that past. His argument is that closeness and, by implication, empathy and connectedness can be best achieved by narrowing the distance between observer and observed. However, our ability to achieve this when dealing with worlds that have gone, and the impossibility of comprehending the essential difference of the past, make this a narrowing of the distance rather than its abolition. In contrast, for de Vivo microhistory's value lies not so much in exchanging one perspective for another but the study of the small in terms of large issues, combining focus and vision, relating the micro and the macro. Instead of replacing one perspective with another, we should perhaps conceptualise microhistory as combining perspectives, deliberately adopting a plurality of viewpoints in order to uncover what has gone.[4]

Braudel once called everyday life the 'great absentee of history'.[5] The habitual, repetitive, taken for granted quotidian transactions whose routines call for no special comment were nonetheless the warp and weft of experience, the very core of life itself. In fact, here microhistory has offered two contradictory approaches. One branch has been attracted to the strangeness of the past. This works out from exceptional moments of abnormality, from the margins or significant deviations in order to uncover the rule that the exceptions prove. To some extent Italian *microstoria* was pushed in this direction by its reliance on state archives, recording acts and behaviours that challenged the norm and could be characterised as deviant.[6] This focus on 'normal exceptions' contrasts with a concern for the faint traces and the insignificant details of day to day rhythms, in order, rather

3   John Brewer, 'Microhistory and the histories of everyday life', *Cultural and Social History* 7 (2010), 87-109.
4   Filippo de Vivo, 'Prospect or refuge? Microhistory, history on the large scale', *Cultural and Social History* 7 (2010), 387-197.
5   Fernand Braudel, *Afterthoughts on Material Civilisation and Capitalism* (Baltimore: John Hopkins University Press, 1977), p.16.
6   Carlo Ginzburg, *The Cheese and the Worms: the Cosmos of a Sixteenth-Century Miller* (London: Routledge & Kegan Paul, 1980). See also Robert Darnton, *The great cat massacre and other episodes in French cultural history* (New York: Vintage Books, 1984).

grandly, to achieve 'profound illumination'. This has led microhistorians, especially in Britain, to concentrate on the mundane and the banal as much as the exceptional points where choices are confronted and decisions made. In doing so microhistory makes its connection back to the British social history influenced and steered by E.P.Thompson's attempt in the 1960s to recover the experience of the English working classes. As both Brewer and Hudson point out, this stemmed from a humanistic desire to recover the history of a variety of groups memorably described by Thompson as 'rescued from the condescension of posterity'.

The final element of the microhistorical endeavour is a concern with the question of agency. Microhistorians are keen to re-insert agency and ask how much scope there was for conscious human choice in various contexts. How far were historical actors imprisoned by economic, cultural and political structures? Levi stresses that a 'variety of possible outcomes' are discovered once the focus of the historian shifts to the small scale and the perspective of everyday life comes into the frame.[7] What looks like an undifferentiated mass takes on its own colours and shades into a heterogeneity of responses along with shared experiences. This aspect raises a broader methodological issue. The agenda of microhistory, shared with the British social historians of the 1960s and those influenced by the anthropologist Geertz's 'thick description', offers a humanist realism. The further reaches of post-modernism and the death of the subject are rejected in favour of a project that aims to reconstruct the 'reality', or several 'realities', of the past.[8]

No doubt some of the claims of the proponents of microhistory, for example that it is more 'interesting' for the general reader, or that it allows us to attain a state of 'total history' may be overblown.[9] Like all historical methodologies, some will respond with the metaphorical (and literal) shrugged shoulders and ask what's new. And to be sure, many historians

---

7   Giovanni Levi, 'The origins of the modern state and the microhistorical perspective', in Jurgen Schlumbohm (ed.), *Microgeschichte – Makrogeschichte: komplementar oder inkommensurabel?* (Gottingen: Wallstein Verlag, 1998), p.62.

8   Inevitably, by offering microhistory as an explicit method for Cornish historical studies I lay myself open to the charge of contradicting earlier calls for more attention to be paid to discourse theory in Cornish Studies more generally. However, I would hold that these two points are not as contradictory as they may appear. The 'reality' our past actors experienced could not be communicated except via words. Similarly, shared discourses of that reality would structure experience. In short, discourse was a part of the reality that people lived through in the past.

9   István Szijártó, 'Four arguments for microhistory', *Rethinking History* 6 (2002), 209-215.

will discover that their unreflective empiricism, or at least aspects of it, can comfortably shelter under the umbrella of microhistory. Its critics have also accused microhistory of encouraging a folksy voyeurism towards an exotic past (although this would seem more relevantly directed at the significant deviation school than the typical-normal uncovering of quotidian rhythms). Others point out how the category of experience can be reified by microhistorians. In contrast to the idea of the everyday being more 'real', they point out how the everyday is itself ideologically constructed. Finally, some have criticised an overly sympathetic identification with past agents.[10] However, this latter itself seems to veer towards adopting unrealistic notions of scientific objectivity and distance. At this point, the microhistorian would presumably readily plead guilty and admit to a point of view that explicitly tries to reduce that ultimately irreducible distance between now and then, between us and our forebears.

So how might we go about this? What might a microhistorical take on the Cornish in the past look like? At the very beginning of the 1840s two Parliamentary reports appeared. These described the mining districts of west and mid-Cornwall. The first, the Inspector of Schools Seymour Tremenheere's report on the 'State of Education in the Mining Districts of Cornwall', was prepared in 1840.[11] Tremenheere provided a picture of the mining communities, focusing on their hours of labour and their leisure time pursuits and taking particular note of their access to 'collateral aids'. These included the allotments, two or three acres leased on three lives, that up to a quarter of mining households possessed. Collateral aids did not end with smallholdings however. For other families there were potato patches, rented annually from farmers, and gardens and, in the westernmost mining district around St Just, the possibility of renting a cow or a part of a cow or taking shares in a fishing boat. These collateral aids provided a degree of insurance and reduced dependence on wages and the vagaries of either the international mining economy or the geological quirks underground that might raise or destroy the prospects of any single mine.

Tremenheere's account also reminds us of the close intermeshing of mining with agricultural and other non-industrial pursuits in the early nineteenth century, something not confined to Cornwall.[12] Moreover, Cornwall's relatively early industrialisation (the output of copper ore rose at a faster rate than either cotton, coal or iron production in the three decades

---

10 For these criticisms see Brewer, 'Microhistory', pp.103-104.

11 Seymour Tremenheere, 'Report on the State of Education in the Mining Districts of Cornwall', 1840. *British Parliamentary Papers*, 1841 Session 1 [317] Minutes of the Committee of Council on Education, 1840-41, 84-109.

12 Barry Reay, *Microhistories: Demography, Society and Culture in Rural England, 1800-1930* (Cambridge: Cambridge University Press, 1996).

before the 1780s) also produced a particular social balance, one that I have described elsewhere as a society of dispersed paternalism.[13] The combination of rural industrialisation that was not contained within existing urban areas and the growing Methodist allegiance that was slowly taking the mass of the population beyond the confines of the Established Church had produced a society where authority and paternalism was exercised at a remove via mine captains, land agents or Methodist itinerants rather than directly by the socially (and usually geographically) more remote landed and/or clerical classes. In the second report, Truro doctor Charles Barham wrote that 'many circumstances have conspired to give a character of independence - something American - to this population. The miner ... is a man of frank and independent manners. He is not often insolent, but he is usually blunt'. Although, he added, sometimes the younger men went beyond that.[14]

Tremenheere and Barham's reports were examples of a prospect point of view, surveying the contours of the mining districts from a social, if not geographical, distance, albeit with considerable sympathy. Yet they offer valuable descriptions of the mining districts just at the point where the industry was about to enter on a 20 year rising trend of output (punctuated nonetheless by harsh years, notably in the later 1840s).[15] The real value of Cornish mining had doubled between 1815 and the 1840s. It then rose by another 60% by the end of the 1850s to reach a plateau of production. This rise however put pressure on the dispersed rural-industrial society of collateral aids that had emerged over the course of the eighteenth century. As mining spread in the 1840s into east Cornwall and Devon the Cornish mining region began to converge - socially and to some extent culturally and politically - with industrial regions elsewhere, before the crises of the later 1860s and 1870s heralded mining's long drawn out and painful decline.

---

13 Bernard Deacon, 'The reformulation of territorial identity: Cornwall in the late eighteenth and nineteenth centuries', (unpublished doctoral thesis, Open University, 2001).

14 Charles Barham, 'Report on the employment of children and young persons in the mines of Cornwall and Devonshire, and on the state, condition, and treatment of such children and young persons', 1841. *British Parliamentary Papers*, 1842 [380] [381] [382] Royal Commission on Children's Employment in Mines and Manufactories. First Report (Mines and Collieries), 731-854.

15 Bernard Deacon, 'Proto-industrialization and potatoes: A revised narrative for nineteenth-century Cornwall', in Philip Payton (ed), *Cornish Studies Five* (Exeter: University of Exeter Press, 1997), 60-84 and 'Mining the data: What can a quantitative approach tell us about the micro-geography of nineteenth-century Cornish mining?', in Philip Payton (ed.), *Cornish Studies Eighteen* (Exeter: University of Exeter Press, 2010), 15-32.

Tremenheere and Barham's reports therefore came at an interesting time in the history of Cornish mining communities, at the end of a period of expansion but just before the spatial extension and social convergence that marked the middle decades of the nineteenth century. They also just preceded the onset of mass emigration, a movement of people that was given a considerable boost by the temporary hardships of the late 1840s.

However, the productive ground for the microhistorian lies not in the accounts of the mining districts offered by Tremenheere and Barham, even though these provide valuable descriptions of conditions for mining families and the socio-economic parameters of their lives. The potential gems lie in the 35 pages of evidence taken by Barham from 125 individuals across mining districts from St Just in Penwith in the west to St Blazey and Tywardreath in the east. In the months of March and April 1841 Barham conducted his 'examinations', asking questions about the organisation of surface work, the hours worked and the health of the workers. Nineteen mine agents and other professionals associated directly with the mines were questioned at length about the workforce. Another 17, including three magistrates, two Wesleyan Ministers, the Rector of Camborne, a rate collector, a surgeon and a schoolteacher, were also asked their opinions of the mining population. But Barham also interviewed and examined 89 working miners. Of these, 28 were children of 15 years old and under, 18 female surface workers and 43 other miners, the majority working underground.

The familiar problems of evidence provided to parliamentary commissions recur here. Those questioned were selected, the questions could be leading, the summaries biased in order to sway a commission in a certain direction. The intention of Barham's report was clearly to construct an argument for an improved system of education in the mining districts. However, there is no reason to conclude that the evidence of everyday activities gathered by him was biased in any obvious direction. Some of the questions asked of the gentry and professional respondents more predictably concerned the respectable fears of the time about gender boundaries and attempts to police them. Questions about the extravagance of dress, the moral conditions of the miners and the coarseness of their language crop up, but not regularly. One is left with the impression that Barham asked these because the Commission expected them rather than such questions being central to his investigation. The answers he obtained seem in any case to have been ambiguous. The principal agent at Wheal Vor thought there was 'room for improvement' in relation to the 'coarseness of language of females at the mine', but also at Wheal Vor a captain of tin dressers responded 'I think that (the girls) are pretty well spoken here generally'.[16]

---

16 Barham, 'Report', 1842, pp.841 and 848.

The voice of the people?

How close can this source take us to the authentic voice of Cornish people in the spring of 1841? Often, Barham's summaries of the examination of his interviewees are terse and almost entirely couched in the third person. Samuel Tippet for example was ten years old and worked at the dressing floors of Trethellan Mine near Lanner. His work for the previous fortnight had been 'washing up', cleaning the stones in wooden troughs prior to their dressing. Before, he was at the slimes but gave that up 'because the slimes was knacked'.[17] After this brief glimpse of Samuel's Cornu-English dialect the account becomes more impersonal.

> He lives with his grandfather about a mile off. He pays his wages to his grandfather. Had seven shillings a month on his first 'spurs' and now gets ten. He sometimes feels tired when he leaves work; chiefly in the back and legs. He brings potato 'hobban' with him for dinner. For breakfast he gets milk and water and bread, barley and wheat mixed. For supper baked potatoes, with pork sometimes. Goes to bed at eight; likes to stay up longer. He goes to school in the New Church (Lanner); has gone to Sunday-school two years. Learns to read and spell. Heard him read the Testament; he reads pretty well.

Other interviews were more revealing of the thoughts and feelings of the workers themselves. Fanny Francis, a 17 year old bal maiden at United Mines, Gwennap, had suffered from fits after a fall when carrying ore three months earlier, an accident that had presumably brought her to Barham's notice. She attended a Bible Christian chapel and had been at day school before starting to labour at the mines at 11 years old. Her mother was a widow left with five children, all of whom had some schooling before being 'put' to the mines. Yet, according to Fanny, 'they did not complain of the work', although one can glimpse a senses of regret at lost opportunities in her final words – 'but poor people cannot do all they could'.[18]

Sometimes, adult miners gave vivid accounts of their work underground. Richard Williams was a 45 year old miner at Wheal Jewell. He'd not suffered one illness since commencing underground work 'at about 11 years of age', until the Christmas of 1840. Then he was working in an end 170 fathoms from a draught of air. 'The air was so bad you could not burn a candle for four hours together'. He 'felt the air scalding down his throat; burning as though it had been hot water in his stomach'. Claiming that none of his comrades could stand the work more than two weeks, he did so for five, 'on account of his four children being employed in the mine, and his

---

17   Barham, 'Report', 1842, p.822.
18   Barham, 'Report', 1842, p.831.

being afraid of their being turned off if he did not continue', which might shed a different light on the much-vaunted independence of the Cornish miner. Since working there, Richard had 'brought up blood since, and now suffers from cough and weakness. He has expectorated black and slate coloured stuff'.[19]

Possibly the most poignant oral testimony to emerge from the evidence was that of John Penhall, a 50 year old miner working at Fowey Consols. John was obviously an intelligent man, teaching his nine children to read and write and paying for them to attend evening classes. He recounted to Barham that he'd taken one of his boys underground at the end of 1840. 'He was 12 years old, a very fine and strong boy of his age'. But about five weeks after starting work his son had fallen off a ladder and broken his leg and collar bone. At the time John was working in a 'distant part of the mine'.

> I travelled as fast as I could to the place; and I seemed to see, every few fathoms as I went, the body of my poor boy all crunched together; it was so clear I stopped and rubbed my eyes and asked myself whether I was in my right mind or no. When I got to the place, the boy was sitting upon a man's knee, looking up quite cheerful, only crying a little'.[20]

Most boys went underground with their fathers or other relatives. Even here, when more unusually his son wasn't working physically close to him, the concern of father for son is clearly evident.

Yet this could be seen as one of those examples of the extraordinary event, the microhistorian's significant deviation that, if it illuminates reality, does it rather indirectly. How far does the evidence enable us to take a close-up perspective on the more mundane daily rhythms of life?

Sleep, eat and ache. Everyday life at the mines
The working day for surface workers in 1841 was generally seven in the morning to five or five thirty, or daylight hours in winter. This could be longer when ores were being prepared for sampling. Occasionally fixed piece rate tasks were set and the bal maiden or boy could go home early. But this happened only at some mines and even then irregularly. If ten and a half hours work with just half an hour for dinner (at some mines this was an hour and at one mine two hours) was not enough, the surface worker was sometimes faced with a considerable walk to work.

---

19 Barham, 'Report', 1842, p.840.
20 Barham, 'Report', 1842, p.854.

Martha Buckingham began work at Consolidated Mines, Gwennap in 1837 at the age of ten. She lived at Bissoe Bridge, about two miles and a steep hill away. In order to get to the mine by seven she had to rise at four. She left work at 5.30 (apart from sampling when the days were extended from six in the morning to eight at night) and would presumably normally be home by seven. After supper she went to bed 'as soon as she can', around 9.30 or ten. Apart from Sundays therefore, Martha's employment left little room for activities other than sleeping, walking to work and selling her labour, just two or three hours a day and none at all at sampling times. Martha's mother was widowed, her father having died in Scotland in 1833 and her three older siblings, a sister and two brothers, all worked 'to the mines'. She clearly had little choice in the matter. On the other hand, Martha told Barham that 'there is not regular work for all in the summer; but in the winter all come, or very nearly all'.[21]

Data collected by Barham from mines across the mining districts show a considerable variation in the wages actually paid to girls like Martha, from a high of 4/6 a week down to less than a shilling. The variation in boys' wages was even greater, ranging from ten shillings (at Wheal Friendship in Devon) to less than a shilling. The principal agent at United Mines reported that girls of Martha Buckingham's age could earn 18/6 a month, 'if constantly employed'. In fact, their wages across the previous twelve months averaged 15/6. This might suggest that they worked around 84% of the days available. Younger girls earned 93% of the maximum possible, while boys earned 87%. Irregularity of attendance could be voluntary as well as involuntary. Barham observed that

> in many mines it is left very much to the choice of the labourer to come to the mine or not; in others, again, illness or some other urgent call elsewhere, interrupts the regularity of attendance, and substitutes are sometimes provided when business or pleasure causes the absence of the young people from the mine.[22]

Moreover, not everyone would have lived so far from the mine as Martha Buckingham. Christiana Pascoe, another surface worker at Consolidated Mines had graduated to cobbing, breaking stones with a short-handled hammer in a seated position, in order to reject the worthless rock. Christiana only lived 'a mile off' and could stay in bed until six. Nonetheless, she didn't get to bed again until from 10 to 11 as her father had died after an accident at Wood Mine the previous year and 'her mother

---

21 Barham, 'Report', 1842, p.845.
22 Barham, 'Report', 1842, pp.784-785.

being a widow ... [there was] household and needlework to be done after she gets home'.[23]

Working hours were shorter for underground miners, although no concessions were made for age, with boys working a full shift or 'core'. By 1841 eight hour cores seem to have become the norm. Although Henry George revealed that when he was in his 20s in the 1810s and a miner at Treskerby 'they worked six-hour courses [sic] at that time'. This was corroborated by Nicholas Tredinnick, agent at East Crofty. Nicholas was born in 1786 and began underground mining before the end of the eighteenth century. He stated that 'he did not often work then more than six hours at a time'.Thomas Moyle, underground agent at Trevascus Mine also reported that in the 1810s 'it was usual for the tutworker to work only six-hour courses'.[24] Longer cores could have been accompanied by other changes that had effectively lengthened the working day of underground miners. Richard Thomas, a 50 year old miner at the Charlestown Mines in mid-Cornwall in 1841, could remember no changes in his hours of work since he started around 1800. Yet he remembered that 'at that time it was usual to relieve "up" (i.e. at surface), rather than "down" [underground], as is now done, in the eight-hour cores, so that he thinks the work-hours were not really so long as at present'.[25] Barham observed that relieving 'in place' in the deeper mines might add an hour or two to the notional eight hour day. It took 'about 40 minutes' to descend to the deepest parts of the mines (1800 feet) and twice that time to climb back up the ladders.[26]

Despite the evidence for the intensified exploitation of underground labour since the turn of the century (although this was at times colluded in by the miners themselves, working 'double stem' or 'double core' when a contract unexpectedly turned in their favour, or substituting for a workmate unable to attend), respectable opinion was sometimes unimpressed by the amount of spare time miners enjoyed. A 'gentleman' in the west complained of miners 'meeting on Saturdays and at other times, provincially termed holding "choruses"'. These he regarded as an 'evil influence', In the Gwennap district a magistrate drew attention to the 'circumstance of miners congregating in large numbers on market days' and 'the crowds of idle youths you may at any time see about our roads, in blacksmiths' shops, and such like resorts'. Further east, in mid Cornwall, another magistrate warned of the consequences 'when people of any age congregate in large masses, without efficient discipline'.[27] Fears of the crowd may have been heightened

---

23 Barham, 'Report', 1842, p.846.
24 Barham, 'Report', 1842, pp.851 and 832-833.
25 Barham, 'Report', 1842, p.851.
26 Barham, 'Report', 1842, p.772.
27 Barham, 'Report', 1842, p.761.

in 1841 by the presence of Chartism and the ever-present possibility of food riots in Cornwall, as indeed occurred a few years later in 1847.

From the perspective of some miners, it seems that little energy was left to cause mischief even after a 'mere' eight hour working day. James Stevens, 15, was examined at Tresavean Mine. He'd been working the six a.m. to two p.m. core at the 146 fathom level and lived in Redruth. The walk necessitated him getting up at four, for which he went to bed about seven in the evening. Barham reported him as 'by no means robust in appearance', even though he only worked four or five days in the week and never on a night core.[28] It was the night work that concerned the Reverend Thomas Jewell, Wesleyan Methodist Minister at St Just. He thought the 'uncertainty of their hours of meals and sleep, and their making little or no distinction between day and night' was not conducive to 'domestic regularity'.[29] Even surface workers could sometimes work through the night. William Rowett, just 13, reported that at the Charlestown Mines

> once or twice a month we work as long as we can see, and then go to supper; we are allowed one hour for supper; then we work by candlelight till 12, we are then allowed till one and we eat some pasty, do not go home. After this we work till two in the afternoon. I am paid for this a day and a half. I put this into my own pocket. Sometimes I feel sleepy, sometimes very well.[30]

This labour was sometimes done on what might appear to our eyes to be a very insubstantial calorific intake. John Henry Martin, a 12 year old miner at Trethellan and lame from an infection in his hip in infancy, for breakfast had 'hot tea' and barley or wheat bread and treacle before walking the mile or two from his home at Menherion in Wendron to the mine, where his task was 'washing up', cleaning the ore stones preparatory to their dressing.[31] On arriving home John Henry would 'get potatoes boiled or baked for supper', while he generally 'dine[d] on potato-pasty'. John survived to the age of 38, living long enough to father at least four children still alive in 1861.[32] Thomas Knuckey, also working at Trethellan, went to work on a barley bread and butter breakfast and ate boiled potatoes 'with fish at times' for

28 Barham, 'Report', 1842, p.825.
29 Barham, 'Report', 1842, p.849.
30 Barham, 'Report', 1842, p.852.
31 Barham, 'Report', 1842, p.822.
32 Census enumerators' books, Wendron, 1861.

supper.[33] Thomas was still alive in 1881, aged 53, widowed and living with his brother in law and family at Penstruthal in Gwennap.[34]

John Martin's dinner of potato pasty was the norm both in the central mining district around Camborne and Redruth and to the east. Francis Barrett, one of the principal agents at Charlestown United, reported that the usual food brought to the mine by the surface workers was 'potato pasty with a little meat for the most part, as often mutton as pork, not much beef'.[35] Pasties co-existed with the less exciting hobbans 'a coarse kind of cake, prepared by incorporating pieces of potato ... with a sheet of dough which is then rolled up and baked'. The sweet version of hobbans was fuggans, hobbans with raisins, figs or plums added. At Consolidated Mines Mary Verran claimed that 'the girls bring hobban-plum and potato more than pasties ... A hobban is not so good as a pasty. Some are made with barley'.[36] While Mary, who lived at Cusgarne, got for supper fish and potatoes, sometimes stew, roast potatoes or broth, the simple and unvarying diet resulted in some of her companions occasionally being 'obliged to give up their work from being sick or faint'. Hobbans were less commonly taken underground although even there they could be resorted to by those too poor for pasties. William Trethewy at Consolidated Mines was a 13 year old living at St Day, presumably an orphan or at least not living with his parents. William had been employed turning the borer at the 110 fathoms level for a month or two but did not complain of tiredness despite surviving on potato hobbans.[37]

To the west, at Wheal Vor in Breage and at Balleswidden in St Just, it seems to have been the practice for surface workers to have their dinners brought to them by friends or family rather then bringing pasties, hobbans or fuggans with them to work. Warm stews were reported by one of the principal agents at Wheal Vor, while at Balleswidden Edward Carthew, surface agent, observed that around half of the surface workers had 'fish and potatoes, or stew with a little meat in it for their dinner'.[38] The ubiquitous fish and potatoes at St Just did not satisfy everyone however. An anonymous adult miner was quoted as saying 'here there is nothing but fish and potatoes ... If I could raise a sufficient sum to buy a horse I would travel and sell fish, and give up mining altogether'. This miner had suffered

33 Barham, 'Report', 1842, p.823.
34 Census enumerators' books, Gwennap, 1881.
35 Barham, 'Report', 1842, p.850.
36 Barham, 'Report', 1842, p.845.
37 Barham, 'Report', 1842, p.846 and census enumerators' books, Gwennap, 1841.
38 Barham, 'Report', 1842, pp.841 and 847.

an 'asthmatic affection, which he cannot throw off', ever since he was sent to clean the adit at Balleswidden after a rare fall of snow –

> there was so much water that they were immersed to the breast, often to the chin; the stream was so powerful, that they were not able to make head against it, so as to return in the same direction in which they entered, but were forced to go along the adit with the stream into another mine; so that they were altogether six hours in this icy, cold water; and when they got to the surface they had to walk two miles back to their own mine before they could get their dry clothes. His comrade, who was a stronger man than himself, took to his bed and died.[39]

Such events were clearly traumatic, but the miners and bal maidens Barham spoke to reported a variety of minor aches and pains and physical ailments, the constant background to their lives of toil. Elizabeth Curnow was a 24 year old who had been coming to the mines since she was 16 but not on a permanent basis. Elizabeth alternated mine work with domestic service. 'Sometimes she goes to the mine and sometimes she goes into service when her health is more established', which might suggest domestic work was more taxing. She complained of being 'taken with a gradual loss of strength and appetite once or twice a year, and finds the harder she works the less she can eat'. When working at the mine she was employed at cobbing, but like other bal maidens, complained that 'she gets very cold about the legs with the broken stones', while the workplace 'runs with water; most complain of it'. Elizabeth's testimony also reminds us of those days before amalgam fillings when the half hour allotted for dinner 'is not long enough ... especially for those who have bad teeth'.[40]

The youngest person interviewed by Barham was Richard Jeffery, aged just nine years and a month and employed at Consolidated Mines at the picking tables, a task he had performed for the previous eight months. Richard 'has had very good health' although 'his hands get sore when he is long at the "shambles" (the heap to which the stones rejected by the pickers are taken)'. When he was interviewed Richard was working until eight in the evening and said he was 'tired with his day's work'. Tired or not, he then faced a two and a half mile walk home at the end of the day. As his father had died in Mexico of cholera, his mother could not 'afford to give him clothes to go' to school in, so he and his three sisters (two working at Consolidated and one as a dressmaker) had little choice but start to earn at

---

39 Barham, 'Report', 1842, p.848.
40 Barham, 'Report', 1842, pp.845-846.

as young an age as possible.[41] John Spargoe had also started work at nine, at Fowey Consols in the east. He was employed at jigging, described by Barham as 'perhaps more fatiguing and injurious than any other performed on the surface'. It involved agitating the mineral-laden water in a sieve in a stooping posture.[42] While described as 'a healthy boy' John Spargoe nonetheless 'finds his back aches a little'.[43] In contrast, several of the girls interviewed stated that they had few complaints. Caroline Coom, an eleven year old picker at Fowey Consols, found it 'easy and pleasant work' and 'does not feel tired at the end of the day'. At the same mine Mary Buller reported 'pretty good health' during her time (six years) working there, mainly cobbing. 'Most of the girls whom I know of, and I know a pretty deal of them in the mine, are strong and hearty', even though she mentioned one exception who was 'terrible weakly, and looks very earthy'.[44]

When it came to underground miners the story tended to be different, with many complaining of occasional poor air and reporting coughing up 'nasty black trade' and of exhaustion after climbing to surface 'which makes him pant a good deal'. Nevertheless, 13 year old Absalom George, an underground miner at Fowey Consols, still 'likes it better than to grass, because the days are shorter'.[45] Older miners tended to be more jaded. Henry Roberts, 36 and a miner underground for 23 years, 16 of them spent in Gwennap mines and then in the St Agnes district, complained that his mine, where he worked at the 75 fathom level, was 'unhealthy. Finds it cold. The water is very cold. Most of the men complain of having colds, and the boys the same'. Barham observed that 'he has a tumour in the neck and feels pains about the side'.[46] The mine in question was Wheal Coates, now possessing one of Cornwall's best known engine houses, its silhouette and the backdrop of blue ocean and golden sands gracing many a postcard, although hiding a rather less alluringly romantic reality in its hidden depths.

Restoring agency

These oral testimonies collected by Charles Barham help to provide us with a picture of everyday life for the labouring miners of 1841. They enable us to approach a little nearer to the lives of the individuals who made their living from the Cornish mines. By shifting our perspective closer in this way, we gain a better impression of the everyday experience of those who produced Cornwall's copper, tin and lead. While the experienced reality of

---

41 Barham, 'Report', 1842, p.846.
42 Barham, 'Report', 1842, p.776.
43 Barham, 'Report', 1842, p.854.
44 Barham, 'Report', 1842, p.854.
45 Barham, 'Report', 1842, p.854.
46 Barham, 'Report', 1842, p.835.

the subjects of Cornwall's mining past takes on a more detailed shape, their individuality can also be grasped. Some appear resigned to their fate, others more cheerful and optimistic. In their words we glimpse the possibilities of agency. As their individual shapes cohere out of an undifferentiated mass of miners and mine labourers we can see that, although facing similar financial constraints, family backgrounds and employment opportunities, these gave rise to subtly different outcomes. But how can this historical perspective, concentrating on the details of individual experience, be related back to the macro? How do the micro-details of everyday life fit into the slow-moving social and economic structures that contained them?

Clearly, the details of the evidence collected by Charles Barham help to shine a light on the working out on the ground of processes that have long been noted. For example, several of those interviewed reported that in 1841 children were being offered for work by their parents at a younger age than formerly. Thomas Moyle, underground agent at Trevascus mine, stated 'I think they did not go to work so early formerly, and that a younger set are employed at the same work'. Richard Lanyon, a surgeon at Camborne, also had the impression that 'they are put to work at an earlier age than they were formerly'. Meanwhile Joseph Jennings, one of the principal agents at Tresavean, thought he knew the reason. He was sure

> the children are younger now than formerly; this is to be attributed in part to the difficulty of obtaining relief under the New Poor Law. In the course of a month we send back many, thinking them too small for the work, being from seven to eight or nine; they are brought by the mothers, who complain that they cannot get bread for them.[47]

We have already seen that some miners reported shorter hours when remembering the 1810s. All this, and the infrequent holidays – at most mines limited to Christmas Day and Good Friday and occasionally the parish feast day – reinforces generalisations about tightening labour discipline at the most heavily capitalised mines and an intensification of women and children's labour participation.[48]

On the other hand longer cores underground necessitated the miner taking food with him, something that did not happen a generation earlier. This was regarded by several as an improvement. Henry Warren, a 60 year

---

47 Barham, 'Report', 1842, pp.831, 834 and 823-824.

48 Eric Vanhaute, 'Between patterns and processes: Measuring labor markets and family strategies in Flanders, 1750-1990', *The History of the Family* 2 (1997), 527-545; John Rule, 'The labouring miner in Cornwall, c.1740-1870: A study in social history' (unpublished doctoral thesis, University of Warwick, 1971), pp.72-89.

old miner at North Roskear, singled out 'the taking food underground' as 'a great improvement'. He 'used not to take anything to eat underground with him and then often felt unable to eat after his return, from faintness'. This was corroborated by Thomas Moyle, who remembered that in the 1820s 'nobody took any [food] down with them, and the feeling of exhaustion was very great', especially when double shifts were worked.[49]

Yet this corroboration of broader generalisations does not seem very different from any social historian's use of evidence to support their propositions. In contrast, one of the key characteristics of microhistory is argued to be approaching a small scale study in its own right rather than as a case study for testing propositions or hypotheses drawn from macro- or structural history.[50] To an extent this relates to the direction of inter-scalar connections. While the macro-historian drills down from generalisations to utilise the more detailed evidence in support of or in order to refute that generalisation, the microhistorian works outwards from observations at the micro-level in order to set the details within a broader context.

However, there is another dimension which can sometimes be lost. Szijarto calls on microhistorians to reconstruct life in more than one context,[51] but a lot of microhistorical work has rested on reconstructing a snapshot at one point in time. If the aim is to reconstruct lived experience from a number of points of view then space and scale need to be supplemented by flow. Only then can the reaction of individual social actors to structural change be teased out and examined for similarities and contrasts.

From spaces to flows; the possibilities of longitudinal study
Of the 96 mine workers and agents whose age is given in Barham's report, it is possible to trace 50 of the males (68%) and 11 of the women (50%) to the 1841 census enumerators' books. Another 11 men and two women were found in later censuses but were not clearly identifiable in the 1841 census. While undertaking this exercise it became obvious that sometimes there was a marked discrepancy between the oral evidence given to Barham and the census record. James Harper, a 35 year old miner at Creegbrawse, stated that he 'had four girls; if he had 50 he would never allow one to go to a mine; they are exposed to corruption by bad conversation'.[52] Yet, in the 1841 Census, James, who died in the 1850s, had two daughters of 10 and 12 who were both described as copper miners. Conversely, there were several cases where those interviewed reported siblings also working at the mines

---

49 Barham, 'Report', 1842, pp.834 and 832.
50 Hudson, 'Closeness and distance', 2010.
51 Szijártó, 'Four arguments', 2002.
52 Barham, 'Report', 1842, p.829.

and yet the occupational column of the 1841 Census remained silent. For instance, Eliza Evans said she had a sister at Budnick Consols in Perranzabuloe, employed at racking.[53] There was no occupational entry for her sister Maria in the 1841 census books. Jane Sandow, a bal maiden at Wheal Gorland, said that all the elder children in her family 'were employed at the mines'.[54] Yet according to the census none were. Recurring instances of this might imply that we have to be extremely wary about the quality of the occupational data in the 1841 census beyond that of the household head.

Eliza Evans was 17 in 1841 and described by Barham as 'delicate', someone who found even the simplest task of picking too hard.[55] Yet Eliza survived and in a small way even prospered. In 1851 she was the eldest of five children still living with her parents - her father was a copper miner - in Perranzabuloe. The census informs us that she was not then employed at the mine, presumably sharing the domestic tasks with her mother. In 1858 she married William May, a local man 13 years her senior, but one described in the 1861 Census as a miner and grocer. He died in 1863 aged 55, leaving Eliza the grocer's shop and two small children, one aged two and the other four months. Eliza appeared in both 1871 and 1881 Censuses, described as a shopkeeper and with her widowed mother – 81 in 1881 – living with her and her children.

Another who survived the crises of the Cornish mining economy that occurred in the 1860s and 1870s without resorting to geographical mobility was William Rowett. William watched the buddles at Charlestown United in 1841. Then 13, he had been at the mines for four years. Although he had attended Mount Charles Wesleyan Methodist Sunday School, he'd 'forgotten what he learnt'. He 'cannot read. Did not give his thoughts to it'.[56] His father was a timberman at the mine with nine children, six of them, according to William, working at the mine. But his father crucially also had a smallholding. Although this was not referred to in the census enumerators' book, William stated that he helped his father after he finished work and returned home to Boscoppa Downs. In 1851 William had left the St Austell district for the first and only time in his life, working as a lead miner in the newly opened mining district at Menheniot near Liskeard in east Cornwall, and lodging with a mining family. In early 1861 he married Mary Hobba back at St Austell and in the census a few months later they were found living in the town at Old Hill. By 1871 William and Mary were back at Boscoppa. In 1871 he was described as a miner, but by 1881, now aged 53,

53 Barham, 'Report', 1842, p.831.
54 Barham, 'Report', 1842, p.831.
55 Barham, 'Report', 1842, p.831.
56 Barham, 'Report', 1842, p.852.

he was a carter and ten years later was called a farmer. Again, it is likely that this was a smallholding - perhaps that of his father - already occupied before 1891, but with the apparent shift from miner to farmer disguising a more gradual change of emphasis in the balance of his working life. While mining and farming at Boscoppa, William and Mary brought up nine children of their own. Their youngest son - Albert - was a solicitor's clerk in 1891, an indicator of intergenerational social mobility, from William, the illiterate buddle boy of 1841, to the professional status of his son over the course of half a century.

While these biographies show that some individuals could survive the seismic shifts that were ravaging Cornwall's mining economy in the second half of the nineteenth century, many others chose instead to leave. A more mysterious case was that of Nicholas Sampson Cloak. In 1841 Nicholas was a 31 year old mine clerk at Carnon Consols and before that a clerk at other mines.[57] He was then living at Perranwell, but with two young children and no adult woman present other than a young servant, it seems Nicholas was a widower. This is confirmed by his marriage in the summer of 1841 to Elizabeth Downing, also from Perranarworthal parish, but a marriage that took place in the Stourbridge Registration District of Worcestershire. Nicholas and Elizabeth then disappear from view for 30 years, to reappear in Aberavon in Glamorganshire in 1871. By then, aged 60, Nicholas is curiously described as a retired carpenter living off interest. How and when his career change from mine clerk to carpenter took place is unclear, although the move from a metal mining to a coal mining district implies a continuing link with the mining world. Perhaps Nicholas and Elizabeth spent time overseas like so many of their Cornish contemporaries.

To sum up, a minority of those interviewed by Barham – 14 men and boys and two women – were traced across the censuses for at least a generation to the 1871 census or later. These were presumably less mobile than the average miner living through this period. They had also by some method - either fortunate contracts or through inheritance - been more likely to succeed in gaining access to small amounts of capital or land, with a tendency to become grocers or small farmers in middle age. Alternatively, this may just reflect a change in description, mirroring the cessation or reduction of the mining component of an earlier dual or mixed economic portfolio.

Conclusions

Those historians who favour the adoption of a microhistorical mode of enquiry are adamant that the end product should be the re-creation of the life of a small area rather than using that area to illustrate generalisations. It

---

57   Barham, 'Report', 1842, p.836.

should be seen as an experiment that can change interpretations rather than an example confirming or rejecting hypotheses.[58] This implies that drawing grand generalisations about the nature of Cornish mining communities from the evidence provided to the Children's Employment Commission is invidious. In this case I shall resist the temptation to do so and leave further interpretation of the words of those who spoke to Charles Barham in 1841 open-ended.

At another level however, how much does the micro-historical approach offer the Cornish Studies practitioner? I would argue that this perspective can add value to the picture of Cornish labouring communities in 1841 already drawn by the work of John Rule and, earlier, A.K.Hamilton Jenkin. It adopts and extends their humanist realism. By injecting a longitudinal perspective and placing our historical actors in the flow of time before and after their appearance in the historical record we can perhaps extend the social history of nineteenth century Cornish communities. For in this phase of classic industrial Cornwall a real choice was indeed emerging. The generation that lived through the mid-nineteenth century was presented with a fundamental choice – to go or to stay. They could join other family members, workmates or neighbours in a journey across the oceans or to the coalfields of England and Wales, either with the intention to remake their future in another place or to make sufficient cash to return and make it in their native place. Or they could stay in the locality their forebears had built and scrape a living from its resources. The question of how far that fundamental choice was the result of conscious, rational thought or how far it was taken out of habit or routine is still an under-researched one. Microhistory and the close study of individuals and localities in the nineteenth century might offer us one more tool to help unravel this.

Moreover, there is a final aspect of the microhistorical approach that carries particular resonance for those engaged in the Cornish Studies project. This project has been marked by its explicit engagement with a past Cornwall and a kernowcentric view that, while deferring to evidence and the normal methods of scientific enquiry, also asserts the right of the Cornish and Cornwall to be a suitable case for serious study in their own right both in the present and the past.[59] The close investigation of the lives of those who came before us helps to restore them and their place to the historical gaze, potentially generating respect not just for them but for their descendants. In the quest to narrow the distance between subject and object, microhistory can fall into the assumption that it is only the subject that is on the move. The historical actors remain trapped in time. Yet perhaps the

---

58 Szijártó, 'Four arguments', 2002; Hudson, 'Closeness and distance', 2010.

59 Philip Payton (ed.), *Cornish Studies, second series* (Exeter: University of Exeter Press, 1993-2013).

reduction of distance between us and them, between now and then, is not quite so unidirectional as this implies. In striving to get closer to historical agents and their everyday lives, those people take on a less ethereal shape and in doing so become more familiar to us. The object is on the move, both literally and figuratively responding to our re-creation. In doing so historical consciousness is somehow being re-shaped. The historical exercise does not deal with static unmoving objects; the past is not a laboratory. By uncovering the details of past Cornish communities we are also inevitably shifting not just our perspectives but our consciousness. In saying this I sense I've come full circle, raising issues about the ownership of the past which have been central to Cornish Studies and hinting at the continuing role of discourse and constructivism even in an explicitly realist perspective on the past.

Chapter Six

'Nothing but pilchards and mackerel?' Re-thinking Chartism in Cornwall

In 1838 the Chartist movement began to demand male universal suffrage, a demand backed by three massive petitions between 1839 and 1848. Since Asa Brigg's groundbreaking *Chartist Studies*, work on its geographical diversity has comprised an important strand of research on Chartism. The fundamental lesson of these studies, however, is that, although its message was heard in all parts of early Victorian Britain, the influence of Chartism 'varied from place to place'.[1] For instance, despite the presence of the largest metal mining workforce in Britain, the traditional view is that west Cornwall's rural industrial population remained largely unmoved by Chartism.[2] Enquiring whether there were any radicals at St Ives, the Chartist missionary Robert Lowery is supposed to have been told 'No ... they catch nothing but pilchards and mackerel'.[3]

There are several reasons why this might be surprising. According to Jon Bohstedt, Cornish miners in the eighteenth century were a prime example of a semi-rural industrial workforce beyond paternalism, living in communities that possessed the shared norms arising from a relatively homogeneous occupational structure, with horizontal solidarities yet sufficient vertical patronage ties to engender a vigorous independent culture of everyday resistance. This was not dissimilar from the social contexts in which Chartism was supposed to flourish. That movement found its most fertile ground in the small and medium sized towns of manufacturing and mining districts, places with a high degree of mutual knowledge and trust, according to Robert Hall.[4] Yet the horizontal solidarities of Cornish

---

1   Asa Briggs, *Chartist Studies* (London: Macmillan, 1959); Robert Fyson, 'Late Chartism in the Potteries, 1848-1858', *Labour History Review* 74 (2009), 111-29; Michael Turner, 'Local politics and the nature of Chartism: the case of Manchester', *Northern History* 45 (2008), 323-45.

2   For Cornwall's early industrialisation and place at the forefront of technological change see Alessandro Nuvolari and Bart Verspagen, ''echnical choice, innovation, and British steam engineering, 1800-1850', *Economic History Review* 62 (2009), 685-710; Bernard Deacon, *Cornwall: A Concise History* (Cardiff: University of Wales Press, 2007), pp.104-11.

3   *The Weekly Record of the Temperance Movement*, 11 October 1856.

4   Jon Bohstedt, *The Politics of Provisions: Food riots, moral economy, and market transition in England, c1550-1850* (Farnham: Ashgate, 2010), pp.135, 163, 268; Robert G. Hall, *Voices of the People: Democracy and Chartist*

communities, while allowing the emergence of an active politics of provisions, failed to foster strong support for Chartism.

Perhaps other factors held back Chartism. For instance, Emma Griffin directs attention to the importance of voluntary associations in raising the cultural capital of working men after the 1820s. Mutual improvement societies, Sunday schools, the co-operative and temperance movements were the training grounds for the working class activists of the 1830s and 1840s, places where they could hone their organisational, management and leadership skills. For Griffin this occurred primarily in an urban milieu. She cites William Lovett, born in Newlyn in 1800, who left for London in 1821, and 'had to admit that his efforts at self-improvement had not come to much while he remained in Cornwall, "I had hitherto made very little intellectual progress"'. She also mentions John Passmore Edwards as one of 'only two rural autobiographers (who) were actively involved in a mutual improvement society'. But what she doesn't explicitly note is that the mutual improvement society in question was at Truro, where Edwards, born in Blackwater, gained his interest in the Anti-Corn Law League before leaving for Manchester in 1844.[5]

In fact, west Cornwall was far from being a desert when it came to voluntary associations. In addition to the thriving Methodist infrastructure and the temperance movement after 1838, Cornwall was well stocked with friendly societies. John Rule claimed that 'miners lacked the experience of the independent mutual funds which played a clear role in the development of artisan trade unions'. But the evidence contradicts this. In 1839 there were five miners' friendly societies in Cornwall, two of these being formed before 1825. This was at a time when there was only one similar society in the south Wales coalfield.[6] Moreover, friendly society membership in Cornwall was relatively high. In 1815 the number of members in Cornwall was equal to 10.4% of the population.[7] Only the industrial counties of

political identity, 1830-1870 (Monmouth: Merlin Press, 2007), p.1.

5   Emma Griffin, 'The making of the Chartists: popular politics and working-class autobiography in early Victorian Britain', *English Historical Review* CXXIX (2014), 578-605; A. J. A. Morris, 'Edwards, John Passmore (1823–1911)', *Oxford Dictionary of National Biography* (Oxford: Oxford University Press, 2004).

6   John Rule, 'The perfect wage system? Tributing in the Cornish mines', in John Rule and Roger Wells, *Crime, Protest and Popular Politics in Southern England 1740 to 1850* (London: Hambledon, 1997), p.59; Humphrey Southall, 'Towards a geography of unionization; the spatial organisation and distribution of early British trade unions', *Transactions of the Institute of British Geographers* NS13 (1988), 466-483.

7   Calculated from P.H. Gosden, *The Friendly Societies in England 1815-1875* (Manchester: Manchester University Press, 1961), p.22.

northern England, plus Monmouthshire and Devon, had higher rates of friendly society membership. Martin Gorsky's detailed analysis of membership at parish level also indicates that the mining parish of Illogan had one of the highest densities of friendly society membership. Significantly, in 1841 Seymour Tremenheere noted in relation to independent benefit clubs that people in the mining districts were 'strongly inclined to their formation' but 'the population is strongly averse to the interference of gentlemen in their concerns'.[8]

All of which brings us back to the puzzle that labour historians were wrestling with in the 1960s and 1970s; why did a tradition of collective action and a society otherwise conducive to plebeian political action, plus a network of voluntary associations, not produce stronger support for Chartism in the late 1830s and 1840s?

Unearthing the story of Chartism in Cornwall was largely the work of one historian. John Rule's 1971 PhD thesis on the labouring miner in Cornwall contained a chapter on Chartism in Cornwall and its influence, or more properly lack of influence. Rule focused on the Chartist mission of 1839 and explained the feebleness of the response to it by reference to the strength of Wesleyan Methodism in west Cornwall. Methodism provided positive opposition, competitive opposition (in competing for potential personnel) and a more generalised negative effect, all of which John Rule described as a 'configuration of quietism'. He later added other elements to this, such as the miners' wage system of tribute and tutwork.[9] Cornwall's specific configuration of quietism and the failure of Chartism to attract the support of its principal workforce – the miners – implied a Cornish exceptionalism. Here was an industrial region that did not respond in the way one might expect.

Others put less emphasis on the role of Methodism. The usual alternative was to argue, as Eric Hobsbawm did, that the failure of the mission was due to factors such as the 'Cornish industrial and social structure', which

---

8   Martin Gorsky, 'The growth and distribution of English friendly societies in the early nineteen century', *Economic History Review* 51 (1998), 489-511; Seymour Tremenheere, 'Report on the State of Education in the Mining Districts of Cornwall', *British Parliamentary Papers* 1841 (317) XX.97, pp.92-93.

9   John Rule, 'The labouring miner in Cornwall c.1740-1870: A study in social history' (unpublished doctoral thesis, University of Warwick, 1971), pp.369/370. See also John Rule, 'Methodism and Chartism among the Cornish miners', *Bulletin of the Society for the Study of Labour History* 22 (1971), 8-11; " "Configuration of quietism"? Attitudes towards Trade Unionism and Chartism among the Cornish miners', *Tijdschrift voor Sociale Geschiedenis*, 2/3 (1992), 248-62 and 'The Chartist mission to Cornwall', in Rule and Wells (eds), *Crime*, 1997, 67-80.

Hobsbawm viewed as backward or 'archaic'.[10] In an early debate following the presentation of Rule's configuration of quietism thesis at a meeting of the Society for the Study of Labour History in 1971 Alf Jenkin offered a new insight on this. He agreed that Cornwall's role as a pioneer industrial area had 'something to do' with its 'archaic character'.[11] But Jenkin's intriguing point was that Cornwall failed to respond to the call of Chartism not because of its remoteness, backwardness or slowness to embrace modernity, but because it was one of the UK's first industrial regions.[12] Early industrialisation had produced a rural industrial society with unique socio-economic dimensions, including a high nominal allegiance to a revivalistic Methodism and a greater access to land and other collateral aids than the more urbanised industrial regions that were emerging in the late eighteenth century.[13]

Both the configuration of quietism and the model of early industrialisation and its resultant socio-economic context reinforce the notion of Cornish exceptionalism, a trope attractive to Cornish Studies practitioners. However, giving primacy to exceptional aspects of the Cornish experience of modernization might prevent us noting those features that Cornwall shared with other regions and localities. It's my contention here that one such feature is the history of Chartism in Cornwall after the mission of early 1839. In 1971 John Rule tended to view the subsequent progress of Chartism in Cornwall as merely a postscript. There were 'glimpses of a continuance of Chartist activities' as 'small groups of Chartists persisted in some of the towns'. Yet these ephemeral groups 'had no significant support'.[14] In what follows I challenge this interpretation, revealing that a consistent level of Chartist activity can be traced through the 'Chartist decade' to 1848. This was comparable with the experience of Chartism across southern and non-industrial England, although clearly it never matched the intensity of Chartist activity in its northern heartlands of Lancashire and West Yorkshire.

There is another aspect to consider. Perspectives on Chartism in Cornwall may have been unwittingly reinforced by modern stereotypes of Cornwall as an apolitical leisure periphery and a place for holidaying and relaxation, rather than industry and politics. Hitherto, there has been an

---

10 E.J.Hobsbawm, *Labouring Men: Studies in the history of labour* (London: Weidenfeld and Nicolson, 1964), p.30.

11 Rule, 'Methodism and Chartism', 1971.

12 See also Sidney Pollard, *Peaceful Conquest: the Industrialisation of Europe 1760-1970* (Oxford: Oxford University Press, 1981), p.14.

13 Bernard Deacon, 'Proto-regionalisation: the case of Cornwall', *Journal of Regional and Local Studies* 18 (1998), 27-41.

14 Rule, 'Labouring miner', 1971, p.373.

over-emphasis on the Chartist mission of 1839 and a focus on the arrival of Chartists from across the Tamar who then proceeded to 'discover' Cornwall, as so many have done before and since. This is overdue for correction by adding a Cornish perspective on this movement for democratic reform. A Cornish Studies approach would seek out the active role of Cornish men and women in Chartism rather than foreground the role of the missionaries who, discovering Cornwall, bring the Chartist message to an essentially passive population. Such a perspective permits us to regain a more balanced perspective on Cornish Chartism as well as adding to the corpus of local Chartist studies. With this in mind, the rest of this essay reviews the historiography of Chartism in Cornwall since Rule's initial thesis, both within Cornwall and outwith, before rethinking the course and context of Cornish Chartism. The active agency of Cornish Chartists will be recovered as we move from Chartism in Cornwall to Cornish Chartists, a group that has hitherto been rendered invisible, victims, in E.P.Thompson's classic phrase, of the 'condescension of posterity'.[15]

The historiography of Chartism in Cornwall
John Rule added a short study of the Truro Chartist Richard Spurr in 1977 and revisited the question of Chartism in Cornwall in 1997. In this, he basically reiterated his analysis of 1971, concluding that, although 'Chartism did not end in 1839' and 'some level of activity' persisted in the towns of west Cornwall, 'the real failure of 1839 was that it built no bridge to the 20,000 miners'. In the meantime, in an under-recognised contribution in 1982, Alf Jenkin had discovered evidence of continuing Chartist activity into the 1840s and the arrival of a succession of further Chartist speakers over the course of that decade. However, its lack of comparison with other localities and its appearance in a journal well outside the mainstream labour history literature meant that Jenkin's work was largely ignored. More recently, there has been some re-assessment of Cornish Methodism's relations with Chartism by Daniel Simpson, who claims that, far from being a failure, Cornish Chartism experienced a 'greater than acknowledged success in Cornwall'. But his re-reading of the reception of the Chartist missionaries in 1839 is based on relatively thin evidence and more concerned to align Methodism in Cornwall with the ideas of moral and social improvement inherent in the Charter than with the course of Chartist activism in Cornwall.[16]

---

15 E. P. Thompson, *The Making of the English Working Class* (London: Gollancz, 1963), p.12.

16 John Rule, 'Richard Spurr of Truro – Small town radical', *Cornish Studies* 4/5 (1976/77), 50-55 (republished in Rule and Wells, *Crime*, 1997, 81-90 and John Rule, *Cornish Cases: Essays in Eighteenth and Nineteenth Century Social*

Since Rule's pioneering work, more 'mainstream' labour historians have added little to our understanding of Chartism in Cornwall, or done much to dent Rule's conclusion that Cornwall's miners were 'hardly involved in the working class industrial and political movements of the first half of the nineteenth century'. In his comprehensive recent account of the regional history of Chartism, Richard Brown has reviewed the course of Chartism in Cornwall. He emphasises Rule's initial conclusion that the 'significant factor in preventing the formation of a "grass-roots" political ideology' was Wesleyanism's anti-political influence. Brown does, however admit that 'Chartism in Cornwall had a more significant history ... than previously suggested'. 'Given the regularity with which some leading Chartists visited the county in the early 1840s it was clearly regarded as worth evangelising and agitating'. These observations contain the seeds of a retrieval of local Chartist organisation from obscurity, although Brown concludes it consisted of 'words rather than actions'. Other factors, such as a lack of 'effective leaders', are then cited as an explanation for the lack of impact on manual workers. Nonetheless, Brown implies that a dominant Methodist culture could not prevent the formation of Chartist groups in the towns, even though their message had difficulty penetrating the rural mining communities.[17]

This is a welcome corrective to most accounts of Chartism in Cornwall, which dismiss its weakness as a simple function of the strength of Methodism. John Rule was of course heavily reliant on E.P. Thompson's interpretation of Methodism as a deleterious influence on working class politics, this itself restating Halevy's classic thesis. The alternative, as we have seen, was to argue that, while Wesleyans in Cornwall did oppose Chartism, the failure of the mission was 'not due to the moderating influence of the Wesleyans' but to Cornwall's 'archaic' social structure.[18] While the role of Methodism has over-influenced the way historians think about Chartism in Cornwall, implying that little need to be said about the movement after the events of 1839, it's a short step from the assertion of

---

History (Southampton: Clio, 2006), 190-201) and Rule, 'Chartist mission', 1997, p.78. (This was also republished in *Cornish Cases*, 2006, 202-221); Alf Jenkin, 'The Cornish Chartists', *Journal of the Royal Institution of Cornwall*, NS9 (1982), 53-80; Daniel Simpson, 'Chartist failure and Methodist madness in nineteenth century Cornwall: a re-analysis', in Garry Tregidga (ed.), *Cornish Studies One* (Penryn: Institute of Cornish Studies, 2015), 123-45.

17 Rule, 'Configuration', 1992, p.248; Richard Brown, *Chartism: Localities, Spaces and Places, the Midlands and the South* (Dunstable: Authoring History, 2015), pp.103-05.

18 Thompson, *Making*, 1963; Emile Halévy, *History of the English People in the Nineteenth Century* (London, Benn, 1934); Hobsbawm, *Labouring Men*, 1964, p.30.

'archaism' to a model of backwardness that neatly lines up with unstated assumptions of Cornwall as a remote periphery.

Such assumptions can too easily generate an insufficiently critical stance towards the disdainful and patronising attitudes towards the locals sometimes expressed in 1839 by the two Chartist missionaries – Robert Lowery and Abraham Duncan. Moreover, their caricature of the Cornish, and particularly the miners, as people 'unused to political agitation' who 'know nothing of political principles' has been too readily taken at face value.[19] Although popular politics in Cornwall before the Chartists awaits its historian, a considerable number of clues exist that suggest working people in the villages and especially the towns of late eighteenth and early nineteenth century Cornwall were hardly entirely inured to the questions that periodically convulsed industrialising Britain.

Alf Jenkin cited letters in the minute book of the London Corresponding Society in 1795 and 1796 from a Timothy Martin of Stithians, while other letters also indicate the existence of societies of reformers at Helston and Truro. At the same time, the St Just miners were reported as planting a 'tree of liberty' (to the alarm of a local land agent), while a man at Redruth, in the heart of the mining district, was heard toasting Tom Paine. After the Napoleonic wars there were meetings in Cornwall to protest Peterloo in 1819. Although the extent of working class involvement in these is unknown, it is unlikely that working men and women in Cornwall were entirely unaware of events upcountry. In addition to the growing circulation of the two Truro newspapers, the *Royal Cornwall Gazette* and the *West Briton*, the readership of Hetherington's unstamped *Poor Man's Guardian* extended to Bodmin and Penzance in the 1830s, and there was an agency at Falmouth for the radical 1819 newspapers *The Republican* and *Black Dwarf*. Meanwhile, women at Truro organised a meeting in support of Queen Caroline in 1820, such meetings being viewed as occasions for the expression of anti-government sentiment.[20]

More generally, Ed Jaggard points to the influence of the active gentry and farmer-led reform movement that arose in Cornwall in the 1810s and

---

19 Rule, 'Labouring miner', 1971, p.365.
20 Jenkin, 'Cornish Chartists', 1982. See also Roger Wells, *Wretched Faces: Famine in Wartime England 1763-1803* (Gloucester: Sutton, 1988), pp.153/54; A.K.Hamilton Jenkin, *News from Cornwall* (London: Westaway Books, 1951), p.33; Charles Gilbert, *An Historical Survey of the County of Cornwall* (London: Longman, Hurst, Rees, Orme and Brown, 1817), p.98; Edwin Jaggard, *Cornwall Politics in the Age of Reform 1790-1885* (Woodbridge: Boydell, 1999), p.35; Patricia Hollis, *The Pauper Press: A Study in Working-Class Radicalism of the 1830's* (London: Oxford University Press, 1970), map at p.337; Malcolm Chase, *1820: Disorder and stability in the United Kingdom* (Manchester; Manchester University Press, 2015), p.175.

1820s. He comments that this 'must have stirred a growing political awareness among not only farmers but also shopkeepers, miners and fishermen'. Jaggard details a 'surprising level of popular political activity' in the borough politics of Truro and Liskeard in the early decades of the nineteenth century, while the issue of parliamentary reform in 1831-32 'convulsed the entire Cornish population'. It is extremely unlikely that Cornish working people remained blithely unaware and uninfluenced by this 'vibrant political milieu'.[21]

As we have seen, the density of friendly societies in Cornwall speaks of organisational abilities in labouring communities. Even trade unions were not entirely absent. Branches of the Operative Stonemasons were active at St Blazey, Penryn and Constantine and Luxulyan in 1831. Moreover, trade unions were not necessary for collective action. In December 1830 the Earl of Mount Edgcumbe wrote to the Home Secretary that 'around Callington and Launceston there have been meetings of labourers in bodies for the purpose of demanding an increase of wages'. Around the same time William Cocks was arrested at Stratton Fair for reading out a broadsheet attacking the corruption of the aristocracy.[22]

A few generations earlier Cornish labouring folk had shown that an ability to combine was not restricted to the miners, whose predilection for food rioting had made them 'the most remarkable of the many semi-rural workers' adopting this tactic over the course of the eighteenth century. In 1766 masons working at Mousehole quay had struck work while women working in the fish cellars there were making 'exorbitant demands'. Two years later, the owners of the fish cellars were intending to bring in other women from a distance 'in order to break the back of all those wicked combinations at Newlyn and Mousehole'. Even miners could combine food rioting with demands for wage increases and strike action, as at Lanescot and Fowey Consols in 1831. St Austell clay workers also struck work for higher wages in 1836 while anti-New Poor Law riots convulsed the north Cornish towns of Stratton and Camelford in 1837.[23]

This background noise of collective action in Cornwall tends to reduce the presumed gap between the reactions of labouring communities in Cornwall and those elsewhere to hardship and restructuring. This takes on more significance in the light of the observation of Robert Hall, in his study

---

21 Jaggard, *Cornwall Politics*, 1999, pp.49, 60, 73, 86.

22 Alf Jenkin, *Cornwall Association of Local Historians Magazine* 8 (1984), 6-7; National Archives HO 32/6, fol. 208; HO 52/6, fol. 209.

23 Bohstedt, *Politics of Provisions*, 2010, p.135; Letters from Thomas Carlyon to William Veale, 10 July 1766 and 26 May 1768, CRO DDML/781 and DDML/793; *West Briton*, 25 February 1831 and 5 February 1836; *The Champion and Weekly Herald*, 19 and 26 March and 5 March 1837.

of Chartism in Ashton under Lyne. He comments that activists 'all over' Britain drew men and women into Chartism who knew 'nothing of political principles'.[24] If those ignorant of political principles in Ashton were able to make the town a leading centre of Chartism then the apparent ignorance of the Charter encountered in Cornwall by the Chartist missionaries seems less of an insurmountable obstacle.

While mainstream labour historians offer little to explain apparent Cornish exceptionalism other than resorting to the strength of Methodism or an 'archaic' economic structure, there are two more promising recent trends in social history. First, histories of collective action have moved away from class and its emergence as the dominant organising principle. Detailed examination of the archive has led Carl Griffin to reject the binary distinctions that have in the past bedevilled labour history, such as that between pre-industrial food rioting and 'modern' trade unionism and strike action, or that between industrial and agrarian communities. He also plays down the idea that the rural worker was 'isolated from the wider social and political currents' of the time. Instead, in his study of collective action in western England (Devon, Somerset, Dorset and Wiltshire) in the late eighteenth and early nineteenth centuries, he claims to find a vigorous and multifaceted culture of resistance that cannot be confined to traditional categories. One example of this is food rioting. The older view is that resort to food riots declined after 1800, but Griffin claims that industrial communities in the west of England continued to turn to this strategy until the late 1820s. This echoes Peter Gurney, who argues that the strikers in the north and midlands of England in 1842 also adopted 'traditional' forms of consumer action, including food riots, in addition to strikes.[25] Even those who hold to the view that food rioting underwent a change after 1800 and became restricted to the peripheries now argue that this was not because of some failure of working class modernization and the inertia of tradition, but because of the persistence of a 'political opportunity' that enabled the continued success of this tactic.[26] These conclusions clearly have implications for the notion of Cornish exceptionalism.

---

24 Hall, *Voices*, 2007, p.7.

25 Carl Griffin, 'The culture of combination: Solidarities and collective action before Tolpuddle', *The Historical Journal* 58 (2015), 443-480; Peter Gurney, '"Rejoicing in potatoes": The politics of consumption in England during the "Hungry Forties"', *Past & Present* 293 (2009), 99-136.

26 Bohstedt, *Politics of Provisions*, 2010, p.250. Food rioting occurred as late as 1867 in Devon and Oxford but Jon Bohstedt argues these late examples were a 'demoralized version', lacking the negotiations and ritual that characterised eighteenth century 'riots'. For the 1867 events see Pamela Horn, 'Food riots in Devon, Somerset and Dorset in November 1867. HO 45/7992', *Bulletin of the Society for the Study of Labour History* 42 (1981), 22-26.

The second interesting direction that histories of collective action are taking is methodological. Peter Jones places the rural disturbances in England from 1815 to 1830 within a 'complex web of local social relations'. This heralds the return of place and locality to a more central role in social history. Malcolm Chase proposes that the 'redrawing of the map of social identities that has accompanied the demotion of class points to a need for greater attentiveness to local and regional variations in workers' lives'. This is echoed by Katrina Navickas' call for a grounding of histories of collective action in a longitudinal regional historical or micro-historical approach. These shifts in emphasis back to local and regional studies potentially bring mainstream social history and Cornish Studies, with its attentiveness to space and place, closer together. However, Navickas also notes that, while there has been a move away from class, 'attention to other identities [apart from gender] is, however, still limited, especially those of race and ethnicity'.[27] So how did Chartism affect Cornwall and Cornishness influence Chartism?

It is time to re-visit Chartism in Cornwall. What follows rounds out John Rule's pioneering work and Richard Brown's extension of that story into the 1840s. After briefly recounting the course of early Chartism in Cornwall, Cornish Chartism in the 1840s becomes the focus of attention, revealing a far greater level of activity than hitherto recognised. The relation between Chartists and Methodists is then re-assessed, supporting the contention that the two were not as incompatible as Rule and others claimed. A number of named Chartists are identified, their occupational backgrounds discussed and their post-Chartist biographies uncovered. The picture is rounded out by examining other aspects of Cornish Chartism, its recreational subculture, the role of women and its spatial discourse.

Chartists in Cornwall
The visit to Cornwall of the two Chartist missionaries in March/April 1839 has been well covered. Robert Lowery and Abraham Duncan arrived by sea at Falmouth and then perambulated around west Cornwall before the mission ended with a meeting at the spiritual home of Cornish Methodism, Gwennap Pit. The contradictory contemporary accounts of what happened

---

27 Peter Jones, 'Swing, Speenhamland and rural social relations: The "moral economy" of the English crowd in the nineteenth century', *Social History* 32 (2007), 271-290; Malcolm Chase, 'Twentieth-century labour histories', in Christopher Dyer, Andrew Hopper, Evelyn Lord and Nigel Tringham, *New Directions in Local History since Hoskins* (Hatfield: University of Hertfordshire Press, 2011, 54-65; Katrina Navickas, 'What happened to class? New histories of labour and collective action in Britain', *Social History* 36 (2011), 192-204.

there reflect broader contrasts in attitudes towards the Chartist mission. The missionaries themselves adopted a determined tone of resolute though qualified optimism, reporting to the General Convention of the Industrious Classes in London that they had 'succeeded in arousing the people, beyond their most sanguine expectations' despite 'the sinister proceedings adopted to thwart them, by Whigs, Tories and local authorities'. Their meetings had attracted 'large numbers of people' and they concluded that 'Cornwall would, ere long, become one of the strongholds of democracy'.[28] That assessment clashed markedly with reports from Cornish elite sources, however.

The Whig *West Briton* vied with its Tory competitor, the *Royal Cornwall Gazette*, to fulminate against 'these misguided men' and their dangerous notion of democracy. According to the former newspaper, the 'grand field day' at Gwennap Pit was 'a complete failure', producing no 'other effect upon their audience than disgust, and a determination to have no fellowship with men whose proceedings are so dangerous to the peace of society. We congratulate our mining population on the good sense they have shown'.[29]

Even opponents admitted the existence of a certain level of curiosity about the Chartist mission, as evinced by the numbers attending, but they denied it had any long-term effect. The Reverend Philpotts wrote to the Home Secretary from his vicarage in the sleepy churchtown of Gwennap, safely distant from the mining villages, about the final Chartist meeting. Although he admitted that 'a large crowd was certainly collected ... very few converts were made'. For Philpotts 'the sole effect of the meeting has been to prove the weakness of the Chartists, and the absence of any sympathy with them on the part of our miners'. In stark contrast, John Carne of Fraddam, between Hayle and Camborne, wrote to his brother in law William Lovett that 'the people have responded to their call for they have assembled together in their thousands'; the missionaries had collected a 'large number of signatures' and local sympathisers were 'forming Associations'. Carne enthusiastically claimed that 15,000 had attended the final meeting at Gwennap Pit and had elected Lowery and Duncan to represent them at the Convention.[30]

Taking his cue from the Vicar of Gwennap, John Rule agreed that the mission was ultimately a failure. The miners had remained committed to 'a

---

28 Rule, 'Chartist mission', 1997; Brian Harrison and Patricia Hollis (eds), *Robert Lowery: Radical and Chartist* (London: Europa, 1979), pp.129ff; *The Charter*, 31 March 1839.

29 *West Briton*, 5 April 1839.

30 Dorothy Thompson, *The Early Chartists* (London: Macmillan, 1971), pp.189-90; Jenkin, 'Cornish Chartists', 1982; *The Chartist*, 14 April 1839. See also Harrison and Hollis, *Lowery*, 1979, p.237.

prior political economy, rather than the potential for political radicalism'. In addition, he pointed out that 'large crowds ... meant little if there was no permanent organisation on which to build a solid movement'. Instead, Rule interpreted the Chartist mission as telling us more about the strength of Methodism in Cornwall than of Chartism. He cited Lowery's complaints about the 'pharasaical cant ... omnipotent in every teetotal committee in Cornwall' and the rhetorical question of the *West Briton* - 'what but our religious light is it that has kept our working classes at peace and free from Chartism'.[31]

Yet, complacent and/or hostile utterances by members of the local elite need to be approached with a little more caution. If Cornish people had too much 'good sense' to be deluded into supporting the demands for democracy contained in the Charter's six points then why was there such a noticeable degree of panic from some local leaders on the arrival of the Chartists? H.S.Graham, Rector of Ludgvan, write to the Home Office on March 16th, 1839, warning of the possible inflammatory effect on the district, 'swarming with miners, who are at present happy and contented, but easily excited'. In a similar vein, Richard Moyle, the Mayor of Penzance, claimed that Cornwall was a place 'in which the labouring classes are in constant employment' and 'where loyalty is proverbial and contentment near universal'. Yet his confidence in the depth of this contentment turned out to be rather shallow: 'all this desirable order of things is threatened to be overturned and society disjointed by a party of itinerant politicians - who style themselves Chartists'. Meanwhile, Lowery reported that at their second visit to Penzance upwards of 7,000 people waited in readiness and claimed they had caused a 'great sensation in the town', with police and coastguards mobilised in anticipation of a feared disorder which in the event did not transpire.[32]

While the course and the context of the Chartists' mission are well dug over, its aftermath is less disturbed territory. As we have seen, in John Rule's studies of the Chartist mission, events after the spring of 1839 were relegated to a postscript. In contrast, Roger Wells discovered Chartist activity in many southern English towns in the 1840s, although this was a 'private, almost secretive presence'. The absence of such activity would indeed make Cornwall exceptional. However, just as Roger Burt questions Cornish exceptionalism in relation to industrial relations after the 1850s, so we might question exceptionalism in relation to Chartism in the 1840s.[33] Far from being exceptionally rare, Chartism in Cornwall was present throughout

---

31 Rule, 'Chartist mission', 1997, p.80 and 'Labouring miner', 1971, pp.368 and 371; *West Briton*, 14 February 1840.

32 Thompson, *Early Chartists*, 1971, pp.187-88; Harrison and Hollis, *Lowery*, 1979, p.236.

the 1840s. Moreover, in the earlier part of the decade at least, this was at a level comparable with if not exceeding that of Devon.

Chartism in Cornwall

Far from being marginal to the story of Chartism, Cornishmen and men with Cornish ancestry could be found right at the heart of the Chartist movement. The best known is of course William Lovett, born in 1800 in Newlyn. The son of a captain of a trading vessel out of Hull who died before his birth, Lovett was brought up a Methodist by his Cornish mother and served an apprenticeship to a local ropemaker. At the age of 21 he left Cornwall and moved to London, where he learnt a new trade as cabinet maker. He also threw himself into early efforts at co-operation and the cause of parliamentary reform. It was Lovett, the secretary of the London Working Men's Association, who, virtually single-handedly, drafted the bill for parliament in 1838 and wrote the People's Charter. Arrested for inciting violence after the Bull Ring riot at Birmingham in July 1839, he served a year in Warwick prison. On his release, having refused to be bound over on good behaviour and let out early despite his poor health, he turned to educational improvement. In 1841 he formed the National Association for the Political and Social Improvement of the People as an alternative to the National Charter Association (NCA), which had been established in 1840. This put him at odds with the more charismatic Feargus O'Connor, a dispute which remained unreconciled until O'Connor's death in the 1850s. Although Lovett remained committed to the Charter and immersed himself in radical politics, being involved in several internationalist movements and supporting the anti-slavery agitation in the States, his influence within Chartism waned after 1841.[34]

Lovett was not the only Cornishman active in Chartism. Robert Kemp Philp was on the executive committee of the NCA in 1841 and played a large part in drawing up the second Chartist petition of 1842. Philp was born in Falmouth in 1819, apprenticed at the age of 16 to a printer in Bristol and settled in Bath. Like Lovett, he also argued with Feargus O'Connor and moved away from Chartism in the early 1840s. A third figure, although one

---

33 Rule, 'Chartist mission', 1997, p.80; Roger Wells, 'Southern Chartism', *Rural History* 2 (1991), 37-59; Roger Burt, 'Industrial relations in the British non-ferrous mining industry in the nineteenth century', *Labour History Review* 71 (2006), 57-79.

34 David Goodway, 'Lovett, William (1800–1877)', *Oxford Dictionary of National Biography*, (Oxford: Oxford University Press, 2004); David Stack, 'William Lovett and the National Association for the Political and Social Improvement of the People', *The Historical Journal* 42 (1999), 1027-50; Malcolm Chase, *Chartism: A New History* (Manchester: Manchester University Press, 2007), *passim*.

with a less immediate connection to Cornwall, was Joseph Rayner Stephens. Stephens, who rejected the Chartist label, was not born in Cornwall but his father was a native of St Dennis. Stephens had followed his father into the Wesleyan ministry by 1829. After being appointed to Ashton under Lyne, he made a series of inflammatory speeches in favour of factory reform and then the suffrage. Having resigned from the Wesleyan connexion, much to their relief probably, in 1834, Stephens was eventually arrested in late 1838, charged with sedition, riot and unlawful assembly, and served 18 months in prison. On his release in 1840 he rejected Chartism.[35] However, as Lovett experimented with his 'new moves' towards encouraging education, Philp became disillusioned and Stephens openly rejected it, others in Cornwall were drifting towards Chartism.

In fact, Chartism in Cornwall pre-dated the arrival of the two missionaries. In 1971 John Rule thought that there had been no communication from Cornwall prior to the arrival of the missionaries. This was not the case. The Convention received a letter from John Carne before the decision to send missionaries was taken.[36] Just like the Wesleys, who arrived in Cornwall and met with a pre-existing group of Methodists, the Chartist missionaries were not the first people to articulate this new political doctrine west of the Tamar. John Rule did note the presence of an active and, according to the local press, noisy group of Truro Chartists in his short biography of Richard Spurr, a cabinet maker who led them and established a Working Men's Association (WMA) in the town. At the end of January 1839 Spurr was calling on people to sign the Chartist national petition. A couple of weeks before Lowery and Duncan arrived, Spurr and his associates moved an amendment at an anti-Corn Law meeting in Truro, that the 'exclusive mode of electing the House of Commons should be changed ... so that the productive millions may be fairly represented'. Spurr was supported, as even the unremittingly hostile *West Briton* was forced to admit, by a 'thunder of acclamation'. Despite that, the amendment was eventually lost amidst what appears to be considerable tactical confusion among the Chartists present.[37]

Undeterred, after the missionaries had come and gone, Spurr and 'a large assemblage of Chartists' succeeded in transforming a meeting at Truro

---

35 Charlotte Fell-Smith, 'Philp, Robert Kemp (1819–1882)', rev. Stephen Roberts, *Oxford Dictionary of National Biography* (Oxford: Oxford University Press, 2004); Eileen Groth Lyon, 'Stephens, Joseph Rayner (1805–1879)', *Oxford Dictionary of National Biography* (Oxford: Oxford University Press, 2004).

36 Rule, 'Labouring miner', 1971, p.362; Jenkin, 'Cornish Chartists', 1982, pp.56-57.

37 Rule, 'Richard Spurr', 1976-77; *West Briton*, 1 February 1839 and 22 February 1839.

Town Hall to address the Queen in support of the restored Whig Government into a debate on the Charter. In doing so he launched a widespread attack on the Whigs and their policies on Jamaica, Canada, church rates and Chartism. Despite insisting that 'the people had a right to arm; they would arm - and that by the power that the constitution gave them they would obtain their rights ... a great number of hands were held up in favour' of Spurr's amendment, although the mayor 'declared the show to be against it'. These accounts from a distinctly unsympathetic source suggest that the Chartists could mobilise considerable numbers in Truro and tend to contradict the *West Briton*'s own earlier picture of Cornish Chartism as a 'complete failure', when 'the muster they made in Truro was miserable in the extreme'.[38]

Just before the meeting on the loyal address Spurr had spent a month in Bodmin Jail after being sentenced for rioting against a church rate in 1838. On his release he and his fellow prisoners were drawn into Truro on a 'chaise and four preceded by flags and music'. Despite popular support for Spurr's stance against church rates, if not the People's Charter, Spurr left Truro in the summer of 1839, harassed by the borough police - the establishment of which he had vigorously opposed - and under a charge of non-payment of rates as his business paid the price for his political activities. In January 1840 the Mayor of Truro wrote to the Home Office warning officials about this 'suspicious and dangerous person', but claimed that 'there seemed to have been no regular Chartist meetings in Truro after his departure'.[39] The Mayor was being premature. For within months, if not weeks, Chartists were meeting not just in Truro but in several other places as well. While the former picture of Chartism in Cornwall becomes hazy in the extreme after the return of the Chartist missionaries and the departure of Richard Spurr, much more light can now be shed on its continuing presence.

In 1984 Dorothy Thompson provided a list of active Chartist localities in 1839, 1842, 1844 and 1848. These included Camborne, Falmouth, Penzance, Redruth and Truro. Brown adds Hayle to this list when referring to Chartist associations in 1841. However, this only touches on Chartist activity. The Chartist press also notes activity and localities at Padstow, St Austell, St Columb, St Day, St Ives and Wadebridge at various times in the 1840s, with Chartist activism peaking in 1841/42 and 1844/45. Just a few months after the Chartist mission left in 1839 it was reported that the Penzance and Hayle WMAs were holding a meeting on Penzance Green. After giving three cheers for the General Convention, a claimed 5,000 people then proceeded into the town and paraded the streets with a band. Earlier, a run on the savings banks was reported from Truro and a month or

---

38 *West Briton*, 24 May 1839 and 5 April 1839.
39 Rule, 'Richard Spurr', 1976-77, p.54.

two later the same happened in Penzance, the result, the Chartists claimed, of Chartist sympathisers withdrawing their savings in response to the General Convention's manifesto of May.[40]

However, the real trigger for an upsurge of Chartist activity in Cornwall was not the failure of the first petition in June/July 1839 but the sentencing of the three men convicted of leading the Newport insurrection in November 1839 - John Frost, William Jones and Zephaniah Williams - and the wider state crackdown that followed it. This led to the incarceration of around 500 leading Chartists, including Spurr, by now resident in London. The initial sentence of execution passed on the three Newport leaders provoked angry condemnation from Chartists across Britain. Within days, thousands of signatures were collected calling for a pardon, for example 30,000 in six days at Birmingham. Outrage was not limited to industrial cities. In Hayle it was reported that a memorial requesting a pardon had collected 1,100 signatures in two days in the last week of January 1840. This had been forwarded to the Government 'on behalf of the unrepresented masses'.[41] Eventually, the Government backed down and commuted the insurrectionists' sentences to life transportation to Australia.

The affair was to have a postscript. Malcolm Chase, in his narrative history of Chartism, cites Barclay Fox's *Journal*, where Fox recounts his visit to see John Frost on board the convict ship 'Mandarin', which put into Falmouth with storm damage on its way to Tasmania. Yet Chase does not mention the fact that Frost and his compatriots made not one stopover in Cornwall, but at least two and probably three. Moreover, these earlier associations with Cornwall were more significant in the history of Cornish Chartism. On February 14th, 1840, the *West Briton* reported that the steamship 'Usk', carrying the prisoners, had put in at Padstow and Hayle with storm damage, staying at the latter place for two days. Two weeks later it was reporting the 'Mandarin' docking at Falmouth.[42]

The apparent confusion can be cleared up as follows. On the commutation of their sentences of execution on 31st January the three prisoners were taken from Monmouth prison to Chepstow, there they were put on board the 'Usk' for conveyance to the prison hulks at Portsmouth. Going down channel, the steamer's passage was severely delayed by storms and it was forced to put into Ilfracombe and then Padstow and Hayle. It eventually reached Portsmouth around the 15th of February and Frost and

---

40 Dorothy Thompson, *The Chartists. Popular Politics in the Industrial Revolution* (New York: Pantheon Books, 1984), p.345. Brown, *Chartism*, 2015, p.104; *The Charter*, 23 June 1839; *Northern Star*, 18 May 1839; Chase, *Chartism*, 2007, p.72.

41 Chase, *Chartism*, 2007, p.139; *The Charter*, 9 February 1840.

42 Chase, *Chartism*, p.151; *West Briton*, 14 February and 28 February 1840.

company were transferred to a hulk. Ten days later they were put on the 'Mandarin', which then took them to Tasmania via Falmouth.[43]

The presence of Frost, Jones and Williams at Hayle caused a considerable stir among the townsfolk. As the news spread they began to gather on the quayside.

> The unfortunate men are regarded by the inhabitants of this town as martyrs to the cause of liberty. The general conversations of the people turned more particularly on devising plans to rescue the prisoners ... and those who hitherto were opposed to the Chartist movement put forth their plans as freely as any ... the only thing wanting was to circulate the plan amongst the Cornish miners in order that it might be carried into effect.[44]

Even allowing for some hyperbole in this account, it is clear that the state's repression was provoking interest in Chartism. Another petition followed from Cornwall in March 1840, demanding Lovett's release from prison, while donations were received for the prisoners' families from Hayle, Truro and Redruth. At Redruth a few months afterwards a National Charter Association locality was formed. It was reported that 'their numbers are progressively increasing'. At the end of the year a Cornwall delegate conference was held in that town and a Cornwall Central Committee established. More than a year after the Newport Three passed Cornwall on their way to Australia, a meeting could be still be held at Redruth calling for their release. Despite the unremittingly hostile West Briton's scathing assessment of its success, claiming that the crowd 'laughed heartily at them', even that newspaper was forced to admit that the Chartists had attracted 'about 200 or 300 of the working classes and others of the town'.[45]

A meeting at Truro in November 1841 included delegates from branches at Camborne, Hayle, Helston, Padstow, Penzance, Redruth, St Columb, St Day, St Ives, Truro, and Wadebridge. In terms of numbers, this was perhaps the high point of the movement in Cornwall. Yet, as the Northern Star depended on correspondence from Chartists in the localities it is very likely

---

43 The fullest account of their journeys can be found at mongenes.org.uk/crime %26Punishment/thechartisttrial.html (accessed 21 October 2016), although even this misses their stay at Hayle.

44 *The Charter*, 23 February 1840.

45 *Southern Star*, 15 March 1840; *Northern Star*, 25 April 1840. Lovett was released in the summer of 1840, after which, together with his wife and daughter, he arrived in Cornwall 'for the purpose of recruiting his health' (*West Briton*, 21 August 1840.); *Northern Star*, 26 September 1840; 2 January 1841; *West Briton*, 16 April 1841.

its reports from Cornwall understated the Chartist activity taking place in this relatively remote district. Indeed, a list of the 299 localities subscribing to the NCA in December 1841 mentions only Truro, Penzance and Redruth. Yet in early December the *Northern Star* published an address to the 'artisans, miners and agricultural labourers of the Borough of Helston' from the secretary of the Helston NCA, David Jillard, who stated the association was meeting weekly at a local temperance inn. Moreover, a month later the NCA at Wadebridge was nominating its officers. Apparently, formal, paid-up NCA localities in Cornwall were accompanied by other, possibly less permanent and more transient, local groups. This is also suggested by the report of a petition sheet received by the National Convention in April 1842 from Falmouth containing 1,200 signatures (12% of the town's 1841 population). Yet there are few references to any NCA branch at Falmouth and Falmouth delegates were not reported as having attended the Cornwall meeting of November 1841.[46]

Truro was the most consistently reported locality. To some extent this reflected its location as the home of Cornwall's two main newspapers and its strategic location on communication routes. Meanwhile, other localities rose and fell, at first Hayle, then Redruth, followed by Camborne and finally Penzance. When a Chartist lecturer went to Camborne in October/November 1841 it was reported that there was not a single Chartist in the town, but six months later 70 members were claimed, compared with just 20 in Truro. in 1842.[47]

By 1845 the main centre of Chartist activity had switched from Camborne to Penzance. A group was started there in 1839 but by the time of the visit of the Chartist lecturer Thomas Clark, in December 1843, there were only around eight members. By October 1844 when the next Chartist lecturer arrived, this had risen to 23. In November 1844 the Chartists succeeded in getting John Read, a currier and 'a sterling democrat ... always identified with the working classes', elected to the town council from its east ward. The Penzance Chartists hailed this as a blow to the Whigs, a 'set of mongrels who do not remain quiet like the old Tory Corporation, but was daily doing mischief'. This electoral success, unique in Cornwall, was followed up in the following spring when the Chartist list was elected to the Board of Highways in Penzance. By this time, 'we now number about fifty uncompromising Chartists - men who fear not the frowns of the haughty aristocrat, nor yet the dastardly threats of the body-grinding employer'.[48]

---

46 *Northern Star*, 13 November 1841 and 27 November 1841, 22 January 1842, 23 April 1842.

47 *Northern Star*, 16 April 1842.

48 *Northern Star*, 3 April 1842; 9 November 1844; 12 April 1845.

Camborne, along with Truro, Hayle, Redruth and Penzance were the epicentres of Cornish Chartism. From these centres of Chartism, lecturers ventured out, creating temporary groups at various times at places such as Helston, St Ives, Falmouth and Wadebridge, from where notices of Chartist activity were more spasmodic. There were even occasional forays into less promising territory. In 1842 a Chartist lecturer descended on the farming village of Tregony to speak on 'the rights of the working classes'. This was followed up by speeches at Gorran Haven (where the coastguards said 'he deserved banishing') and Mevagissey, where he was 'received by the fishermen in a most generous manner'.[49]

After 1845, reports in the *Northern Star* of Chartist activity in Cornwall subsided. Only Truro and Penzance seem to have formed branches of the Chartist Cooperative Land Society. Nevertheless, it has been claimed that 'women joined the Land Company in Cornwall and Kent, thus lending support to a Chartist venture in counties in which the movement had traditionally been weak', even though no-one from Cornwall is named in the lists of Land Company ballots in 1845-48.[50] The declining mentions of Cornwall in the *Northern Star* may just reflect the general falling away of Chartist coverage in those years. Only 13 delegates from the whole of the UK handed in their credentials at the Annual Convention of 1845 in London. Nonetheless, one of them was from Camborne. Later, in 1848 when excitement had mounted again, fuelled by events in France, the Chartists organised elections to a National Assembly. There was to be one delegate from Cornwall. Ten English counties had no delegate at all, including Somerset and Dorset, while there was only one from the whole of Wales.[51] Cornwall clearly was not comparable with the great centres of Chartist agitation in the industrial regions of Lancashire and Yorkshire. But it was not that exceptional when compared with rural south and east England. Indeed, it's been claimed that there were 500 identifiable Chartist locations in England.[52] If that was the case, then, in relative terms, the 13 identified Chartist locations in Cornwall amount to a 20% higher incidence of Chartist localities in relation to population that that of England.

Even as late as 1848 a new Chartist locality could emerge. A reported 1,500 people at a great reform meeting at St Austell in May of that year (a

---

49 *Northern Star*, 16 July 1842.
50 Jutta Schwarzkopf, *Women in the Chartist Movement* (London: Macmillan, 1991), p.84. See also Thompson, *The Chartists*, 1984, pp.341ff; Chartist ancestors website, www.chartists.net/chartist-land-plan/chartist-land-plan-1845-50/#ballot (accessed 13 September 2016).
51 *Northern Star*, 26 April 1845; 15 April 1848.
52 Malcolm Chase, *The Chartists: Perspectives and Legacies* (London: Merlin, 2015), p.100.

month after the Chartist demonstration at Kennington Common) carried a resolution in favour of the Charter. The mover, Sam Barlow, stated that 'all the evils were centred on class legislation' and the meeting dispersed with 'three cheers for the Charter'. In the same month a meeting at Penzance to express loyalty to Her Majesty after the Chartist threat had been seen off had produced a 'tirade of abuse' against Chartists 'who were still active in the town'. At the same time, further petitions were still being presented to Parliament in favour of the People's Charter and one of those was from Truro. Moreover, a letter from the secretary of the Truro Charter Association in 1850 mentioned the existence of other groups at Penzance, Helston and St Austell.[53] This was the last appearance of Cornish Chartists in the Chartist press, but provides evidence for its survival even after the failure of the third petition of 1848.

Chartism and the Methodists

John Rule's conclusion that the strength of Methodism and temperance agitation in Cornwall acted to limit support for Chartism has been widely accepted.[54] Chartist leaders themselves were well aware of the competing pull of Methodism. At the General Convention in July 1839 a delegate stated that Cornwall could be 'a great acquisition to the cause', if only 'they could have their religious prejudices removed'. There is also evidence that on occasion teetotal leaders could be less than obliging to Chartists. In 1841, the chairman at a Rechabite meeting at Truro refused to allow 'a Chartist agitator' to address the meeting, at which the Chartists 'retired uttering murmurs of disappointment'.[55] Yet the evidence for a continuing level of Chartist activism through the 1840s should give us cause for reflection.

The relationship between religious feeling and Chartist allegiance was not inevitably antipathetic. There were Christian Chartists and even Chartist churches, though mainly in Scotland. Chase argues that Chartism, in its ideology and its actions, shared considerable common ground with nonconformity. In Cornwall too there was hardly automatic opposition from teetotallers. In fact, Lowery related how, after a meeting at St Ives, 'a number of very intelligent working men came to us at the Temperance House, whom we found to be mostly teetotallers ... they assured us [that] the people were very much pleased with what they had heard'. The fiery Richard Spurr at Truro was described as a teetotaller in May 1839 while three Chartist leaders at Truro, together with the Christian Chartist

---

53 *Northern Star*, 20 May 1848; 6 May 1848; 13 April 1850; 24 June 1848.
54 Brown, *Chartism*, 2015, p.24.
55 *Northern Star*, 13 July 1839; *West Briton*, 23 April 1841.

missionary Edward Mead, signed the total abstinence pledge in 1841 and called on all NCA members in Cornwall to follow their lead.[56]

If Chartism and teetotalism were not incompatible then neither were Chartism and Methodism. After all, regular itinerant Chartist lecturers were tapping into a model very familiar to Cornish Methodists. A lecturer called Powell from the north of England took the Chartist message to mid-Cornwall in November 1841, visiting Padstow, where he engaged in a dispute with a local Methodist. While the clash with a more quietist Methodist approach to material difficulties was evident here, other speakers used the religious feelings of the people to their advantage. In a short trip in the summer of 1839 William Cardo claimed that when he demonstrated 'that the principles of the Charter were synonymous with the principles of Jesus Christ and the objects of both was to better the condition of the people ... very soon the whole of the people were with him'.[57] Lecturers could and did appeal to a Christ who spoke for the poor and dispossessed.

Finally, Chartism could also benefit from a broader anti-establishmentarianism in Cornwall. This found periodic expression in the 1830s and 1840s in the form of opposition to the imposition of a church rate. We have already seen how the emergence of Chartism in Truro closely followed riots around the distraint of goods for non-payment of church rates in 1838. Richard Spurr, the most visible local Chartist at that point, clearly gained popularity (and notoriety) by his association with that campaign. In 1843 too, there was 'very great excitement' at Camborne when a church rate was proposed. The local Chartist leader, James Skewes, moved to postpone the question for twelve months and a show of hands supported him. Edward Pendarves, MP for West Cornwall, demanded a poll of ratepayers but after three days the churchwardens gave up the attempt to impose the rate when it became clear there was a substantial majority against it. Seizures of goods for non-payment of church rates were also critical in the late flowering of Chartism in St Austell in 1848 and it was the attempt to levy a church rate there that triggered the formation of a Chartist association.[58] This suggests nonconformists and Chartists shared some ground, even in Cornwall's Methodist strongholds.

Chartism and the miners

For John Rule, 'the real failure of 1839 was that it built no links to the 20,000 miners' of Cornwall. It is certainly the case that miners were less likely to be found in the ranks of Chartist activists in Cornwall than their

---

56 Chase, *Chartism*, 2007, pp.141-42; Harrison and Hollis, *Lowery*, 1979, p.132; *The Operative*, 5 May 1839; *Northern Star*, 29 May 1841.

57 *Northern Star*, 27 February 1841; 4 December 1841; 6 July 1839.

58 *Northern Star*, 6 May 1843; 20 May 1848.

numbers warranted. In the 1840s over a quarter of the male labour force were employed directly in the mines, but fewer than one in ten of identified Chartists were miners. Philip Howell has pointed out how the occupational background of Chartists 'represented the dominant trades in the localities', for example framework knitters in Nottinghamshire, woolcombers in Bradford, colliers and iron workers in Gwent.[59] On the surface therefore, it would seem as if Cornwall was an exception to this, with the dominant group less involved. But not if the spatial focus is shifted from the Cornish scale to that of the actual Chartist localities. Evidence for the local leadership comes largely from lists of the committees at Truro, Penzance, Camborne and Wadebridge. Of these, only at Camborne was a majority employed in mining and there we do find three miners among the eight named Chartists. This is admittedly rather fewer than might be expected given their numbers in the town. But it is also evidence for more than a negligible involvement of miners in Camborne Chartism. When the church rate was defeated in 1843 it was claimed that its supporters lost because of the miners, who 'mustered most strongly against it'.[60]

There are other hints of occasional participation by miners. John Rule relates a report that miners at St Agnes 'turned out' to attend a meeting that transpired to be a hoax. Yet the significance of this is surely that they had 'turned out' rather than stay at home and ignore the whole business. Visiting Chartist lecturers throughout the 1840s held meetings regularly in mining towns and villages. Following the visit of a Chartist lecturer to Camborne in October/November 1841, there was a reported surge in Chartist membership in the town. Towards the end of 1843 'large and enthusiastic meetings' were also reported at Camborne by another itinerant lecturer. Meetings in 1842 at the mining villages of St Day and St Agnes were said to hold the 'prospect of having an abundant harvest' and a branch of the NCA was temporarily established at the former place.[61]

Some individual miners may well have supported the Chartists in nearby towns, although not being involved in branch organisation. At Penzance for example, 'William Davy, a miner, who after a hard day's toil, walked eight miles to meet the friends of Democracy, replied to the sentiment "Oppression, may it soon cease"'. Miners were clearly at times involved in Chartism although in an intermittent manner, preferring to migrate when traditional working rights and customs were threatened rather than stay and

---

59 Rule, 'Chartist mission', 1997, p.80; Philip Howell, 'The local background of Chartism revisited: a note on the geography of popular politics in early Victorian Britain', *Area* 28 (1996), 150-159.

60 *Northern Star,* 6 May 1843.

61 Rule, 'Labouring miner', 1971, p.373; *Northern Star,* 2 April 1842; 6 January 1844; 23 April 1842.

organise. It may also be significant that the temporary upsurge of support for Chartism in the mining districts in the winter and spring of 1841/42 coincided with unrest over wages and reports of strikes in Cornish mines. At Consolidated Mines in Gwennap there was a strike over a fine for absenteeism and miners marched to Illogan, intending to organise a union. The *West Briton* reported that a meeting was to be held and, significantly, 'a Chartist delegate is expected to attend'.[62]

Talk of unionism in 1842 came to nothing. Nevertheless, the less active role of the miners in Cornish Chartism becomes less unusual when we consider the role of coal miners in Chartism. Twenty-five years ago Roy Church summed up historians' equivocation over the miners' role in the movement and found that 'on balance ... evidence for mass Chartist support among miners is minimal and far from persuasive'. Miners' leaders, particularly those involved in the formation of the Miners Association of Great Britain and Ireland in 1842, were familiar with Chartist views and supportive of them, but reluctant to foreground Chartist demands. They gave precedence instead to their own sectional interests, using Chartism if and when it suited them. Given the general lack of mass involvement by miners and the specific absence of trade union organisation among miners in Cornwall, their lack of involvement in formal Chartist organisations was therefore hardly exceptional.[63]

In general, Chartism was an important factor in the spread of trade unionism in the 1840s outside the most skilled trades, which tended to keep their distance from the movement.[64] In parts of the Cornish labour force trade unions were established and in the 1840s these were invariably linked to Chartism. Sometimes, this was merely paranoia on the part of employers unable to distinguish between trade unionism and Chartism. In Penryn in 1842 granite masons were locked out because of their refusal to dress stone destined for London, where the stonemasons were on strike. This dispute spluttered on for a couple of months with one merchant announcing that 'this evening any Chartist unionist of the Tradesmen's Society in my employment shall no longer be in my service'. Yet there is no evidence for any organised Chartist locality in Penryn. On the other hand, shoemakers

---

62 *Northern Star*, 4 January 1845; Burt, 'Industrial relations'; *West Briton*, 1 April 1842.

63 Roy Church, 'Chartism and the miners: a reinterpretation', *Labour History Review* 56 (1991), 23-36; Chase, *Chartism*, 2007, pp.243-244; Brown, *Chartism*, 2015, p.382. For closer relations between Chartism and unionism among Cornish miners in South Australia see Philip Payton, *One and All: Labor and the Radical Tradition in South Australia* (Mile End, SA: Wakefield Press, 2016), pp.72-73.

64 Chase, *Chartism*, 2007, p.210.

were active as Chartists and were also likely to be unionised. The Cordwainers' Society at Penzance was described in December 1844 as 'recently formed', although it is unclear whether Chartism led to trade unionism, or vice versa. At the same time, 'the tailors of Penzance are uniting, as also are the stonemasons'.[65] Nonetheless, trade unionism, limited to a few crafts, was relatively weak in Cornwall, and could not provide the base for widespread support for the Charter.

Who were the Cornish Chartists?

John Rule's small groups of anonymous Chartists who struggled into the 1840s can, with the aid of the Chartist press, be given life. Sixty seven Cornish Chartists were named in the sources consulted. Of these, many are untraceable because of misspelt names, the provision of surnames only or difficulties in distinguishing between a number of people with similar names. However, the occupations of 45 are known and 41 can be found in either the 1841 or 1851 census enumerators' books.[66] Two groups in particular stand out. A third of Chartists worked in the building trade - carpenters, cabinet makers, masons and painters. Most of these were journeymen, employed by others. But not all. Joseph Wallis was a master carpenter at Penzance. There were other owners of small businesses. Also at Penzance John Paul was a master currier and Alexander Davies a master shoemaker, by 1861 employing six men and three boys. Overall, Penzance appears to have had a more middle class component in its Chartist Association.

Shoemakers were the second group that appears to be over-represented in Cornish Chartism, making up almost a quarter of the total. They were especially prominent at Truro. Though less represented among the leaders of Penzance Chartism, the 'truly independent cordwainers of the town' were singled out as 'the bravest of the brave among labour's sons' in 1845. The large proportion of shoemakers is typical, shoemakers being the archetypal artisan radical of the early and mid-nineteenth century.[67] John Endean, from Truro, who toured mid-Cornwall in December 1840, agitating the towns there for the Chartist cause, was later an organiser of the Cordwainers'

---

65 *Northern Star*, 29 January 1842; 26 March 1842; 28 December 1844.

66 The biographical details in this section are based on the relevant entries in the nineteenth-century census enumerators' books.

67 *Northern Star*, 12 April 1845; Eric Hobsbawm and Joan Scott, 'Political shoemakers', *Past & Present* 89 (1980), 86-114; This occupational breakdown, with its preponderance of building workers and shoemakers, does not vary markedly from that of activists in Ashton-under-Lyne. See Robert Hall, 'A united people? Leaders and followers in a Chartist locality, 1838-1848', *Journal of Social History* (2004), 179-203.

General Mutual Assistance Association in 1845, even though described as a bookseller in 1841. Endean moved to St Ives where for a short time he led a Chartist group in 1845 before leaving for Bethnal Green in London by 1849.[68] There, he became a life insurance agent before changing occupation again to become a florist and moving out into what was then the growing rural town of Edmonton by 1871. Endean was however, unusual. Most of the Chartists traced retained the same occupation throughout their working lives. These occupations included a wide range - butchers, woolcombers, a tinplate worker, a brushmaker, printer, dealer in hardware, even a farmer.

Given the difficult circumstances - the lack of large urban centres, relatively weak trade unionism, opposition from Wesleyan ministers and the watchful vigilance of the local authorities - the men who agitated for the Charter in Cornwall must have sometimes despaired of their thankless task. Yet they stuck to it in the face of apathy and occasional persecution. One such was John Longmaid, who was Richard Spurr's right-hand man in his interventions at Truro in early 1839. When Spurr left for London, Longmaid took over as secretary of the Truro group. At an anti-corn law meeting at Truro in March he was moving an amendment of 'no confidence in any agitation that shall not have for its object the six points of Radical Reform'. Within a month it was being reported he had left the town, 'compelled to leave ... in quest of employment elsewhere ... persecuted by the liberal middle classes' of this 'Whig and Tory-ridden town', according to the *Northern Star*. Longmaid was a skilled tailor and had moved just a few miles west to Redruth. This seems to be temporary as he was back in Truro by October 1843. However, by 1851 he had quit Truro again for Redruth, the age and Truro birthplace of his youngest child suggesting he and his family left Truro for good sometime after 1849.[69] In the second half of the 1850s Longmaid departed Cornwall altogether, making a living as a life assurance agent in St Pancras in 1861 and moving out to Greenwich in the 1860s, where he took up his old tailoring trade again. He died in Greenwich in 1881, aged 69.

Chartists like the cabinet maker Richard Spurr were susceptible to pressure from local elites and vulnerable to persecution. Another in this position was William Guscott, a marble mason and engraver of Penzance. Guscott had been born in Tavistock in 1810 but at some stage moved west and became an enthusiastic member of the Penzance NCA, acting as its secretary for a time in the early 1840s. In 1845 however, it was reported that

---

68 *Northern Star*, 2 January 1841 and 22 February 1845.
69 *West Briton*, 4 March 1842; *Northern Star*, 26 March 1842; 28 October 1843; Longmaid was still vigorously putting the Chartist case at a meeting in Truro on a loyal address following the failure of the Chartist demonstration in 1848 (*West Briton*, 28 April 1848).

he had been victimised and discharged from his job. 'He, noble fellow, though a fond and lovely wife with four lovely children are solely dependent on him, braves all rather than give up one iota of his principles as a Chartist' and was reported as going on the tramp in search of work.[70] However, Guscott was back in Penzance in 1851, living in Camberwell Street with his wife and his 'four lovely children'. Moving to a court off New Street in the town, Guscott outlived his wife and survived to 1897.

The leading light of the Camborne Chartists, James Skewes, was another cabinet maker. Skewes lived in 1841 at College Row in the town, also home to several other local Chartists. In 1845 he was elected to represent Cornwall at the Chartists' National Convention and duly travelled to London, optimistically reporting to the relatively sparsely attended Convention that 'if [Cornwall] were properly agitated it could be the best Chartist district in the kingdom'.[71] Skewes then disappears from the historical record and it has proven impossible to trace either him or the wife and daughter he was living with in 1841. He may well have joined so many of his Camborne neighbours by taking the emigration route in the late 1840s. Other Chartists were already mobile. Patrick O'Brien, born in Limerick, had arrived in Penzance in the winter of 1840/41 from Dublin where he had met and married his wife. O'Brien was a schoolmaster, the only example of such identified in the ranks of Cornish Chartism. At some point after 1845 he left Penzance again. By 1851 he was living in the school house at Rodmarley, Worcestershire and was described as a 'professor of music', although efforts to locate him after that date have proved unsuccessful.

Several of our identifiable Cornish Chartists, aged between 17 and 59 in 1841 at the height of the agitation (their mean age was 32/33 and median age 29), later moved away from Cornwall. Of the 41 who can be found in either the 1841 or 1851 censuses at least eight left Cornwall before their death (although these included two return migrants). But in one way they seem exceptional as most can be traced within the UK and died in these islands. Seven others, like Skewes, drop out of the historical record, and may therefore have emigrated overseas. But even if all seven emigrated, this emigration rate (18 per cent of the Chartists) seems low given the importance of emigration in Cornwall after the 1830s.[72] Two thirds of local

---

70 *Northern Star*, 12 April 1845.
71 *Northern Star*, 26 April 1845.
72 Baines estimated that as many as 45% of Cornish men aged between 15 and 24 ended up emigrating in the four decades from 1860 to 1900. (Dudley Baines, *Migration in a Mature Economy: Emigration and Internal Migration in England and Wales, 1861-1900* (Cambridge: Cambridge University Press, 1986), p.152.)

Chartists ended their days in Cornwall. William Wale, a shoemaker active in the Truro Chartists, was typical. William was 26 years old in 1841 and lived with his parents in Goodwives Lane, a poor part of town. He married in 1847 but his wife was dead before 1851. Never re-marrying, William then lived with other members of his family in Goodwives Lane until the 1880s, before moving to Moresk Road in Truro in that decade and dying sometime in the 1890s.

Chartism and women

The post-activist experiences of Chartists have not figured prominently in Chartist studies of other localities. Another aspect, until recently 'comparatively neglected' has been the role of women in the movement.[73] For the greater part, female supporters of the Charter in Cornwall remain anonymous. That does not mean they were not present. In April 1840 the 'patriotic females of Hayle' donated 2/6 to the fund for the wives and families of prisoners. This was the same amount as was raised by the Working Mens' Association of the town. Later in the year 'a few females' at Hayle Copperhouse repeated this, donating to a fund to provide imprisoned Chartists with clothing.[74]

Women remained unnamed, with one exception. In July 1842 two letters appeared in the *Northern Star* from Caroline Maria Williams of College Row, Camborne. They were addressed to 'Chartist sisters everywhere'. Caroline argued that

> the Charter will never become the law of the land until we women are
> fully resolved that it shall be so ... Talk of freedom, whilst the land is
> reeking with oppression, might make a devil blush ... depend upon it,
> women, our influence and exertions will soon pull oppression down.
> Unity is strength. Our aid added to the men's, will soon make our
> tyrants yield to us our rights, or perish.

In her second letter, she admitted that she used to collect for Wesleyan missions. Although the influence of a Methodist rhetoric is plain in her letters, she now called on women not to give to foreign charities, organised by 'well-fed, well-clothed hypocrites'. This stirring call to arms had its limits however. Her call to her sisters to act ended rather tamely not in a call to the barricades but an appeal to 'make dolls' bonnets, ironholders, pin

---

73 Joan Allen and Owen Ashton, 'New directions in Chartist Studies', *Labour History Review*, 74 (2009), 1-5.

74 *Northern Star*, 25 April 1840 and 26 September 1840.

cushions ... and sell them for the cause', activity that did little to disturb the boundaries of the everyday sexual division of labour of the 1840s.[75]

Strangely, despite clearly giving her address as College Row, Camborne, Caroline Williams is consistently described by Jutta Schwarzkopf in her history of Chartist women as an 'independent-minded Bristol Chartist'. This is based on an earlier indirect mention of Williams in the *Northern Star* as 'having recently opened a school in Bristol', a place from which she had submitted a poem dated 24th May 1841 to the *Star*. Schwarzkopf follows David Jones, who described Williams as 'of the middle or lower middle class'.[76] However, no evidence for this is cited, other than the reference to the school. This seems to have been short-lived, with Caroline Williams writing a few months later from College Row, not a street particularly associated with the 'middle or lower middle class' at this time, but a well known centre of Camborne Chartism. Perhaps the school was a dame school and Caroline an example of a woman from a working class family who had followed a traditional migration route from Cornwall to Bristol. By 1842 she had returned to Camborne and to a terraced row that housed other Chartist activists.

Chartist culture

The role of women in making and selling things to help raise money reminds us that Chartism was not merely a political programme aimed at legislative change. It was a movement of democratic ideas and practice. This practice accompanied the emergence of a vigorous Chartist recreational culture in the early 1840s.[77] Although on the periphery of the Chartist movement, aspects of wider practice and ideas, culture and language can all be found in the Cornish Chartism of the 1840s.

Chartism was not just an endless round of political meetings. At Christmas 1844 a reported crowd of 125 sat down to tea at Penzance after a 'soiree' and listened to the National Chartist anthem sung by 'a select choir'. This followed another Chartist soiree at Camborne, attended 'by Chartist friends from Truro, Penzance and other places'. A couple of years earlier 60 men and women were attending tea and listening to a Rechabite band organised by the Camborne Chartists. This meeting was held to celebrate the christening of two local Chartist leaders' children at Camborne

---

75 *Northern Star*, 23 July 1842 and 30 July 1842. Unfortunately, Caroline Williams cannot be traced in the census enumerators' books of either 1841 or 1851.

76 Schwarzkopf, *Women*, 1991, pp.175, 195, 217, 230; *Northern Star* 30 April 1842, 23 July 1842, 4 June 1842; David Jones, 'Women and Chartism', *History* 68 (1983), 1-21.

77 Hall, *Voices of the People*, 2007; Chase, *Chartism*, 2007, pp.140-48.

Church. The boys were named James Fergus O'Connor Skewes and George Bronterre O'Brien Watts. They were not the only examples of the phenomenon of activists naming their children after prominent Chartist leaders. The Truro Chartist John Endean also named his son James Fergus O'Connor Endean in 1844 while one of John Longmaid's sons was given the name John Frost O'Connor Longmaid in 1842.[78]

Soirees and naming practices are local examples of a more general practice among Chartists. They suggest that a Chartist sub-cultural network existed across some Cornish towns exactly as it did in other parts of the UK. Its participants drew strength from their companionship and adopted a healthily suspicious view of the authorities. This could lead to passive civil disobedience, as at Penzance where Charles Reynolds refused to complete his census schedule in 1841. Even the *Northern Star* deemed this was going too far: 'C.Reynolds ... acted very foolishly in refusing to fill up the schedule. We love an adherence to principle; we like to see it holden with prudence', it rather primly reported.[79]

While in terms of its practice and attitudes to authority Cornish Chartism therefore exhibited characteristics familiar to students of Chartism in other localities, the language of local Chartism contains some evidence of attempts to give a general oppositional and democratic rhetoric a specifically Cornish flavour. Howell has pointed out how Chartism was implicated in the construction of a national sense of community rather than a local one.[80] Here, a Cornish Studies perspective alerts us to the more subtle spatial meanings inherent in the Chartist message. It was not that an ideology of English/British nationalism shared by Chartists was inapplicable or rejected in Cornwall; it was more that such ideas had an ambiguous purchase in a peripheral region where local identities also exerted a powerful pull.

When appealing for support local Chartists usually deployed language that would have been recognisable anywhere. For example, in 1839 the Truro WMA appealed to the people's 'inalienable rights ... basely robbed by a selfish and plundering aristocracy and a covetous set of vile swindlers and grasping money-mongers'. The Helston Chartists in 1841 called on the artisans, miners and agricultural labourers of Helston to rescue 'the land of your birth from degradation and ruin' as 'we find ourselves surrounded by poverty, destitution and distress to an extent unparalleled in the annals of British history'. A month earlier the Redruth Chartists had called on their 'friends and brethren' to 'join in the great national struggle in all parts of

---

78 *Northern Star*, 4 January 1845; 21 December 1844; 26 March 1842; Census enumerators' books, 1851 and 1861.
79 *Northern Star*, 26 June 1841.
80 Howell, 'Local background', 1996.

England, Ireland, Scotland and Wales, in order that we may gain for ourselves a fair share of political power'. This was the familiar call to the people 'in the name of humanity, to come forward and help us to get rid of such a set of devouring droves that keep you in subjection ... and a Frenchified police, to carry out their black designs, to swear away your lives and liberty if it suits their purposes'. People were reminded of the 'base, bloody and brutal laws' carried through by that 'set of noodles', the 'Whig faction' that had given them 'a most abominable Poor Law Amendment Act which punishes poverty as a crime, separates husband from wife, and tears the weeping mother from her offspring', recently replaced by 'a bolder set of public plunderers' in Peel's new Tory Government of 1841.[81]

However, in addition there were efforts to hook this discourse into local tradition. Richard Spurr had not hesitated to refer to the 'the Cornish motto "One and All"' at meetings in Truro in 1839. He also took care not to cede the ground of local patriotism to his opponents, interpellating his listeners regularly as 'Cornishmen'. The Helston Chartists warned that if people 'look tamely on' while the battle for freedom was being waged, 'you deserve not the name of Cornishmen'. They appealed to the 'patriotic spirit that fired the breasts of your brave sires ...and that you still cling to your ancient admirable motto 'One and All'". Reference was also made to 'One and All' at a meeting at Chacewater in the same year, when William Lovett was significantly referred to as 'one of their own country'. Meanwhile, the Redruth Chartists went furthest in linking the struggle for the Charter to historical memories circulating in Cornwall. They called on men to 'come forward with the same united petition as you did when you petitioned for the release of your countryman, Trelawny'. Here was a plain invitation to 'Cornish boys' to do 'their duty' and as a result 'reap the benefit of an upright government which will make equal laws and equal rights'.[82]

Conclusion
Adopting a Cornish Studies perspective has allowed the traditional story of Chartist missionaries in Cornwall to be rounded out to include those groups of Cornish Chartists who, often in the face of considerable hostility from local elites and the press, sustained a fluctuating but ever present level of activity throughout the 1840s in the towns of west Cornwall. The strength of Wesleyan Methodism in this district did not prevent the emergence of a Chartist sub-culture in several towns, notably Truro, Camborne and Penzance, a culture that echoed the vibrant Chartist-led self-organisation

---

81 *The Operative*, 16 June 1839; *Northern Star*, 26 November 1841 and 16 October 1841.

82 *West Briton*, 22 February 1839; *Northern Star*, 27 February 1841 and 16 October 1841.

that suffused working class communities across Britain in those years. As elsewhere, Chartists in Cornwall collected signatures for petitions, encouraged trade unionism, condemned the landed class's monopoly of politics, joined in a Chartist recreational culture and even helped to elect borough councillors sympathetic to the cause. In all this, Cornwall was less exceptional than some have asserted.

At the same time, however, the persistence of Chartism in Cornwall's larger towns was not sufficient to make it the 'great acquisition to the cause' that some of the more optimistic Chartists had hoped.[83] West Cornwall remained on the periphery of the Chartist movement, while east Cornwall, like rural southern England, was hardly touched. Moreover, although Cornish miners did get involved in some places, notably Camborne, and at some times, as in 1842, John Rule's conclusion stands: Cornwall's metal miners, its pre-eminent occupational group, were largely unmoved by the campaign for the People's Charter. On the other hand, this again was less exceptional than has sometimes been made out, with miners in Britain's coalfields also only sporadically involved in formal Chartist organisation.

Having rescued the history of Cornish Chartism in the 1840s from its previous obscurity, a number of potential research questions remain. From a Cornish Studies perspective, the relations between the British national discourse of Chartism and local strategies and discourses need teasing out. There are, for example, hints of tactical disagreements revolving around centre-local relations. A delegate meeting was convened at Penzance in June 1845 to 'consider the best means of establishing the democratic principle throughout the county'.[84] Debate revolved around whether to raise funds to send a representative to the forthcoming Chartist Convention in London or raise money for a 'lecture fund ... independent of the executive; still tendering our support to that body'. In the event the former option, supported by delegates from Penzance and Camborne, was agreed and the more independent line argued for by those from Truro and Falmouth rejected. This report hints at broader disagreements over relations with the central Executive and reminds us of the difficulties experienced in marrying the 'national' project of the Charter to local sensibilities.

The period of the Chartist Land Company from 1845 to 1848 also requires more work. Is it really the case that the Chartist Land Plan attracted little support in Cornwall? If so, was this connected with the greater access to smallholdings, allotments and collateral aids in the far west?

The 'mainstream' historiography on Chartism has in recent years focused on longitudinal studies that take Chartism beyond the decade from

---

83 *Northern Star*, 13 July 1839.
84 *Northern Star*, 11 Jan 1845.

1838 to 1848.[85] First, the earlier history of collective action and everyday life in Cornish labouring communities needs unravelling to establish the context in which some seeds sown by the Chartists flowered in the 1840s while others wilted. This can now break free from the confining and artificial distinction between categories of 'pre-modern', consumer-oriented food rioting and 'modern', producer-focused action that has for so long bedevilled the social history of labouring communities in this period.

Second, there is now increasing emphasis on Chartism as a training ground for democracy, linking it to the growth of mid-century radicalism.[86] No more is Chartism seen as a dead end, a proto-revolutionary campaign for liberation that failed, to be superseded by an unconnected moderate and respectable path to parliamentary democracy. Chartists and Chartist activism melded into the emergence of Victorian Liberalism. In Cornwall for example, the next generation of those miners that in 1839 were supposed to have shunned the Chartists were at the leading edge of British radical politics, described as 'neatly, precisely and completely Democratic', even though Methodism still held sway over the majority of Cornish communities.[87] Times had clearly changed by the 1880s. But how? And why?

Cornish Chartism in the 1840s deserves a lot more than the postscript devoted to it hitherto. Never on a scale comparable with other industrial regions in the north of England or in Wales before the disaster of the Newport rising in 1839, Cornish Chartism nonetheless compared favourably with other rural parts of Britain. John Rule ended his account of the Chartist mission of 1839 with a teetotal meeting in Gwennap in 1840 when people signed the pledge rather than the Charter.[88] But a more telling ending would be the events of 1847 when a crowd of food rioters at Redruth led attacks on the market and grain stores. And not just at Redruth, as protesting crowds gathered across Cornwall. Support for the Charter in the 1840s overlapped with a continuing commitment to the customary protests of the moral economy. The 1840s was a decade of transition in Cornwall - a decade when faith in traditional protest with its roots in the eighteenth century overlapped with the more modernist demands for political reform voiced by the Chartists. It is that combination and not the absence of Chartism that made Cornwall unique.

---

85 Chase, 'Twentieth-century labour histories', 2011, pp.58-59.
86 Chase, *The Chartists*, 2015, pp.1-13; Griffin, 'Making of the Chartists', 2014.
87 *West Briton*, 24 September 1885.
88 Rule, 'Chartist mission', 1997, p.80.

Chapter Seven

Bishops and teetotallers: Cornish identity politics in the later nineteenth century

Two decades ago David Cannadine warned that a potentially 'excessive concentration on "Britishness"' ran the risk of ignoring the 'many alternative, individual identities, sometimes complementary, sometimes contradictory, which are more locally - but no less purposefully – articulated'.[1] Since then the flood of writing on Britishness has continued unabated and been joined by a growing academic literature on Englishness.[2] Cabinet ministers queued up to make speeches about Britishness and journalists hastily scribbled about Englishness, as an end-of-century angst about Britishness converged with the insecurities of an English intelligentsia made uneasy by post-colonialism, devolution to Scotland and Wales, the European project and globalisation.[3] However, whereas Englishness has now become a fit subject for polite conversation, further scales of identity within England are less explored, despite the observation that unevenness at the regional scale 'will continue to complicate the

1 David Cannadine, 'British History as a "new subject": Politics, perspectives and prospects', in *Uniting the Kingdom? The Making of British History*, ed. Alexander Grant and Keith Stringer (London: Routledge, 1995), p.26.

2 This had already been triggered by Linda Colley's *Britons: Forging the Nation 1707-1837* (New Haven, CT: Yale University Press, 1992). It has been continued by, among others, Keith Robbins, *Great Britain: Identities, Institutions and the Idea of Britishness* (Harlow: Longman, 1998), Norman Davies, *The Isles: A History* (London: Macmillan, 1999) and Richard Weight, *Patriots: National Identity in Britain 1940-2000* (London: Macmillan, 2002). For an early examination of Englishness in the past see Gerald Newman, *The Rise of English Nationalism: A Cultural History 1740-1830* (London: Weidenfeld and Nicolson, 1989). This was belatedly followed by such works as Robert Colls, *Identities of England* (Oxford: Oxford University Press, 2002); Krishan Kumar, *The Making of English National Identity* (Cambridge: Cambridge University Press, 2003) and *The Idea of Englishness: English Culture, National Identity and Social Thought* (Farnham: Ashgate, 2015); Michael Kenny, *The Politics of English Nationhood* (Oxford: Oxford University Press, 2014). The relationship between British and English identities is explored in Rebecca Langlands, 'Britishness or Englishness? The historical problem of national identity in Britain', *Nations and Nationalism* 5 (1999), 53-69; Ben Wellings, 'Empire-nation: national and imperial discourses in England', *Nations and Nationalism* 8 (2002), 95-109.

3 Jeremy Paxman, *The English: A Portrait of a People* (London: Penguin, 1998).

collective representation of England'.[4] Now that Britishness and Englishness are firmly ensconced in academic consciousness and political debate, it's high time to go beyond them, to the localities and regions of England (and Scotland and Wales).

This chapter pursues the issue of identity onto an apparently sub-national terrain, investigating the case of Cornwall. Cornwall makes intriguing though fleeting appearances in the literature on British history and nationalism.[5] Its small size, only 1.5% of the land area of the UK, has ensured its lack of visibility. Yet scale has not been the only factor. Tom Nairn, in his polemic *After Britain*, points out how

> beyond the familiar Scotland-Ireland-Wales triad there now lies the question of Cornwall, and of the very small territories, the Isle of Man, Jersey and Guernsey, which were simply ignored by traditional all-British political reflection – too insignificant to figure, as it were, in its dazzling image of greatness and global reach.[6]

But Cornwall has not been consistently ignored. Rather, its categorisation within Britain seems to present a puzzle. In the 1920s A.K.Hamilton Jenkin, Cornwall's mining historian, recounted an apocryphal story from the nineteenth century:

> "Hes Coornwall a nashion [nation], hes a a Hiland [island], or hes a a ferren [foreign] country?", an old school dame, Peggy Combellack, would ask.

> "He hedn't no nashon, he hedn't no highlan, nor he hedn't no ferren country," the brightest of the scholars on one occasion answered.

> "What hes a then?" asked Peggy.

---

4   Christopher Bryant, 'These Englands, or where does devolution leave the English?', *Nations and Nationalism* 9 (2003), 393-412.
5   See for example Davies, *The Isles*, 1999, p.477; Hugh Kearney, *The British Isles: A History of Four Nations* (Cambridge: Cambridge University Press, 1989), pp.1 and 105; Eric Hobsbawm, *Nations and Nationalism since 1780* (Cambridge: Cambridge University Press, 1992), p.178; Robbins, *Great Britain*, 1998, pp.8-9; Weight, *Patriots*, 2002, pp.598-603.
6   Tom Nairn, *After Britain: New Labour and the Return of Scotland* (London: Granta, 2000), p.4.

"Why, he's kidged [joined] to a furren country from the top hand",
was the reply.[7]

Peggy Combellack's conundrum is, according to Cornish historian Philip
Payton, 'as significant today as it was in Peggy's time'. For Payton,
Cornwall and the Cornish 'remain together an enigma – not falling neatly or
happily into the new categories that are appearing, a battleground perhaps
for conflicting visions, constructions, imaginings of Cornishness, Celticity
and Britishness'.[8]

If this is the case, it is somewhat surprising that Cornwall and its identity
are largely overlooked in the academic literature on Britain and Britishness.[9]
Here is an instance of an identity from within which some people claim
national status, but, uniquely, from a marginal location at the edge of
Englishness. This emplacement guarantees Cornwall's uncertain place in
popular categories and academic discourses. Both 'of England' and 'not of
England', it defies easy analysis. Cornwall and the Cornish teeter on the
brink of a conceptual and historiographical crevasse, neither county nor
nation. As a result of this conceptual indistinctiveness, its identity remains
unfathomed. In addition, another possibility ignored by Peggy Combellack
was that of region. While regions have a long pedigree in the lexicon of
geographers and historians, the concept rarely surfaced in popular
discourse. The intention here is to restore Cornwall and Cornishness to a
more visible place in the British mosaic by investigating its 'regional
moment' in the second half of the nineteenth century. Two campaigns
demanding special treatment for Cornwall are examined to reveal the
discourse of Cornishness that underpinned them. I argue that these
campaigns and their associated discourses offer lessons for twenty-first
century campaigners for greater recognition of Cornwall's distinctiveness
and the right of its people to equal treatment with the other nations of these
islands.

The region in the English academy
Despite a growing hunt for regional identity in England since the 1980s
historians agree that it remains a 'difficult and elusive entity'.[10] Perhaps this

---

7   A.K.Hamilton Jenkin, *The Cornish Miner* (London: George Allan and Unwin,
     1927), pp.274-275.
8   Philip Payton, *A Vision of Cornwall* (Fowey: Alexander Associates, 2002),
     pp.47 and 65.
9   Cornwall gets no mention in Kumar, *Making,* 2003 and *Idea,* 2015 or Kenny,
     Politics, 2014.
10   Edward Royle, 'Introduction: regions and identities', in Edward Royle (ed.),
     *Issues of Regional Identity (*Manchester: Manchester University Press, 1998),

is because in the past as much as the present English regions were 'in large degree simply ghosts'.[11] If regions have little meaning beyond lines on the map serving political and administrative convenience then it is hardly a surprise that English regionalism was a 'dog that never barked'.[12] Yet it has long been assumed that regions are not just the perceptions of historians and geographers; they could also be 'conscious regions', places where the inhabitants had a sense of their own identity.[13] Edward Royle emphasised that the term 'region' was one of convenience. A region might be an administrative unit, but equally it could be a 'zone of human activity' or even 'a feeling, a sentimental attachment to territory shared by like-minded people'. He urged historians to jettison an over-rigid attachment to one definition of region or to twentieth century templates and concern themselves primarily with the view from the bottom, what a region meant (if anything) to the person living there.[14] John Marshall echoed this, arguing that the growth of regional consciousness in many parts of Britain was 'almost totally unexplored'.[15] Yet Marshall's inference that regional identities waxed and presumably also waned over time has itself been largely unexplored. This reflected a wider phenomenon, as the work of regional historians occurred in isolation from a growing body of literature from geographers and regional scientists on regions and their evolving and increasingly elastic definition of this contested and ambiguous term.[16]

The majority of historical work on regional identities in England is confined to the north of that country. Indeed, the absence of work on other regions speaks volumes. Even in the north, after an ambitious (and unlikely) comparison of the North West with the Basque Country, John Walton concluded that the idea of a 'North West' lacked any real meaning until the 1970s.[17] However, other northern regions are claimed to have deeper roots.

---

p. 1.

11 Vernon Bogdanor, *Devolution in the United Kingdom* (Oxford: Oxford University Press, 1999), p.271.

12 Christopher Harvie, 'English regionalism: the dog that never barked', in Bernard Crick (ed.), *National Identities: The Constitution of the United Kingdom* (Oxford: Blackwell, 1991), 105-18.

13 Alan Everitt, 'Country, county and town: patterns of regional evolution in England" *Transactions of the Royal Historical Society* 29 (1979), 79-108.

14 Royle, *Issues*, 1998, pp. 4-5.

15 John Marshall, *The Tyranny of the Discrete. A discussion of the problems of local history in England* (Aldershot: Scolar Press, 1997), p. 104.

16 See John Allen, Doreen Massey and Allan Cochrane, *Rethinking the Region* (London: Routledge, 1998).

17 John K. Walton, 'Imagining regions in comparative perspective: the strange birth of North-West England', in B. Lancaster, D. Newton and N. Vall (eds), *An Agenda for Regional History* (Newcastle: Northumbria University Press, 2009),

The North East is sometimes singled out by scholars of contemporary English regionalization as the only region with a discernible territorial identity.[18] This is partly because its academics have constructed a powerful narrative of regional identity, claiming that remoteness from London, an early medieval legacy provided by the bishopric of Durham and the kingdom of Northumbria, and an identity based on heavy industry and mining are taken as evidence that 'North East England has had a marked political identity for centuries'.[19] Yet the conclusions of extended work on the historical identity of the North East clash sharply with the received wisdom. Far from a coherent regional identity with continuity over the centuries Adrian Green and A.J.Pollard conclude that the North East has 'not been a coherent and self-conscious region over the longue durée'.[20]

If the North East only enjoyed an intermittently visible historic identity then other English regions have been virtually invisible. With one exception. Historians of English regionalism often note Cornwall as a second example of a 'strong' regional identity.[21] Cornwall is prone to be viewed through a prism of exceptionalism, both by its own historians and by others.[22] Eric Hobsbawm pointed out that 'the Cornish are fortunate to be able to paint their regional discontents in the attractive colours of Celtic tradition, which makes them so much more viable'.[23] For Bryan Ward-Perkins Cornwall 'remains the one part of England where not all indigenous inhabitants automatically describe themselves as "English"'.[24] This claim is extended into the past. Green and Pollard observe that Cornwall 'was, and still is' the most distinctive county in England, 'with an identity as strong as that of Brittany'.[25] David Neave, while dismissing the possibility that

---

289-302.

18   Mark Sandford, *The New Governance of the English Regions* (London: Palgrave, 2005), p. 34.

19   John Tomaney, 'In search of English regionalism: the case of the North East', *Scottish Affairs* 28 (1999), 62-82.

20   Adrian Green and A.J.Pollard, 'Finding North-East England', in Adrian Green and A.J.Pollard (eds), *Regional Identities in North-East England, 1300-2000* (Woodbridge: The Boydell Press, 2007), 209-26.

21   Christopher G.A. Bryant, *The Nations of Britain* (Oxford: Oxford University Press, 2006), pp. 226-30.

22   Philip Payton, *The Making of Modern Cornwall* (Redruth: Dyllansow Truran, 1992).

23   Eric Hobsbawm, *Nations and Nationalism since 1780* (Cambridge: Cambridge University Press, 1992), p. 78.

24   Bryan Ward-Perkins, 'Why did the Anglo-Saxons not become more British?', *English Historical Review* 115 (2000), 513-33.

25   Adrian Green and A.J.Pollard, 'Introduction: identifying regions', in Adrian Green and A.J.Pollard (eds), *Regional Identities in North-East England, 1300-*

counties in England could also be regarded as regions in the nineteenth century, noted the exception of Cornwall, which he defined as a 'culture region' notwithstanding its county administrative status.[26]

Of course others, especially in Cornwall, would hesitate to describe nineteenth century Cornwall as a region, and most certainly not as an 'English' region. After all, the descriptor 'region' was not applied to it by contemporaries, who preferred either 'county' or, almost as commonly, 'Duchy', with its hints of a special status, a vestige of 'Cornwall's constitutional accommodation'.[27] Some observers have been over-influenced by the existence of a cultural and political nationalist movement in twentieth century Cornwall, enthusiastically asserting that Cornwall is 'a historic nation whose claims to statehood have never really disappeared'.[28] Others see Cornwall 'sitting ... somewhere between region and nation'.[29] Conversely, another version of 'presentism' unproblematically reads Cornwall's current administrative status as an English county back into the seventeenth century.[30] Yet attempts to clarify Cornwall's exact status miss the point. Defining a sense of place related to territory as a county community, a regional identity or a national aspiration is less important than recognising the presence of a spatial identity cohering around the territory of Cornwall. The approach I take here is to recognise this plasticity and resist attempts at a rigid classification, preferring to view Cornwall as a sub-state territory with a de-facto county status, but a potential regional vocation which contains narratives of nationality.[31]

Regions and discourses

Historians of national identity now agree that nations are 'discursive terrains'. Language as rhetoric, narrative and ideology plays a critical part

---

2000 (Woodbridge: The Boydell Press, 2007), p. 14.

26 David Neave, 'The identity of the East Riding of Yorkshire', in Edward Royle (ed.), *Issues of Regional Identity*, (Manchester: Manchester University Press, 1998), 184-200.

27 Payton, *Making*, 1992, p. 65.

28 Amer Hirnis, 'The South West economy: potential for faster economic development', in Irene Hardill, Paul Benneworth, Mark Baker and Leslie Budd (eds), *The Rise of the English Regions?* (London: Routledge, 2006), p. 205.

29 Dafydd Moore, 'Devolving Romanticism: Nation, region and the case of Devon and Cornwall', *Literature Compass* 5 (2008), 949-963.

30 John Morrill, 'The British Problem, c.1534-1707', in Brendan Bradshaw and John Morrill (eds), *The British Problem, c.1534-1797: State Formation in the Atlantic Archipelago* (Basingstoke: Macmillan, 1996), 1-38.

31 For more on this see Bernard Deacon, 'County, nation, ethnic group? The shaping of the Cornish identity', *International Journal of Regional and Local Studies* 3 (2007), 5-29.

in constructing symbolic meanings, re-interpreting cultural practices and building mental boundaries around people and places.[32] Versions of the past are moulded to serve contemporary interests. Luis Castells and John Walton point out how regions also required the invention of 'a distinctive culture that is capable of forging and sustaining a distinct identity of which the inhabitants are conscious'.[33] Like nations therefore, regions can also be viewed as 'imagined communities', constructed through representations, texts and practices and the narratives and discourses adopted by both insiders and outsiders.[34] Regional identities in the past were therefore 'discursive products'. But historians have paid relatively little attention to the mechanics of the discourses that underpinned a regional sense of belonging. In practice there is constant slippage from the 'images and perceptions of territory that contemporaries carried about with them' and the representations and discourses that carry identity myths to post-facto reconstructions of culture zones.[35] Moreover, while a rich body of theory exists around the formation of group identity, historians have focused on identifying those factors determining an individual's consciousness of belonging to a wider group or specifying which identities provided the strongest explanation for collective action and why. This focus on the role of identities in individual agency and action is clearly important but nonetheless detracts attention from the history of the identities themselves, how they function and how they change over time.

In contrast the Finnish geographer Anssi Paasi offers a sophisticated, diachronic framework for understanding how regions emerge over time. In his model regions are institutionalized through an overlapping series of four stages: the acquisition of territorial shape, when a territory is identified as a distinct unit; symbolic shape, when specific symbols and meanings are attached to it; institutional shape, during which institutional practices socialize the inhabitants of a territory, and finally the establishment of a territory in the wider social consciousness.[36] Furthermore, Paasi

---

32 Helen Brocklehurst and Robert Phillips (eds), *History, Nationhood and the Question of Britain* (London: Palgrave, 2004), p. xxvi.

33 Luis Castells and John Walton, 'Contrasting identities: north-west England and the Basque Country, 1840-1936', in Royle (ed.), *Issues*, 1998, 44-82.

34 Dave Russell, 'Culture and the formation of northern English identities from c.1850', in Lancaster, et al. (eds), *Agenda*, 2007, 271-87.

35 Marshall, *Tyranny*, 1997, pp.95-100.

36 Anssi Paasi, 'The institutionalization of regions: a theoretical framework for understanding the emergence of regions and the constitution of regional identity', *Fennia* 164 (1986), 105-46; 'Deconstructing regions: notes on the scales of spatial life', *Environment and Planning A* 23 (1991), 239-56; 'Region and place: regional identity in question', *Progress in Human Geography* 27 (2003), 475-85. Historians have been slow to make use of Paasi's work. Even

conceptualized regions as existing at a variety of scales, always in the process of 'becoming' rather than 'being'. Regions give rise to senses of place and belonging and to spatial identities residing at a scale somewhere between locality and nation-state. Regions can be created and changed by influences flowing from either direction - regionalization, involving state-centred policies imposed on regional problems, or regionalism, 'the aspirations and activism of the concerned inhabitants of a region'.[37] The former, while over the long run capable of creating regional identity, is top-down and exogenous; the latter is bottom-up and relies on the agency of social actors in the region itself. Martin Jones and Gordon Macleod also usefully distinguish between these, which they term 'regional spaces' and 'spaces of regionalism'.[38]

Critically therefore, 'regions' are sub-state territorial entities varying greatly in size and function, but also 'social constructs ... made in broader social practices'.[39] Moreover, in the making of some regions other potential regions are unmade. A wide variety of possible regions exist although only some are established as such in the dominant spatial discourse. Paasi emphasises the role of language in 'spatial socialization', acknowledging that rhetoric plays a part in constructing boundaries and thus otherness and that discourses are 'plays of power' institutionalized via language.[40] More specifically, he proposes that the symbolic construction of space is based on a dialectic between two types of language. The first is a language of difference, distinguishing one place or region from another. The second is a language of integration, homogenising the spatial experiences of a place or region. These two processes, of differentiation and integration, are clearly central to any understanding of identity formation.[41] For Paasi the

---

Celia Applegate's comprehensive account of regional history across Europe, which was alert to both materialist and idealist perspectives, failed to cite his work (see Celia Applegate, 'A Europe of regions: reflections on the historiography of sub-national places in modern times', *The American Historical Review* 104 (1999), 1157-82.

37 Peter Wagstaff (ed.), *Regionalism in Europe* (Oxford: Intellect Books, 1994), p. 4.

38 Martin Jones and Gordon Macleod, 'Regional Spaces, Spaces of regionalism: Territory, Insurgent Politics and the English Question', *Transactions of the Institute of British Geographers* NS29 (2004), 433-52.

39 Anssi Paasi, 'The resurgence of the "Region" and "Regional Identity": theoretical perspectives and empirical observations on regional dynamics in Europe'. *Review of International Studies* 35 (2009), 121-146.

40 See Paasi, 'Region and place', 2003; 'Resurgence', 2009.

41 They are noted in works from a range of disciplinary perspectives, for example Shmuel Eisenstadt and Bernhard Giesenard, 'The construction of collective identity', *European Journal of Sociology* 36 (1995), 72-102; Bernd Simon,

'production and reproduction of the discourses on region are normally crucial in establishing the spatial frames for regional identities'.[42]

All this is intriguing but too often maddeningly imprecise. For instance, Paasi draws our attention to the presence of competing constructions of places and regions and multiple identities jostling each other in shared spaces. Nonetheless, Paasi's use of the concept of discourse remains over-generalized and restricted to a structural level. It is unclear how we might identify the hybrid, interleaving discourses he identifies and there are few signposts as to how discourses are produced and transformed in practice. In short, the mechanisms of the production and reproduction of discourses remain obscure and we are given little guidance on the way in which such competing narratives of place 'vie for hegemony within any given space'.[43] Any one territorial identity can overlap with others, the idea of 'nested identities' being proposed to describe this hierarchy of spatial identities. However, this says little about the relationship between those levels of identity.

Paasi recognises that discourses of place and past only adhere and become potent if there is some connection, however fragile, to experience. Discourses therefore, while central to understandings of place, quarry 'history' for their collective memory (and collective amnesia) and are always located in context. In an important intervention in the debate about social history and poststructuralism Adrian Jones makes the case for an approach to discourse that supplements a concern for rhetoric and narrative with a focus on actions.[44] It is one thing to identify a discourse but another to identify sites of action, those contexts in which discourses become legitimated, taking on a less ethereal shape as they find experience in material action. Jones argues that it is only when we search for this praxis that we discover the limits of a particular discourse as it encounters other discourses. Each identity therefore has to be analysed in specific contexts.

Paasi suggests it is important 'to ask not what regional identities are but what people mean when they talk or write about regional identities'.[45] Qualitative evidence suggests the meaning of the Cornish identity differs markedly from that of local identities in other counties administered as part

Claudia Kulla and Martin Zobel, 'On being more than just a part of the whole: regional identity and social distinctiveness', *European Journal of Social Psychology* 25 (1995), 325-40.

42 Paasi, 'Resurgence', 2009, p. 140.

43 Gordon Macleod, 'In what sense a region? Place, hybridity, symbolic shape, and institutional formation in (post-) modern Scotland', *Political Geography*, 17 (1998), 833-63.

44 Adrian Jones, 'Word and deed: why a post-poststructural history is needed, and how it might look', *Historical Journal* 43 (2000), 517-541.

45 Paasi, 'Region and place', 2003, p.481.

of England. For example, in 1991 the Presidents of the Yorkshire and Cornwall Rugby Football Unions both provided messages before the County Championship final of that year between their respective teams. The Yorkshireman saw county rugby as a stepping stone to English rugby success. But the Cornishman felt moved to refer to Bishop Trelawny's imprisonment in the Tower of London in the seventeenth century, arguing that 'the Cornish have the additional motivation of a Celtic people striving to preserve an identity'.[46] The Cornish can imagine their identity as either a local identity within England, or as an identity which is something other than English, or sometimes both at the same time. This is not new. We can now turn to two campaigns of the later 1800s in order to probe the sites of action and examine the meanings involved in discourses of Cornwall and Cornishness.

Campaigns for regional recognition

Two campaigns open a window into discourses of Cornwall, the Cornish and Cornishness in the second half of the nineteenth century. Moreover, these campaigns are of more than historical significance; they can be read as early salvoes in the long-running struggle for territorial recognition and respect for Cornwall. This involves a rejection of a 'devonwall' region and includes a claim for special treatment for Cornwall. As such, these early campaigns hold lessons for Cornish campaigners of the early twenty-first century who, remarkably, are still being forced to confront the same issues. The first nineteenth-century campaign was the battle to achieve an Anglican diocese separate from Exeter. This was born in the 1840s, peaked in the 1850s and 60s and was crowned with success in 1876 when Disraeli's Conservative government agreed to establish a Cornish episcopate. The second campaign was less successful, although also bound up with and triggered by the religious cultural politics of the time. This was the more short-lived, but also more popular, campaign for a Sunday Closing Bill, launched in late 1881 but narrowly defeated in Parliament in the summer of 1883.

The course of the campaign for a Cornish diocese has been charted in some detail by P.S.Morrish.[47] He notes how demands for a Cornish bishopric surfaced in the wake of the re-structuring of the Established Church in the 1830s and plans for a new diocese of Manchester in the 1840s. However, Cornwall was different. Here, the arguments for a new diocese contained two novel aspects, in addition to the more familiar economic and demographic grounds usually put forward to justify new

---

46 *Camborne Packet*, 13 April 1991.
47 P.S.Morrish, 'History, Celticism and propaganda in the formation of the diocese of Truro', *Southern History* 5 (1983), 238-266.

dioceses in England's growing industrial regions. From the 1840s, a historical case was constructed in Cornwall, claiming a Cornish bishopric was not a novel excursion at all but merely the re-establishment of a former bishopric from the days of an 'independent British church ... refusing obedience to the Roman see'.[48] This cannily tapped into the anti-Catholic sentiments and fears of Romanism stimulated by the contemporary Tractarian movement in the Church of England, even though that movement in turn influenced many of those mooting a separate Cornish diocese.

To this historical argument an 'ethnological' argument was added in the 1850s. This initially took the form of stressing economic and social differences. By the 1860s a further argument was inserted, that of racial difference. This coincided with the rediscovery of Cornwall's Celtic connections on the part of its elite. The point at which Cornwall's 'great and good' adopted Celticity can be dated quite precisely. In 1860 an archaeological paper by Sir Gordon Wilkinson, published in Cornwall's leading antiquarian journal, the *Journal of the Royal Institution of Cornwall*, led to heightened contact with the Cambrian Society in Wales. Enthused by this, members of the Royal Institution rushed to sign up as Celts: 'we are here at the utmost verge of the Celtic system; we want to connect our local antiquities with the antiquities of other Celtic tribes', stated their President.[49] From this point, campaigners for a Cornish diocese began to employ the Celtic dimension explicitly. Celticity and claims to racial difference, according to Morrish, 'flowered' in the Reverend Wladislaw Lach-Szyrma's letter to Gladstone in 1869, which set out the case for a Cornish diocese. It continued to provide background noise through to the consecration of the new bishop in 1877 and the ceremonies surrounding the laying of the foundation stone of the new cathedral at Truro in May 1880. Afterwards, Lach-Szyrma could claim that the cathedral's construction meant 'the meaning of Brito-Celtic antiquity is maintained'.[50]

Morrish compares the historical and ethnological arguments employed in Cornwall with other similar campaigns. While there did exist historical arguments in favour of a Northumberland diocese centred on Hexham, he noted these were 'not pursued with such vigour' as in Cornwall and were ultimately 'discounted'. As he observes, the role of the historical arguments was to 'mould public opinion' and neutralise non-Anglicans, who made up

---

48 John Carne, 'The Bishopric of Cornwall', *Journal of the Royal Institution of Cornwall* 2.7 (1867), p.182.

49 Charles Barham, 'President's Address', *Journal of the Royal Institution of Cornwall* 43 (1861), 15-16.

50 W.S.Lach-Szyrma, *The Church History of Cornwall and the Diocese of Cornwall* (Truro, c.1885), p.125.

the vast majority, over two-thirds, of the Cornish population.[51] Morrish was ultimately more concerned to distinguish historical 'fact' from popular 'fiction' and pursue the accuracy of the ethnological arguments. Their significance however lies more in what they tell us about discourses of Cornwall and the Cornish in the generation from the 1850s to the 1880s, as we shall see below.

Meanwhile, what did that majority of the Cornish population think of the diocesan campaign, one that some might have been viewed as a family affair within the Church of England and irrelevant to the Cornish people? *The West Briton*, mouthpiece of respectable middle-class Cornish Methodist opinion, reported the campaign for a diocese in 1854 but without editorial comment.[52] In 1860, it offered a rather curt view; it was difficult to discover 'what tangible or intelligible advantage is to be gained from carrying out such a project'. The reason for its suspicion lay in the main object of many Anglican reformers. Several of the latter incautiously argued that a bishop on the spot would prevent or even reverse the further spread of dissent in Cornwall, where by the time of the religious census of 1851 the Church of England found itself suffering some of its lowest percentage shares of churchgoers. For the *West Briton* and the majority of Methodist opinion, reversing this was an unwelcome and unnecessary prospect. Examining the objects of those calling for a Cornish diocese, the newspaper stated that

> few of our readers ... will be inclined to envy the feelings of a man who can thus lament over the great religious reformation in Cornwall effected by Wesley and his followers ... So far   from   the   great distance of Exeter being an evil, it has, on the contrary, hitherto been the happiest circumstance that could befall.

Given the contemporary state of the Church of England the editor concluded that a resident bishop was 'quite as likely to be a calamity as a blessing'.[53]

However, by the time the campaign was on the verge of success the *West Briton* had reverted to its former neutral stance. After the Cornish diocese was approved, the reporting of the consecration of the new bishop was more positively supportive as the paper joined enthusiastically in the hyper-loyalist celebrations surrounding the ceremony of laying the Cathedral's foundation stone in 1880. Opposition was by then confined to individual dissenting voices in the letters columns and to some regular correspondents. The author of 'Cornish men and Cornish matters' forthrightly stated that

---

51 Morrish, 'History', 1983, p.259.
52 *West Briton*, 13 Oct 1854.
53 *West Briton*, 13 Jan 1860.

there were some in Cornwall who rejected the flummery surrounding the foundation-stone ceremony. They 'decline to link their loyalty to the State ... with any loyalty to the bishop and the organisation of which he is head', while 'one of them actually wished to know if the Truro people had gone "crack'd"'.[54] Nonetheless, even this scepticism, drowned in the columns of newsprint devoted to the various ceremonies and the visit of the Duke and Duchess of Cornwall, focused more on the role of freemasonry on the day than the presence of the cathedral or its new occupant.

There were others who were more critical. In a letter to the paper, John Lean, a dissenter, described freemasonry as 'puerile' and 'ridiculous humbug'. He denied that anyone wanted a cathedral outside the 'clergy of the Establishment', whose 'teaching is distasteful ... to the majority of the Cornish people'. He went further, suggesting that 'anything in the shape of a building is wanted in Cornwall rather than a Cathedral, and if no other use could be found for the ground on which it is to stand, infinitely better to appropriate it to the growth of cabbages'.[55] The Bible Christians, whose presence had grown faster than the main Wesleyan body over the previous generation, also retained a healthy suspicion of the Anglican project. 'There never was less need of an Episcopal Bishop of Truro than at the present time', wrote J.H.Batt.[56] Nevertheless, the leading lights of Cornish nonconformity willingly participated in the ceremonies and appear to have been thoroughly co-opted into the cathedral project by 1880.

The Sunday Closing movement
Just months later, many of this same group of nonconformist leaders joined with some Anglican churchmen to play a much more direct role in the second, this time less successful, campaign of 1881-83 for a Sunday Closing Bill for Cornwall. This followed hot on the heels of the successful Welsh Sunday Closing Act of 1881, which triggered what was effectively the last throw of the dice from the United Kingdom Alliance, a temperance lobbying group with its headquarters in Manchester. The UK Alliance had been formed in 1853. Its support peaked in the early 1870s, before fading somewhat after Disraeli's Intoxicating Liquors Act of 1874 set statutory and liberal opening hours for pubs.[57] The UK Alliance's full title was United Kingdom Alliance for the Immediate and Total Legislative Suppression of the Traffic in All Intoxicating Liquors, but its original prohibitionist stance

---

54 *West Briton*, 25 Feb 1875; 27 May 1880; 20 May 1880.

55 *West Briton*, 3 Jun 1880.

56 J.H.Batt, 'A new bishop for Cornwall', *Bible Christian Magazine* LVI (1877), 257-261.

57 K.Theodore Hoppen, *The Mid-Victorian Generation, 1846-1886* (Oxford: Oxford University Press, 1998), pp.607-608.

was soon modified in favour of Local Veto, or granting local options to restrict opening times. Sensing an opportunity in the wake of the Welsh Sunday Closing Act, temperance activists set about demanding its extension to parts of England and to Cornwall.

In the summer of 1881 multiple petitions in favour of Sunday Closing were launched in Cornwall, reportedly 138 from the St Austell district alone. Here, Robert Kirton, a draper's assistant living in Menacuddle Street, was the key driver of the campaign. Kirton convened a meeting at Truro in November to discuss the possibilities of a Sunday Closing Bill for Cornwall. Although Kirton himself seems not to have favoured a separate bill, a Cornish Sunday Closing Bill was proposed by Arthur Mason, canon at the new Truro Cathedral. Mason was backed by the Reverend John Morrell, Curate of Madron, and the Reverend J.H.Sampson, a Baptist Minister at St Austell. Although some were sceptical, expressing reservations about 'exceptional legislation for Cornwall', the meeting unanimously carried the motion. and a Sunday Closing Association for Cornwall was formed, its interim committee comprising Bishop Benson, Canon Mason and Robert Kirton, along with the Reverend Philip Newnham, Vicar of Maker, David Bain of Portreath, George J. Smith MP, John Clark Isaac of Liskeard, Samuel Wills, a draper and grocer and Wesleyan lay preacher from Wadebridge, and one of the Fox family. At a later meeting others were co-opted. These included Edwin Tregelles of Falmouth (civil engineer and Quaker), who claimed that it was he and the Wesleyan minister Robert Eardley of Penryn who had first mooted the idea of a Sunday Closing Bill for Cornwall.[58]

The *West Briton* was impressed by the fervour displayed by those participating in the founding meeting but in the new year poured cold water on the idea. Although 'the temperance people of this county have suddenly arisen almost en masse to promote a Bill for closing public houses on Sunday' it was 'strongly of the opinion that no Government would pass a measure for one county of England. It would be piecemeal legislation brought to an absurdity'.[59] By this point however, the *West Briton* editor was unable to rein in a wave of enthusiasm that, in a reminder of the great spontaneous Methodist revivals that had blazed their way across Cornwall in the early part of the century, possessed its own momentum and was seemingly carrying all before it. A rash of local branch committees were formed. These organised meetings in small and usually sleepy villages, such as Blackwater, Pensilva. Upton Cross, Mawnan and even Durgan, with its handful of cottages.[60] Keen and energetic canvassers were dispatched to

---

58 *West Briton*, 3 Nov 1881 and 10 Nov 1881.
59 *West Briton*, 19 Jan 1882.
60 *West Briton*, 19 Jan 1882; 26 Jan 1882; 9 Feb 1882.

obtain signatures on petitions in support of the Bill. Within a month and a half 120,000 had signed up, an astounding 60% of the adult population. Support appears to have been derived from all parts of Cornwall and all social classes, It was claimed for example that 477 of the 549 workmen at Hayle Foundry had signed.[61] Backed by this evidence of support, a deputation from Cornwall met local MPs in February and then waited on the Home Secretary. Sensing the popular mood, in the contemporary East Cornwall by-election in 1882 both candidates – Tory and Liberal – were quick to declare their support for the measure.[62]

A Sunday Closing Bill duly appeared, with Gladstone's Liberal Government guaranteeing parliamentary time, despite ongoing difficulties with the Irish Nationalist MPs who were at this time obstructing parliamentary business in pursuit of Home Rule. The Cornish Sunday Closing Bill reached its second reading by the end of March, but was then continuously blocked by Charles Warton, Conservative MP for Bridport in Dorset. Warton dismissed the strength of feeling on the issue in Cornwall. For him, petitions were not 'free and unfettered opinion' or 'genuine expressions of feeling' but the result of massive coercion by dissenters. The Bill was 'Radical tyranny' and 'parochial legislation for the sake of a parcel of crotcheteers'.[63] In contrast, William Copeland Borlase, newly elected Liberal MP for East Cornwall, was making an explicit link between the desire for the bill in Cornwall and Celticity. At a meeting at Penzance Wesleyan chapel he pointed out that 'it is a very remarkable thing that we in Cornwall should have taken up this movement next to Wales ... it seems to me as if we are part and parcel of that ancient people, that we have part of the Celtic blood in us'.[64]

Not everyone in Cornwall was in favour of the Sunday Closing movement however. In early October 1882 Thomas Hart, a brewer at Penryn, was chairing a meeting of opposition at the Royal Hotel, Falmouth. This followed a meeting organised by Thomas Lukes of the White Hart, St Austell, when 30 or 40 victuallers, according to the *West Briton*, had met at that place. Lukes observed that although it had been claimed that 'the bill had been promoted by the Cornish people, ... that was not so, for it has been to a very great extent promoted by travelling preachers who were only in the county two or three years, and were not Cornishmen at all'.[65] There was some substance to this allegation. Of the nine original members of the Sunday Closing Association Executive Committee, six had been born

61 *West Briton*, 23 Feb 1882; 2 Mar 1882; 17 Aug 1882.
62 *West Briton*, 23 Mar 1882.
63 *West Briton*, 17 Aug 1882.
64 *West Briton*, 28 Sep 1882.
65 *West Briton*, 5 Oct 1882.

outside Cornwall. Several of the most prominent early enthusiasts, such as the Reverend John Morrell, Join Ainge of Liskeard and the Reverend Eadley of Penryn appear to have grown up in Yorkshire or Lancashire.[66]

Although many of the early leaders were not Cornish, as the movement spread through the towns and villages of Cornwall, the more local activists, judging by their surnames, were predominantly so. Moreover, the 120,000 signatories to the petition must indicate a groundswell of native support for the movement, even though the publicans who were opposing the bill, all of whom incidentally were Cornish-born, dismissed the petition as 'signed principally by women and Sunday School habitués'. They launched a counterpetition which collected 20,000 signatures in a month, only to be condemned in turn by the Sunday Closing Association Executive Committee as containing a third of signatures that were not genuine.[67]

After the first bill fell foul of parliamentary wrangling in the 1882-1883 session, another was launched in the following session. At a meeting of the Sunday Closing Association Executive at Truro in February 1882 it was stated that 170 public meetings had been held in support of this bill, and 'all Cornishmen should be proud of their efforts'. The promoters had been 'animated by the same spirit as those hardy miners of two hundred years ago, who joined so lustily in the song "And shall Trelawny die"'. Meanwhile, at Falmouth the Reverend John Morrell was citing letters he had received from all parts of England asking for advice from Cornwall 'and telling of the admiration which the Cornish people were held by temperance reformers throughout England'. 'Was it an insult to Cornwall to be in the van?', he asked.[68]

In July 1883 the Earl of Mount Edgcumbe, the President of the Sunday Closing Association, moved the second reading of the Cornish Sunday Closing Bill in the Lords, but a motion for a third reading was narrowly lost by one vote on 30th July 1883.[69] Like other abortive bills for local option in this period for Durham, Yorkshire and the Isle of Wight, the Cornish bill ultimately failed, even though it came closest of any to success. Unlike those other places however, and in a manner reminiscent of the campaign for a Cornish diocese, the supporters of the Bill had heavily laced their campaign with historical and cultural appeals to a sense of Cornish identity and to Cornwall's uniqueness as a Celtic territory.

66 Census enumerators' books, 1881.
67 *West Briton*, 5 Oct 1882 and 23 Nov 1882.
68 *West Briton*, 22 Feb 1883.
69 *Hansard*, House of Lords debate, 30 July 1883, Vol. 282, cc907-925.

The key moments of Cornishness

The term 'discourse' has become extremely fashionable but many historians tend to apply it in a merely descriptive way, employing the two concepts of narrative and discourse interchangeably. For some, discourse equates to a less politically nuanced or structurally constituted and more free-floating ideology. Furthermore, when it is subject to greater definition the preference of social and cultural historians is to borrow from literary approaches and from Hayden White's reading of Foucault's episteme.[70] Discourse then becomes a linguistic terrain occupied by tropes of figurative language and historians proceed to pick their way through this landscape, on the way dissecting any metaphor, metonymy, synecdoche or irony they might find. However, discourse analysis encompasses a wide range of approaches from the literary through linguistic approaches to critical discourse analysis and discursive psychology, spanning the humanities and the social sciences. Here, I will apply a social scientific approach to discourse, focusing on the discourse analysis of Ernesto Laclau and Chantal Mouffe as a route to a more explicit model of discourse that can help us uncover the discourses found in later nineteenth century Cornwall.[71]

Discourses work to produce meanings for groups and individuals. From such a perspective collective identities cannot exist until they are constituted in discourse; 'it is not until someone speaks of, or to, or on behalf of a group that it is constituted as a group'.[72] Discourses are structured patterns of language that constitute a linked system of meanings, produced and reproduced by social practice. Moreover, drawing from poststructuralism, Laclau and Mouffe assert that such meanings are never fixed, although people constantly struggle to stabilize definitions of society and the individual. Therefore, discourse analysis should be about plotting the course of the struggles to fix meaning. To do this Laclau and Mouffe use a number of key concepts. For them, discourses comprise a collection of 'moments' or signs, the meaning of which is determined by their relation to other signs. Moments crystallize around privileged signs which they term 'nodal points'. When a nodal point is established and meanings become naturalized or taken for granted the fluctuating meaning of signs is temporarily halted. Such a situation establishes 'closure', when signs are brought together in a particular formation that produces meaning. Closure

---

70 Alan Munslow, *Discourse and Culture: The Creation of America* (London: Routledge, 1992), p. 2.

71 See Ernesto Laclau and Chantal Mouffe, *Hegemony and Socialist Strategy. Towards a Radical Democratic Politics*, (London: Verso, 1985.)

72 Ernesto Laclau, 'Power and representation' in Mark Poster (ed.) *Politics, Theory and Contemporary Culture* (New York: Columbia University Press, 1993), p. 289.

can only be temporary however as there is 'always room for struggles over what the structure should look like, what discourses should prevail, and how meaning should be ascribed to the individual signs'.[73] Their interest in how discursive structures are reproduced and transformed makes Laclau and Mouffe's approach of relevance to a historical perspective on the making and unmaking of discourse. Furthermore, their notion of discourse as fundamentally unstable and subject to change exposes the apparent 'objectivity' of dominant discourses as being the result of political processes and struggles.

Laclau and Mouffe's discourse analysis therefore concentrates on identifying the nodal points that structure an identity and the ways these nodal points are filled with meaning by being equated with and contrasted against other signifiers. Meaning is invested through the construction of chains of equivalence (constructing common features of groups) and difference (contrasting these with the features of other groups). This echoes the logics of similarity and difference that underlie accounts of group identity and Paasi's analysis of regional formation encountered above.

The principal nodal point of the mid-century discourse of Cornishness was 'Cornishman'. Cornish people were relentlessly interpellated by this gendered call to identity, best illustrated in the campaign for a Sunday Closing Bill. In a reference to the 'Song of the Western Men' at one of the 170 public meetings in support of the campaign in 1881/2 a working man, William Andrew, stated that 'there was a time when it was said in Cornwall "30,000 [sic] Cornishmen shall know the reason why" and they should now stand as honourable men, and show England what Cornishmen can do today'.[74] The opposition to the Sunday Closing Bill campaign that belatedly emerged during 1882 also adopted a nomination trope of 'Cornishmen'. The meeting of victuallers at St Austell concentrated on the fact that the Bill was promoted by those who were 'not Cornishmen at all'.[75] Such sentiments echoed the words of the mayor of Truro in 1877 who, on the enthronement of the new bishop, congratulated his audience 'as Cornishmen upon the restoration of their ancient rights'.[76]

The sign 'Cornishmen' was linked closely to that of 'one and all' to construct a logic of equivalence within this discourse. In the eighteenth century the crowd in many parts of England and Wales used this slogan to indicate solidarity and determination at times of action over corn prices.[77] However, with the decline of food rioting as a collective response in other

---

73 Louise Phillips and Marianne W. Jørgensen, *Discourse Analysis as Theory and Method* (London: Sage, 2002), p. 29.

74 *West Briton*, 19 January 1882.

75 *West Briton*, 5 October 1882.

76 *West Briton*, 3 May 1877.

parts of Britain after the 1820s and the continuing predilection of Cornish communities for this form of protest, 'one and all' came to be seen as a peculiarly Cornish motto. Already, by the 1830s 'in any matter which recommends itself to the general opinion of the county, a unity of action among all classes appears still to be occasionally manifested. In such cases the Cornish motto "One and All" may be recognized as still possessing some degree of vitality'.[78] The discourse of Cornishness generated during the first half of the nineteenth century adopted and adapted 'one and all' for its own purposes. In doing so it cut across potential class-based identities. On the occasion of the laying of the foundation stone of the new cathedral, among the mottoes chosen for the ceremonial arches set up in Truro in 1880 we find the ubiquitous 'one and all'. After the ceremonies were over it was confidently stated that the Duke and Duchess of Cornwall had 'completely won over the hearts of "one and all"', the phrase now entirely stripped of its insurrectionist connotation.[79]

If the logic of equivalence revolved around the moments of 'Cornishmen' and 'one and all' the logic of difference was constructed around other signs reinforcing Cornish uniqueness. By the 1880s these fell into three types: historical, occupational and racial. The discourse of historical difference was constructed around the historical narratives already discussed. Yet other differences were as prominent. In a sermon, Canon Lightfoot claimed that Cornwall was 'thoroughly unique' in four particulars: the nature of its labouring population, the hold of Wesleyan Methodism on its people, its vegetation and the nature of its coasts and its 'general configuration'.[80] The most common moment in the differentiation aspect of the Cornish discourse was that of occupational uniqueness. Twenty years earlier, in 1854, a newspaper editorial had claimed the Cornish were 'different' because 'the fact of there being a great mining population, and some of them engaged in our fisheries, renders them an independent, and intelligent, and a self-relying people'.[81] Mining, industry and independence in Cornwall were contrasted with farming and, by implication, dependence, in neighbouring Devon. As this argument was deployed in the 1860s to bolster the case for a separate diocese the border

---

77 E. P. Thompson, *Customs in Common* (London: Penguin, 1993), pp. 236 and 238; John Rule, *Cornish Cases: Essays in Eighteenth and Nineteenth Century Social History* (Southampton: Clio Publishing, 2006), pp. 49-50.

78 Seymour Tremenheere, 'Report on the State of Education in the Mining Districts of Cornwall', *British Parliamentary Papers* 317 XX.97 (London: Her Majesty's Stationery Office, 1841), p. 100.

79 *West Briton*, 27 May 1880.

80 *West Briton*, 20 April 1877.

81 *Royal Cornwall Gazette*, 29 September 1854.

between Cornwall and Devon was sharpened in terms of socio-economic structures. Occupational difference was still a moment in the Cornish discourse of the 1880s, although by this time it was being eroded and blurred by the growing economic clouds ominously gathering around the Cornish mines, which were rapidly reducing their workforces.

As occupational differences became a discursive moment increasingly detached from material conditions so a new moment in the logic of difference appeared. The Reverend Reginald Hobhouse wrote in 1860 that the Cornish were 'a different race and of a different tone, habits and disposition, to those of Devonshire'.[82] By the mid-1860s this was overlaid by the distinction between Celt and Saxon. The *Royal Cornwall Gazette* argued that the Church in Cornwall had originally been founded by 'Celtic missionary bishops' and condemned both Saxon influences and the 'Italianate priesthood' of St Augustine that had 'almost extinguished the light of the ancient British church'.[83] Difference was being linked in this instance to the dominant religious discourse of Protestantism and an emerging view in some quarters of a proto-Protestant and 'purer' early 'Celtic' church. Calls for special treatment legitimated by ethnological and racial difference reached their apogee in the Reverend Lach-Szyrma's pamphlet, written in 1869. He asserted that 'no contiguous counties in England contain populations so entirely distinct in race from one another as Devon and Cornwall ... The Cornish ... are mostly Celts ... A distinct race requires a distinct mode of treatment'[84] The borders between Cornwall and Devon were now not merely socio-economic, but racial, dividing Celtic Cornish from Saxon English.

By the 1870s racial difference was firmly established as a moment in the discourse of Cornishness. The mass overseas emigration that began in the 1840s was explained by F.R.S. Jago, President of the Royal Institution of Cornwall, by the 'fact' that Cornishmen were 'a race prone to adventure whose pursuits have taken them into remote lands'.[85] A racial identity was also in this decade being extrapolated back to former times and linked to narratives of historical difference. Lamenting hard times, William Copeland Borlase asked

> where is that proud race of stalwart tinners of whom we have read
> that in ancient days they formed a separate caste above the common

---

82 Morrish, 'History', 1983, p. 247.
83 *Royal Cornwall Gazette*, 24 February 1865.
84 Wladislaw S. Lach-Szyrma, *The Bishopric of Cornwall: a letter to W.E.Gladstone* (Truro: J.R.Netherton, 1869).
85 F. R. S. Jago, 'Presidential address', *Journal of the Royal Institution of Cornwall* 5 (1874), 3-18.

tillers of the soil, and who lived under direct royal protection (though that was another name for royal spoliation) with manners, and customs, and laws all peculiarly their own.[86]

By the 1890s Borlase was even speculating about the 'basis of the Cornish race' and adapting the idea of racial difference to the discovery that the Cornish scored highly on Beddoe's index of 'nigrescence'.[87]

The discourse of Cornishness in the third quarter of the nineteenth century therefore constructed subject positions of 'Cornishmen', linked to 'one and all' and tied back to common myths of origin. These were the master signifiers, organising a collective identity of Cornishness. They comprised the logic of equivalence for the Cornish subject. Moreover, the discourse combined this logic with history, occupation and race as moments in its logic of difference. Such moments were temporarily fixed in the 1870s and gave voice to a collective identity that had been transformed over the course of eighteenth and early nineteenth century industrialization.[88]

Transformed, but not totally. For there were recognizable elements of continuity in the discourse of Cornishness, as for example in its myths of origin. Although discourses could mutate they were never completely fluid. Instead, the notion of hybridity, of two or more discourses mixed in one statement or observation, seems more appropriate. On the other hand, such accounts of group identity can also seem too structural, positing a set of linguistic structures which then possess the power to regulate the individual. The subject becomes an unfinished product and an effect of discourse rather than an initiator of action. This has prompted some social psychologists to challenge this approach to discourse and instead focus on discursive performance, on the production of identity through interaction, moving from discourses as sets of structures with a regulatory power to their use by agents in everyday discursive performance. Therefore, in the final section, I want to move from discourse as a regulatory structure towards rhetoric, or the way in which discourses were actively used as strategies and how they were deployed in argument in order to counter potential or actual challenges. Furthermore, this moves us back to Jones' point that sites of action where discourses become praxis tell us more about discourses than their content.[89]

---

86 William Copeland Borlase, 'Presidential address', *Journal of the Royal Institution of Cornwall* 6 (1879), 151-67.
87 William Copeland Borlase, *The Age of the Saints* (Truro: Joseph Pollard. 1893), p. xvi.
88 Deacon, *Cornwall*, 2007, pp. 94-147.
89 Jones, 'Word and deed', 2000.

The rhetoric of Cornish campaigning

Rhetorical strategies – of nomination, predication (or category construction) and argumentation, help construct an 'us' as opposed to 'them'.[90] We have met nomination and predication strategies already in discussing the discourse of Cornishness. But what argumentation strategies were drawn on to support the campaign for a Sunday Closing Bill for Cornwall in the early 1880s?

Cornish Sunday closing was justified by a range of arguments. Many were part of wider British temperance or teetotal discourses, but some overlapped with the discourse of Cornishness. The latter relied on the discourse of difference: the Cornish 'were the relics of a grand old race which were [sic] in possession of the whole of England before the Saxons came over and the Cornish people preserved characteristics which were recognized as distinct'. Building on this Canon Mason went on to state that 'Cornwall, especially, because of its love of the virtue of temperance, had a claim upon England for a Sunday Closing Bill, which no other county had'.[91] This gave Cornwall a leadership role which the organisers of the campaign were keen to accept. 'What Cornwall does today will echo from far and wide tomorrow'.[92] Another argumentation strategy however was a demand for equality. Supporters of a bill were simply asking 'for the same facilities as have been given to Ireland, Scotland and Wales'.[93] This strategy contrasts starkly with that of the campaigners for local option in the North East. There, the campaigns were explicitly seen as stepping stones to national legislation, 'the North meant to have Sunday Closing for the nation', stated the Venerable Archdeacon Watkins at a meeting in Darlington in 1883. In the North East activists tended to see county bills as second best, but were prepared to try any route to Sunday Closing, 'either by county or national legislation'.[94] A meeting of the Newcastle Temperance Society viewed 'with pleasure the agitation in favour of an entire Sunday Closing Bill for Northumberland; but while giving this our most cordial support, we do not slacken our efforts to promote the national measure'.[95] Unlike Cornwall, campaigners in Northumberland and Durham made no reference of any kind to historical arguments in support of local bills. Instead, newspaper editors concentrated on the implications of 'piecemeal

90 See Ruth Wodak, 'The discourse-historical approach', in Ruth Wodak and Michael Meyer (eds), *Methods of Critical Discourse Analysis* (London: Sage, 2001), pp. 72-73.
91 *West Briton*, 10 November 1881.
92 *West Briton*, 25 February 1883; *Royal Cornwall Gazette*, 23 February 1883.
93 *West Briton*, 17 August 1882.
94 *Northern Echo*, 7 February 1883.
95 *Newcastle Courant*, 22 December 1882.

legislation', agonising over a 'new principle' they were clearly unsure about.

Yet, although campaigners in Cornwall asserted their equality with Ireland, Scotland and Wales rhetorically, here lay the campaign's Achilles heel and the political limits of the Cornish identity. The most insistent counter-argument levelled against it was that such a bill would be 'partial legislation' for an English county. In the Commons in 1882 Cornish MPs were 'simply ask[ing] for the same facilities as have been given to Ireland, Scotland and Wales'. However, this call for equal treatment was dismissed by opponents as 'parochial legislation' for a small part of England; it 'was a national question, and ought to be dealt with comprehensively and not in particular districts'.[96] This objection was echoed even in Cornwall, the *West Briton* stating 'we are strongly of the opinion that no Government would pass a measure for one county of England. It would be piecemeal legislation brought to an absurdity'.[97] Launching the campaign, Canon Mason had asserted that 'most of them were inclined to think there was a good deal of difference between Cornwall and other counties. [But] Cornish people were very happy to be united to England and they did not wish to have home rule (laughter)'. The laughter indicated the hedging that took place around this issue. Arguing for equivalence to Wales on the grounds that it was a 'sister kingdom', Mason and others were quick to play the 'Celtic' card and claim that the Cornish shared 'Celtic blood' with the Welsh. But they stopped short of proposing that Cornwall was not part of England. The latter element existed - the *West Briton* had written that 'whatever may be said in joke about it being out of England, it is still one of England's counties' - but the discourse of Cornishness did not at this point explicitly include it.[98] The reason for the exclusion of this particular rhetorical strategy lay in the power of another discourse of identity – that of Englishness – to achieve a closure and accommodate Cornwall firmly within its boundaries. This was the main reason why the Sunday Closing campaign ultimately failed to achieve success despite widespread public support. It was generally accepted, even by its proponents, that it required 'exceptional legislation'. However, for most observers, that also meant it did not lie 'within the range of practical politics'.[99]

Essentially, those expressing a Cornish identity utilized a regionalist discourse, co-existing and indeed feeding into a national discourse of Englishness. Cornishness and Englishness were not contradictory or incompatible; indeed the former could be the building block for the latter.

---

96 *West Briton*, 22 July 1882.
97 *West Briton*, 19 January 1882.
98 *West Briton*, 10 November 1881; 19 January 1882.
99 *West Briton*, 3 November 1881.

At a meeting in 1819 the Mayor and inhabitants of Truro resolved that 'as true Britons, and, especially, as "the faithful Cornish", we are determined "one and all", to support the just prerogative of the Crown and the authority of the Government; standing firm in defence of the throne and of the altar'.[100] Historical narratives of a close connection between Crown and Cornwall, reproduced via the Duchy of Cornwall, were here part of a conservative, royalist tradition looking back to a golden age in the seventeenth century, albeit mediated by reference to Cornish self-identification in earlier times as 'ancient Britons', like the Welsh.[101] Such a conservative royalist discourse was still very evident in the celebrations surrounding the visit of the Duke and Duchess of Cornwall and the laying of the foundation stone of the new cathedral in 1880. On the 'Cornish arch' were placed the arms of four 'old Cornish families'. These jostled for attention with the county arms, the ducal coronet and the new coat of arms of the Cornish see. At other places in the town the ubiquitous Cornish motto 'One and All' could be seen, but alongside others such as 'Welcome to England's Prince' and 'God Bless our Gracious Queen'.[102]

Opposition to the day's jamborees was aimed at the Bishop and the role of the freemasons, rather than at the royal connection.[103] The alternative Liberal/Radical, progressive and nonconformist discourse that fuelled the later Sunday Closing Bill campaign was also fundamentally an English discourse, locked into the taken-for-granted assumption that Cornwall's status was that of an English county. Rhetoric from within this discourse was even less likely to transcend that status than a conservative Cornish royalist tradition bent on romanticizing the role of the Duchy of Cornwall in Cornish life. Instead, it resisted the urge to look backwards and dream of lost golden ages and was unable to escape the dominant territorial discourse of (Cornish) county, (English) nation and (British) Empire.

Conclusions

In Cornwall, a territorial identity infused campaigns for the devolution of decision-making to a more local level. This spatial identity with its appeal to 'Cornishmen' and 'one and all' and its discourse of differentiation was ubiquitous by the later nineteenth century. But its political limits were met

---

100 Richard Polwhele, *Traditions and Recollections, Domestic, Clerical and Literary* (London: John Nichols, 1826), p. 584.
101 Mark Stoyle, *West Britons* (Exeter: University of Exeter Press, 2002), pp. 157-80; Matthew Spriggs, 'William Scawen (1600-1689) – a neglected Cornish patriot and father of the Cornish language revival' in Philip Payton (ed.), *Cornish Studies Thirteen* (Exeter: University of Exeter Press, 2005), 98-125.
102 *West Briton*, 27 May 1880.
103 *West Briton*, 20 May 1880.

in the campaign for Sunday closing. In that instance, campaigners were unable to come up with an argument which convincingly neutralized their opponents' claim that a bill for Cornwall alone would lead to 'Cornwall being isolated, as it were, from the rest of England'.[104] The presence of a shared discourse of Englishness meant that proponents of the bill could not follow the logic of their own claims for parity with the 'sister kingdoms' of Scotland, Ireland and Wales. A restructured Cornish patriotic discourse had constructed Cornwall and its people as 'different'. It was influential enough within Cornwall to make an appeal to Cornishness an automatic resort of politicians and newspaper leader-writers alike. Yet, strong in the cultural sphere, it was only weakly articulated in the political. Even Lach-Szyrma, the most prominent contemporary Celticist, wrote of Cornwall as being 'of England' at the same time as he was arguing that the Cornish were racially not English.[105] Celtic categorizations and elite narratives of a myth of origin that was non-English had combined with older elements to produce a territorial identity vigorous enough to sustain the campaign for a Cornish diocese in the middle decades of the century. However, in the struggle for a Sunday Closing Bill it came into conflict with a dominant geo-cultural narrative of Englishness, supplying a set of constraining parameters, a 'space of possibilities' and practical limits within which the late nineteenth century Cornish identity was confined.

This inability to transcend an over-arching narrative of Englishness in the late nineteenth century would seem to locate the Cornish identity as an example of an English regional identity. A 'reflective and conscious' region was in the making. But it was not made. Cornwall was also an administrative county and viewed as such within the broader socio-spatial consciousness of British society. Ultimately Cornish regionalism was unable to counter that wider consciousness and a proto-regional identity was consequently unable to escape being represented as a county identity. Later, in the early twentieth century, a more potentially oppositional categorization was furnished by the emergence of a self-consciously 'Celtic' cultural revivalism adopting a national self-representation, quarrying Cornwall's useable past for its material resources.[106] Cornwall's brief heyday as a rare example of a self-conscious English region faded into a hybrid identity as

---

104 *West Briton*, 17 August 1882.

105 Lach-Szyrma, *Bishopric*, 1869.

106 Bernard Deacon, Dick Cole, and Garry Tregidga, *Mebyon Kernow and Cornish Nationalism* (Cardiff: Welsh Academic Press, 2003). For the concept of useable pasts see Terence Ranger, 'Towards a useable African past', in C.Fyfe (ed.), *African Studies Since 1945* (London: Longman, 1976). For its application to Cornwall see Neil Kennedy, *Cornish Solidarity: Using Culture to Strengthen Communities* (Portlaoise: Evertype, 2016).

either (Celtic) nation or (English) county, or sometimes both. It is not that Cornwall was unique in the way appeals to place were mobilised for single-issue campaigns. This could and did happen elsewhere. What made it unique within 'England' was the historicized appeal to a non-English past and the demands for equal treatment with Wales, Scotland and Ireland. This 'trans-Celtic' appeal and a narrative poised at the edge of Englishness and teetering on the brink of rejecting that Englishness, was not – could not be – replicated in other English counties and regions.

The campaign for the Sunday Closing Bill for Cornwall, if successful, would have had untold consequences for Cornish self-respect in the twentieth century. It would have put Cornwall on a par with Wales and symbolised its difference from English counties, firmly grounding a claim to special treatment and a non-English status. However, the campaign was fatally compromised by Cornwall's status within the spatial consciousness of wider British society and the inability of its elite to transcend a discourse of Englishness. The failure lay not in the discourse of Cornishness or the level of its internal coherence but in its context. Remarkably, the majority of Cornwall's early twenty-first century elite are still just as compromised by their attachment to the myths and narratives of Englishness. The lessons of the Sunday Closing movement tell us that unless that discourse is jettisoned, efforts to demand equal treatment for Cornwall, the genuine devolution of power, the protection of the Cornish as a national group, or respect and recognition for the special status of Cornwall are ultimately doomed to failure.

Chapter Eight

Persistence without performance: the case of Mebyon Kernow

The ethnoregionalist party family has spawned a considerable literature over the past half century.[1] Early attempts to explain the emergence of parties seeking to reorganise the territorial structure of the state focused on broad structural socio-economic or cultural factors.[2] Structures were then joined by strategies as scholars focused on political parties' role as agents in the game of politics. Consequently, their performance has been linked to aspects such as their internal organisation or the strategies and tactics they adopt.[3] More recently, the spotlight has turned to the contrasting ways in which the ethnoregionalist party family in Europe has responded to evolving challenges since the 1990s. These are, on the one hand the rise of multi-level governance and the need to compete simultaneously at local, regional, state and European levels and on the other the necessity of forging a position within a multi-dimensional policy space.[4]

Within this burgeoning ethnoregionalist party scholarship, Jeffery claims that the reasons why such parties emerge, reproduce or fail to reproduce

---

1   These political parties can be described in a number of ways, for example as 'autonomist' or, more unwieldy, as 'stateless regionalist and nationalist' (Anwen Elias and Filippo Tronconi (eds), *From Protest to Power: Autonomist parties and the challenges of representation* (Vienna: New Academic Press, 2011); Eve Hepburn, 'Re-conceptualizing sub-state mobilization', *Regional & Federal Studies* 19 (2009), 477-499.) The term ethnoregionalist is preferred here as it neatly combines such parties' minority ethnic base with their call for devolution of power to sub-state units.

2   Stein Rokkan and Derek Urwin, *Economy, Territory, Identity: Politics of West European Peripheries* (London: Sage, 1983); Tom Nairn, *the Break-up of Britain: Crisis and neonationalism* (London: NLB, 1977).

3   Lieven de Winter and Huri Türsan (eds), 1998; *Regionalist Parties in Western Europe* (London: Routledge, 1998); Lieven de Winter, Marga Gómez-Reino Cachafeiro, and Peter Lynch (eds), *Autonomist Parties in Europe: Identity Politics and the Revival of the Territorial Cleavage* (Barcelona: Institut de Ciencies Politiques i Socials, 2006).

4   Hepburn, 'Re-conceptualizing', 2009; Emanuele Massetti and Arjan H. Schakel, 'From class to region: How regionalist parties link (and subsume) left-right into centre-periphery politics', *Party Politics* 21 (2015), 866-886; Emanuele Massetti and Arjan H. Schakel, 'Between autonomy and secession: Decentralization and regionalist party ideological radicalism', *Party Politics* 22 (2016), 59-79.

themselves has been a major theme.[5] In practice however, ethnoregionalist parties which have failed to prosper have been conspicuous by their absence. At first, attention focused on the electorally most successful family members - the *Volksunie*, *Convergència i Unió* (CiU), *Partido Nacionalista Vasco* (PNV), the Scottish National Party (SNP) and later the *Lega Nord*.[6] Over the past two decades, the net has been cast progressively wider and a succession of long-lost relatives rediscovered. The work of De Winter and colleagues introduced cases from Spanish regions, along with Brittany, Friesia, Sardinia and Savoy, while Elias and Tronconi's collection of case studies included examples from Corsica and Galicia. Meanwhile, the chronically under-performing French regionalist parties were re-examined.[7] Nevertheless, Hepburn in 2009 could still note that there had been relatively little work on negative cases, those 'where nationalist and regionalist parties have not succeeded', even though it is 'just as imperative to explain failure as success'. She described this as an 'important shortcoming' in the literature.[8] Yet, her study of the Sardinian *Partito Sardo d'Azione* (PSd'A) has evoked only a relatively muted response. While the ephemeral *Ligue Savoisienne* (LS) in Savoy received attention,[9] subsequent work on ethnoregionalist parties which have not made a successful transition 'from protest to power' remains scarce.

This reminds us of one such absence in the widening literature, an under-studied case on the margins both of the ethnoregionalist party family and of

5   Charlie Jeffery, 'New research agendas on regional party competition', *Regional & Federal Studies* 19 (2009), 639-650.

6   John Coakley (ed.), *The Social Origins of Nationalist Movements: The Contemporary West European Experience* (London: Sage, 1992); Benito Giordiano, '"Institutional thickness", political sub-culture and the resurgence of (the "new") regionalism in Italy – a case study of the Northern League in the province of Varese', *Transactions of the Institute of British Geographers* NS26 (2001), 25-41; Peter Lynch, *Minority Nationalism and European Integration* (Cardiff: University of Wales Press, 1996); Saul Newman, *Ethnoregional Conflict in Democracies: Mostly Ballots, Rarely Bullets* (Westport CT: Greenwood, 1996).

7   De Winter et al., *Autonomist parties*, 2006; Elias and Tronconi, *Protest to Power*, 2011; Frans J. Shrijver, 'Electoral performance of regionalist parties and perspectives on regional identity in France', *Regional & Federal Studies* 14 (2004), 187-210; Igor Ahedo Gurrutxaga, 'Nationalism in the French Basque Country', *Regional & Federal Studies* 15 (2005), 75-91.

8   Eve Hepburn, 'Explaining failure: the highs and lows of Sardinian nationalism'. *Regional & Federal Studies* 19 (2009), 595-618.

9   Emanuele Massetti and Giulia Sandri, 'Francophone exceptionalism within Alpine ethno-regionalism? The cases of the Union Valdôtaine and the Ligue Savoisienne'. *Regional & Federal Studies* 22 (2012), 87-106.

western Europe - *Mebyon Kernow* (MK), the Party for Cornwall. Pursuing the metaphor of a party 'family', MK remains an orphan, outside the family gathering. For instance, Toubeau makes use of a list of 27 'regional nationalist' parties in Belgium, Italy, Spain and the UK to examine the influence of such parties on state structures. MK is not one of them. Szöcsik and Zuber throw their net a lot wider, including 210 parties in 22 European democracies in a dataset on 'ethnonational' party positions. The *Union Démocratique Bretonne* (UDB) and *Partit Occitan* (PO) in France are present, as is the *Progetto Nord Est* in Veneto and in the UK the Scottish Green Party. But there is no MK. Similarly, Massetti and Schakel use a database of 77 regionalist parties active between 1950 and 2010 to discuss the effects of decentralization on their electoral strength and to compare their ideological orientation with the economic structures of their regions. MK is not included, even though their database includes the UDB, the LS and a host of Spanish regionalist parties together with the Frisian National Party.[10]

Yet MK is an interesting case. It is one of the oldest ethnoregionalist parties in western Europe. Formed in 1951, within nine months its founders had added the 'right to self-government in domestic affairs in a federated UK' to its aims. Since then, its core demand has remained self-government for Cornwall, in 2016 in the form of a 'National Assembly for Cornwall'.[11] MK therefore provides us with one of Hepburn's negative cases, a party that has not made an electoral breakthrough. Yet its longevity, when combined with its marginal electoral visibility, demands explanation. Furthermore, as English regionalist parties emerge and appear to be embedding themselves, in the shape of Yorkshire First, now the Yorkshire Party, and the North East Party, the experience of a party in a territory on the administrative edge of England may hold lessons for these new arrivals on a hitherto sparsely populated English regionalist terrain.

In what follows I first identify the usual criteria for success before describing the course of MK's progress within the framework of Pedersen's lifespan model of political parties.[12] However, MK's continuing survival becomes a puzzle in the context of this model, as it predicts that parties

---

10 Simon Toubeau, 'Regional nationalist parties and constitutional change in parliamentary democracies: A framework for analysis', *Regional & Federal Studies* 21 (2011), 427-446; Edina Szöcsik and Christina Isabel Zuber, 'EPAC – a new database on ethnonationalism in partty competition in 22 European democracies', *Party Politics* 21 (2015), 153-160; Emanuele Massetti and Arjan H. Schakel, 'Ideology matters: Why decentralisation has a differentiated effect on regionalist parties' fortunes in Western democracies', *European Journal of Political Research* 52 (2013), 797-821.

11 Richard Jenkin, *40 Years of Mebyon Kernow* (MK, 1991), pp.2-3; *Cornish Nation* 71 (2015-16), p.2.

which fail to cross various thresholds will eventually perish. The issue of durability is thus added before assessing the factors affecting the party's performance and persistence. In doing this a demand and supply side explanatory model is borrowed from studies of other political party families. This has the advantage of directing us towards relationships between the multiple factors explaining variable party success. While, as in Hepburn's study of the Psd'A, a combination of strategic choices and structural factors can be identified, the explanation for MK's poor performance yet stubborn persistence lies more in structural constraints and opportunities than strategic choices such as ideology or positioning. Moreover, extra attention needs to be paid to longer term cultural and historical supply side factors. These are especially useful in explaining the paradoxical location of MK.

Measuring success
De Winter and Tursan identified votes, policy success and office-holding as criteria for ethnoregionalist party success, noting that the less successful parties electorally were also less likely to have achieved policy success, defined as the restructuring of the unitary state. This prefigured the three measures of success employed by Elias and Tronconi – electoral performance, policy impact and government presence.[13]

However, in their study *From Protest to Power* Elias and Tronconi re-introduce a more diachronic framework for studying ethnoregionalist parties. For them, success lies in parties' ability to cross the various thresholds first proposed by Pedersen in his model of party lifespans. Pedersen put forward four thresholds. These are the threshold of declaration, when a party explicitly declares its intention to contest elections; the threshold of authorisation, when it fulfils the legal or organisational requirements necessary to participate; the threshold of representation, when seats are won in representative assemblies; and the threshold of relevance, when a party impacts on other parties and government policy outputs. Elias and Tronconi add a fifth threshold, suggested by Deschouwer.[14] This is the threshold of governance, marking a party's formal entry into government. As they note in their collection of western European case studies, there has been considerable variation in ethnoregionalist parties' ability to cross these thresholds.

---

12 Mogens Pedersen, 'Towards a New Typology of Party Life-Spans and Minor Parties', *Scandinavian Political Studies* 5 (1982), 1–16.
13 De Winter and Tursan, *Regionalist Parties*, 1998, pp.235ff; Elias and Tronconi, *Protest to Power*, 2011, pp.1-22.
14 Pedersen, 'New typology', 1982; Kris Deschouwer (ed.), *New Parties in Government* (London: Routledge, 2008).

MK's lifespan: from protest to protest

To what extent has MK crossed the various thresholds outlined by Elias and Tronconi? The party emerged from a broader cultural revivalist milieu that took on organisational shape in the inter-war period.[15] As an example of a bottom-up party, dating its crossing of the threshold of declaration is not straightforward. Although its first Chair, Helena Thomas, successfully fought a local election in 1953, including a call for regional self-government in her election leaflet, for its first decade and a half MK acted as a pressure group. Membership remained open to members of other parties into the mid-1970s, with prominent Liberal and Conservative politicians who later became MPs joining in the 1960s. This was during the period when MK somewhat hesitantly began more permanently to cross the threshold of declaration.

A parliamentary seat was first contested in 1970 and the party was then present at each state election until 1983. But the decision to abandon a pressure group strategy and seek votes remained open to debate and was periodically re-visited. This occurred in the mid-1970s and in the more difficult context of the late 1980s and early 1990s when the party was at a low ebb, contesting few elections with activists more involved in single-issue and cross-party campaigning.[16] It was not until the early 1990s that doubts were finally resolved and the party can be said to have unambiguously crossed the threshold of declaration.

If dating the crossing of the threshold of declaration is fuzzy, then so is that for the threshold of authorisation. MK faced no legal impediment to contesting elections, but from the 1960s found it difficult to overcome organisational constraints. These took two forms, the ability to find candidates willing to stand and the difficulty of raising sufficient finance to pay for deposits for elections at state and, from 1979 to 2014, European levels. Nonetheless, MK has contested the majority of parliamentary seats between 1997 and 2015 (and in 1979) and all six Cornish seats at the two general elections of 2010 and 2015. However, the party has never been able to contest more than 27% of Cornish wards in local elections. Yet 100% participation in local elections is hardly a necessary condition of crossing the threshold of authorisation. For example, in the last four rounds of elections to Welsh unitary councils from 2004 to 2017, Plaid Cymru contested between 44 % and 49% of Welsh wards, while the Breton UDB has contested between 16% and 26% of cantonal and departmental elections since 2004, a proportion not that different from MK. In Cornwall at the

---

15 Philip Payton, *The Making of Modern Cornwall: Historical experience and the persistence of 'difference'* (Redruth: Dyllansow Truran, 1992), pp.134-135.

16 Bernard Deacon, Dick Cole and Garry Tregidga, *Mebyon Kernow and Cornish Nationalism* (Cardiff: Welsh Academic Press, 2003), pp.51-89.

unitary authority elections of 2009-17 the Labour Party contested around half of wards.[17] All these parties have won seats at state level and all would be regarded as having long ago crossed the threshold of authorisation.

On occasions, MK's absence or presence at elections has been as much the result of a deliberate decision as lack of resources. This was the case when proportional representation in regional constituencies became the system for European elections in 1999. Cornwall was not regarded as a region in its own right and became part of a much bigger multi-member constituency. Although the threshold for retaining the £5,000 deposit was set at just 2.5%, that equated to around 25% of the Cornish vote. This financial penalty resulted in MK choosing not to contest this level of election in 1999, 2004 and 2014. However, in 2009 it did contest the European elections, but specifically because the local elections were being held on the same day and participation in the European elections would 'boost MK's campaign for unitary authority seats'. Similarly, an argument for contesting parliamentary elections, despite the hurdle of the first past the post voting system, was that it raised the profile of the party at local elections.[18] This was particularly relevant in 1997, 2001 and 2005 when general elections were held on the same day as elections to Cornwall County Council, a context that tended to drown out the more local issues that might be expected to figure in the council elections. In the most recent general election of 2017, closely following local government elections, MK took the decision not to stand, citing weariness after fighting the local elections and the difficulty of raising sufficient money to mount a credible campaign.[19]

Although Henig and Baston could conclude in 2002 that MK was 'a serious and committed presence on the Cornish scene with potential for growth',[20] a major breakthrough continues to elude the party. As can be seen in Table 1 on the next page, MK has increased its electoral presence at the state level since the 1980s although there has been no advance in its vote share. However, like other ethnoregionalist parties, MK performs considerably better at second-order elections. In particular, in the European elections of 1979 and 2009 its vote was a lot higher than in state elections,

17 Cornwall Council, 'Election results',
    https://democracy.cornwall.gov.uk/mgManageElectionResults.aspx?bcr=1
    (accessed 23 July 2016); Local Elections Archive Project,
    http://andrewteale.me.uk/leap/ (accessed 23 July 2016).
18 *Cornish Nation* 51 (2009), p.4; *Cornish Nation* 14 (1999), p.3.
19 BBC News, 'No candidates from Mebyon Kernow in 2017 general election',
    11 May 2017, http://www.bbc.co.uk/news/uk-england-cornwall-39880934
    (accessed 12 May 2017).
20 Simon Henig and Lewis Baston, *The Political Map of Britain* (London:
    Methuen, 2002), p.50.

where it struggles to surpass 2%. In the first European election, fought on a first past the post basis, a major issue revolved around the constituency boundaries, which combined Cornwall with the city of Plymouth in neighbouring Devon. MK campaigned against this refusal to give Cornwall sole, direct representation and benefited from a wider protest against the breach of territorial integrity. The 9% of the Cornish vote attained at that election remains MK's best result outside local elections.

Table 1. MK electoral performance by governance level[21]

Europe		State			Local (County)		
year	% vote	year	% vote in seats contested	% seats contested	year	% vote in seats contested	% seats contested
		1970	2.0	20			
		1974(F)	1.5	20	1973	32.6	3
		1974 (O)	0.7	20	1977	17.1	9
1979	9.5	1979	2.9	60	1981	16.6	11
1984	-	1983	1.2	40	1985	35.9	4
1989	3.0	1987	-	0	1989	26.9	4
1994	2.1	1992	-	0	1993	19.0	9
1999	-	1997	0.8	80	1997	14.6	16
		2001	2.1	60	2001	12.2	27
2004	-	2005	1.7	80	2005	12.6	23
2009	6.8	2010	1.9	100	2009	17.0	27
2014	-	2015	1.9	100	2013	24.1	21
		2017	-	0	2017	22.2	15

By 2009 the electoral system had changed to a proportional South West region-wide list system, in which Cornwall comprised just a tenth part. At that election in Cornwall MK won 6.8%, outpolling Labour, the party of

---

21 Calculated from electoral statistics at Richard Kimber's Political Science resources, available at http://www.politicsresources.net/ (accessed December 8 2015) and The Electoral Commission, available at http://www.electoralcommission.org.uk/find-information-by-subject/elections-and-referendums/past-elections-and-referendums (accessed December 8 2015); author's database of local election results.

government (although not doing as well as the United Kingdom Independence Party or the Greens).

How does this compare with other west European regionalist parties? The most direct comparator is France, which has a similar plurality voting system (although with two ballots) at legislative and cantonal (since 2015 departmental) elections. As Table 2 on the next page indicates, at the parliamentary level some parties, notably the Basque *Abertzaleen Batasuna* (AB), then *Euskal Herria Bai* (EH Bai) and the Corsican parties, poll considerably higher. However, most French ethnoregionalist parties command levels of support not that different from that of MK, even at the parliamentary level. The apparently higher score of the UDB is accounted for by elections where the party has been given a free run by *Les Verts* and, as in the case of their first deputy Paul Molac in 2012, the *Parti Socialiste* as well. In fact, the median UDB vote at the parliamentary level since 2000 has ranged between 1.23% and 2.01%, which is very close to that of MK (from 1.56% to 2.26%). Moreover, in the most recent 2017 legislative elections the electoral alliance of the UDB and the *Mouvement Bretagne et Progrès* scored a mean vote of 1.84% and a median of just 1.18%

At the local level, MK's performance is better than all French ethnoregionalist parties. In Brittany for example, in 2008, 2011 and 2015 the mean vote for UDB candidates was 5.8%, 8.5% and 4.4%, far lower than MK's mean vote in either 2009 or 2013 (17.0% and 24.1%). Regionalist parties elsewhere in France fare no better. Support for the *Ligue Savoisienne*, the *Partit Occitan* or the *Bloc Catala/Unitat Catalana* was lower still. Only the *Abertzaleen Batasuna/EH Bai* and the Corsican parties poll at levels near to MK. In 1999 a record number of MK candidates contested the District elections and after that year MK began regularly to win seats at this level. In 2009, when unitary local government was imposed and the district level abolished, MK also won seats on that authority. However, its number of councillors remains small, three in 2009 and four in 2013 and 2017, and the proportion of seats contested is around a quarter or less. Indeed, although the number of councillors has slowly grown and the vote share held up, the number of candidates flatlined after the growth surge at the turn of the last century. At the most recent local elections in 2017, the mean vote of its candidates held up at above 20% and it retained its four seats, but the proportion of seats contested fell noticeably from its peak in the 2000s.

Table 2. Mean vote of MK and French ethnoregionalist parties compared[22]

	Legislative elections, 1993-2015	Local elections, 2001-2015
	% votes in seats contested (% of seats contested)	% votes in seats contested (% of seats contested)
MK	1.7% (72%)	17.0% (24%)
UDB	2.1% (48%)	5.5% (25%)
AB/EH Bai	5.7% (100%)	12.4% (93%)
Catalan parties	1.2% (80%)	1.9% (35%)
PO	0.8% (14%)	7.7% (1%)
LS	2.0% (25%)	5.0% (34%)
Alsace d'Abord	3.9% (36%)	6.8% (20%)
Union du peuple alsacien/Unser Land	1.9% (11%)	11.7% (15%)
Moderate Corsican parties	9.1% (80%)	16.6% (24%)
Radical Corsican parties	12.3% (45%)	10.3% (19%)

For ethnoregionalist parties the key level of electoral competition is that of the region. In the absence of a regional level of government MK has no choice but to focus on the local level. In Cornwall local elections are clearly regarded as second order elections, with mean turnouts of 37-38% at both European and Cornwall Council levels contrasting with 69% at Westminster elections. No direct comparison can therefore be made with the performance of Massetti and Schakel's dataset of western European ethnoregionalist parties at a regional level, at which they tend to perform the best.[23] Nonetheless, it is worth noting that at the European election of 2009 MK won 6.8% of the votes in Cornwall. Of the 53 western European parties in Massetti and Schakel's dataset that were still active, 29 polled a higher mean over their last four regional elections. Yet 24 did not manage to attain

---

22 French Ministry of the Interior election results (http://www.interieur.gouv.fr/Elections/Les-resultats, accessed December 8, 2015); L'Ouest France; party websites.

23 Massetti and Shakel, 'Class to region', 2015.

a mean of 6.8%. MK's electoral performance, while feeble at a parliamentary level, does not appear to be too dissimilar from many members of the European ethnoregional party family.

MK's primary and secondary policy dimensions

Meanwhile, crossing the threshold of representation at a local/regional level has had little effect on MK's positioning or strategy. Indeed, throughout its fluctuating fortunes since the 1970s MK's position on the centre-periphery cleavage has undergone only relatively minor change. De Winter identifies five types of ethnoregionalist party – protectionist, autonomist, federalist, independentist and irredentist.[24] Adopting this typology MK started life as a protectionist party, with its founding aims encouraging aspects of Cornish culture and promoting Cornwall's status as 'one of the six Celtic nations'. This stance, developing cultural identity within the state, gradually morphed into autonomism in the 1960s and 70s when MK's central political demand became greater autonomy for Cornwall. Massetti and Dandoy employ slightly different categorizations, distinguishing decentralist, autonomist parties, those seeking reforms to the state's political structure, from secessionist parties, those that have an aim of independence, albeit in the background.[25] On these criteria MK can be located on the borders of an assertive autonomism and ambiguous secessionism, moving from the former to the latter in the later 1970s but since the 1990s reverting towards its starting position. In practice however, it is difficult to draw a clear distinction between these categories.

As we have seen, in its very first contested election in 1953 the MK candidate included 'regional self-government' among her demands'.[26] When the party re-appeared in the electoral arena in the mid-1960s its position remained unchanged – 'independence in domestic affairs'. In advance of its first parliamentary foray in 1970 policy was re-affirmed as 'domestic self-government', while at the election itself the party campaigned on the formula 'internal self-government'. 'Internal' and 'domestic' self-government remained official policy although full self-government was adopted as the ultimate aim in 1979.[27] In practice, party activists recognised that this was a long-term aim and the 1980 party conference proposed that

---

24 De Winter and Tursan, *Regionalist Parties*, 1998, pp.205-207.

25 Emanuele Massetti, 'Explaining regionalist party positioning in a multi-dimensional ideological space: A framework for analysis', *Regional and Federal Studies* 19 (2009), 501-531; Régis Dandoy, 'Ethno-regionalist parties in Europe: a typology', *Perspectives on Federalism* 2 (2010), 194-220.

26 Deacon et al., *Mebyon Kernow*, 2003, p.34.

27 Colin Murley, election leaflet, 1967; *Cornish Nation* 2.1 (1970), p.6; *Cornish Nation* 36 (1979), p.2.

the 'first step' to self-government should be a Secretary of State for Cornwall and a Cornish Office, taking its cue from the Scottish Office. As the party moved to the left in the early 1980s however, the demand for self-government tended to take a back seat and was replaced by the more generalised aim of 'autonomy'.

By the time MK began to contest elections less sporadically again in the later 1990s its position on the centre-periphery cleavage had returned to 'self-government', although this time, again shadowing the SNP and Plaid Cymru, the formula 'self-government within the European Union' became official policy by 1994. Even this was not foregrounded, its immediate demands at the 1997 campaign being a Cornish Assembly or Parliament and the replacement of combined Cornwall and Devon governance bodies with Cornish institutions. As the new millennium unfolded self-government was postponed as MK retreated to a more clearly autonomist position. Its 'vision' agreed at the 2006 conference was the 'same right to self-determination as Scotland and Wales' with a long term aim of a 'Cornish Assembly with powers broadly similar to the Scottish Parliament'. In the shorter term it recognised 'the need to be pragmatic' in order to 'build campaigns which can unite Cornish communities and work towards Cornish self-government'. This reflected its involvement in the cross-party Cornish Constitutional Convention, set up in 2000 to demand a devolved regional assembly for Cornwall. Within this campaign MK maintains a distinctive position by recognising Cornwall as a 'distinct national community for all forms of governance and administration'.[28]

Interest has recently shifted to the ideological position of nationalist and regionalist parties on matters other than independence and devolution.[29] While, in its first few years and again in the early 1960s, MK undertook research into such things as education, unemployment and transport policy, the party adopted no clear position on such issues, declaring in 1972 that 'left, right and centre are irrelevant'. The organisation was not so much centrist in orientation as apolitical. It was with the leadership of Len Truran from 1968 that MK moved to a broadly progressive, left of centre position. Truran, a local schoolmaster, regarded the Liberals as the main competition for 'patriotic' Cornish voters and supported a strategy to 'seek to occupy the radical middle ground that they [the Liberals] once occupied'.[30] The party

---

28 MK, *The Real Future for Cornwall* (Manifesto for European election, 1993), p.1; *Cornish Nation* 6 (1997), p.7; MK, 'Our vision for Cornwall', *Cornish Nation* 42 (2006), p.2; 'Self-government for Cornwall', *Cornish Nation* 45 (2007), p.2; *Towards a National Assembly of Cornwall* (Truro: Cornish Constitutional Convention, 2014), p.4.

29 Massetti and Schakel, 'Class to region', 2015.

30 *Cornish Nation* 2.9 (1972), p.67; *Carn* 8 (1974).

manifesto *What Cornishmen Can Do*, written by Truran in 1968, adopted a number of policies dependent on active state intervention, reflecting the dominant, Keynesian social democracy of the time.

During the late 1970s an influx of younger members began to push for a more socialist stance, influenced by the UDB and developments within Plaid Cymru. This had the effect of shifting party discourse more explicitly leftwards. Truran adopted the language of internal colonialism in 1978 – 'we are England's oldest colony, suffering from the chronic effects of that colonisation'.[31] After a period of factionalism following the 1979 general election, MK was consolidated as a party of the left, by the early 1990s calling for self-determination, local democracy, environmental sustainability, internationalism, social justice and peace. In 1996 the party adopted a set of policies that included state intervention on health, housing, education and welfare, 'tailored to the needs of our people'. The formula was vague but an election leaflet the following year rejected a 'Cornwall sacrificed to market forces'. It fought the general election on a platform of Cornish values, green commitments, left of centre policies and decentralisation of power. These remained its four cornerstones into the 2010s. At each election a full set of policies was unveiled, for instance in 2015 promoting such aspects as an end to austerity, fairer taxes, decent public services, stronger action on climate change and a reformed EU along with the constant refrain of greater self-government for Cornwall and institutional recognition.[32]

MK's ideological focus and its positioning on issues has remained consistent over the past three decades. Its core demands for the accommodation of Cornish territorial interests and the Cornish identity had for some time been bracketed with economic policies seeking more resources (in the shape of the highest level of European grant aid, which arrived after a long campaign in 1999) to improve competitiveness and more Cornish-based institutional structures to bring economic development into line with local tradition. The timing of its emergence into electoral politics in the 1960s and 1970s has bequeathed a broadly left of centre, social democratic heritage, one that was not seriously eroded by the re-assertion of a dominant neo-liberal discourse after the 1980s or the growth of populist and Eurosceptic views among the electorate.

MK and policy impact
MK has clearly not yet reached the final threshold of government but is it anywhere close to the threshold of relevance? Its core demand has been the

---

31 Len Truran, 'A booby prize for Charlie', *Cornish Nation* 35 (1978), p.12.
32 MK, *Real Future*, 1993; *Cornish Nation* 3 (1996), p.11; MK, *Cornwall 2000 – The Way Ahead*, 1997; *Vote for Cornwall … a new approach to politics*, 2015.

devolution of power to Cornwall. However, especially in its early days, much energy has been expended on more defensive campaigns to prevent the dissolution of Cornwall-based institutions into wider 'regional' administrative units based on the larger planning region template employed by the UK Government for England. For example, in 1999 a South West Regional Development Agency was made responsible for an area of which Cornwall was only a small part, rather than the Cornish Development Agency MK and others had been calling for. In 2011 the coalition government's Parliamentary Voting System and Constituencies Act legislated for equal-sized constituencies but treated Cornwall, unlike Wales or Scotland, as part of a South West region, an assumption that inevitably produced a cross-border constituency and the equally inevitable campaign against it.

These ongoing defensive campaigns were joined by more pro-active campaigning for a Cornish Assembly when, in 1998, MK launched a Millennium Convention.[33] This however coincided with the closure of Cornwall's last working tin mine and the appearance of Cornish Solidarity, a short-lived direct-action orientated group that overshadowed MK's less newsworthy efforts. In quieter times, in 2000, a second cross-party campaign was launched for a Cornish Assembly, establishing a Cornish Constitutional Convention.[34] MK activists led the collection of a petition of 50,000 signatures while its leadership worked as part of a cross-party group, including Liberal Democrat MPs and prospective parliamentary candidates, a few Conservative politicians and others.

While the campaign for an Assembly has yet to bear fruit, some long-standing MK core policy demands have been met in recent years. These are claimed to be evidence of the 'significant impact of Cornish identity in the local political landscape'.[35] In 2003 the Cornish language was recognised under the European Charter for Regional or Minority Languages. In 2014 central government followed this up by recognising the status of the Cornish as a national minority under the Framework Convention for the Protection of National Minorities. In 2015, following the Scottish referendum, the Government also signed a 'devolution deal' with Cornwall Council and the unelected Cornwall and Isles of Scilly Local Enterprise Partnership. This transferred a few powers over bus services, further education training, business support and health and social care, while

---

33 *Cornish Nation* 9 (1998), p.8.

34 *Cornish Nation* 18 (2000), p.3.

35 Joanie Willett and John Tredinnick-Rowe, 'The fragmentation of the nation state? Regional development, distinctiveness and the growth of nationalism in Cornish politics', *Nations and Nationalism* 22 (2016), 768-785.

insisting the transfer had to be 'fiscally neutral'.[36] There was no direct MK input into this very limited devolution, one quickly followed by similar deals with rural regions and counties in England. Indeed, MK was quick to criticise it as putting 'power into the hands of unelected private sector companies ... It is cynical and destructive'.[37]

However, direct impact on constitutional reform by ethnoregionalist parties is relatively uncommon. Of more relevance is the ability to influence the programmes and behaviour of party competitors or to set agendas. Elias and Tronconi suggest that the 'mere presence' of an ethnoregionalist party may be sufficient to influence agendas, although they add the significant rider that this is 'with significant share of support' for the ethnoregionalist party and that vote maximisation is the usual prerequisite for influence.[38] However, Herzog suggested that regardless of vote share, the presence of minor parties can force a reaction from mainstream parties.[39] In the case of Cornwall and MK, the party's greatest influence on party competitors may actually have occurred even before it began to contest parliamentary elections, as long ago as the 1950s and 1960s, before the limitations of its electoral support at that level became transparent. The threat of vote maximisation, as opposed to vote maximisation as such, was enough to encourage the regional branch of the Liberal party to strengthen its accommodative, pro-Cornish devolution stance.

Overall therefore, the extent of MK success is limited. In terms of electoral salience, the party is more visible than it was before the 1990s and succeeds in getting a handful of local councillors elected. Moreover, its vote share is comparable with that of other fourth parties in the UK at local level and with the UDB in neighbouring Brittany. But it has yet to make a breakthrough at state level and its performance at that level shows no progress since 2001. The party's failure to mobilise voters means of necessity it has failed in terms of government incumbency. Even at local level it has no 'blackmail potential' and remains a party of protest. Its effect on policy outcomes is at first sight also marginal, with no direct impact on recent very cautious moves to devolve powers to local government or central government recognition of the Cornish identity and language. That said, the official recognition of the Cornish language and a degree of central government funding from 2005 (although removed in 2016), and the

36 www.gov.uk/government/publications/cornwall-devolution-deal, accessed July 22, 2016.

37 *Western Morning News*, 20 May 2016.

38 Elias and Tronconi, *Protest to Power*, 2011, pp.365 and 361.

39 Hanna Herzog, 'Minor Parties: The Relevancy Perspective', *Comparative Politics* 19 (1987), 317–29.

recognition of the Cornish people as a national minority followed long campaigns in which MK's voice had been the most consistent one.

Yet, MK's survival over a period of half a century is not explained by the lifespan model, which is stronger on description than explanatory power. Studies based on Pedersen's lifespan model have been criticised in terms of their case selection.[40] Pedersen dismissed smaller parties that were unable to challenge the policies of mainstream parties or wield coalition potential. Additionally, he predicted that if parties failed to cross the thresholds they would eventually wither away in the long term and die. In MK's case, having survived for over 65 years, the 'long term' would appear to very long term indeed. In addition, MK's persistence echoes the 'puzzle' noted by Sloan. There has been an increase in the UK of minor parties fighting elections at all levels in a context where the voting system penalises them severely. Following Herzog, Sloan calls for a wider definition of relevance, to include opening up political debate beyond the familiar issue spectrum. This can be 'regardless of vote share or the number of minority candidates'. If that is so then presence becomes a necessary condition for forcing reactions from other parties and durability becomes a prior condition of success. Indeed, Harmel goes further, positing durability as an explicit criterion of party success, along with votes and policy impact.[41]

Demand and supply models of party success
If the lifespan model fails to explain the combination of persistence with a marginal electoral appeal at statewide elections, we have to move beyond that model. In explaining the variable success of radical right parties a demand and supply conceptual framework is often employed. This splits factors into the demand side, including the grievances that create demand for the parties, emanating from socio-cultural and socio-economic breeding grounds for voter disaffection, and the supply side. Supply-side factors are subdivided in turn into external determinants, such as the electoral system, the structure of party competition and aspects of the broader social context - and internal factors - such as organisation, strategy and positioning. This demand and supply framework has been extended to radical left parties and is potentially applicable to any party family.[42]

---

40 Emanuele Massetti, 'Review of Elias and Tronconi, *From Protest to Power'*, *Party Politics* 20 (2014), 143-148.
41 Elias and Tronconi, *Protest to power*, 2011, p.19; Luke Sloan, 'Can we feel their presence? A new framework for investigating minor parties in English local government', *Local Government Studies* 40 (2014), 621-641; Robert Harmel, 'On the study of new parties', *International Political Science Review* 6 (1985), 403-418.

Indeed, it closely echoes some familiar frameworks long adopted to explain ethnoregionalist party performance. Taking his cue from Tarrow's previous work on party resources, Muller-Rommel proposed a model whereby electoral success depended on the capacity of the ethnoregionalist party to mobilise internal and external factors.[43] Endogenous factors were party organisational structure, leadership capability and the presence or absence of factionalism, while exogenous factors were the level of centralisation of the state structure, the stability of the party system and the presence of influential allies. This combination of internal and external factors, political opportunity structures and strategic agency, with or without the specific factors noted by Muller-Rommel, has continued to hold sway in explanations of the variable success of ethnoregionalist, and indeed other parties. This was operationalised more recently by Elias as the external operating environment on the one hand and internal ideological and organisational factors on the other, in her study of parties in Catalonia.[44] These various frameworks map closely onto a demand and supply model. However, the advantage of the demand and supply conceptual framework is that it enables us to pay more attention to groups of factors and their interaction, while offering space for the cultural factors that are more relevant for explaining persistence.

Demand-side factors
Hepburn suggests that ethnoregionalist parties can tap into public disaffection with traditional politicians and, along with Greens and the radical right, be the main beneficiaries of voter discontent.[45] However, macro-level issues such as globalisation or modernisation apply across a state's territory. It is not clear therefore how such general factors translate into micro-level voting preferences or why they should lead to support for different party families in different places.[46] There is no comparable data on levels of voter disenchantment with modernisation or feelings of

---

42 Cas Mudde, *Populist Radical Right Parties in Europe* (Cambridge: Cambridge University Press, 2007); Luke March and Charlotte Rommerskirchen, 'Out of left field? Explaining the variable success of European radical left parties', *Party Politics* 21 (2015), 40-53.

43 Ferdinand Müller-Rommel. 'Ethnoregionalist parties in Western Europe: theoretical considerations and frameworks of analysis', in De Winter and Tursan (eds), *Regionalist Parties*, 1998, 17-27; Sydney Tarrow, *Power in Movement* (Cambridge: Cambridge University Press, 1994).

44 Anwen Elias, 'Catalan Independence and the Challenge of Credibility: The Causes and Consequences of Catalan Nationalist Parties' Strategic Behavior', *Nationalism and Ethnic Politics* 21 (2015), 83-103.

45 Hepburn, 'Re-conceptualizing', 2009.

46 Mudde, *Populist Radical Right*, 2007, p.230.

disempowerment in Cornwall as opposed to other places. Proxies, such as the vote to leave the European Union in June 2016 or support for Ukip, suggest voters in Cornwall are slightly more likely to vote for Brexit or Ukip than the English average, but not as strongly as in eastern England. (In Cornwall 56.5% voted for Brexit, compared with 53.3% in England and 52.5% in Wales). This might be expected, given the age and skills distribution of the Cornish electorate, with higher proportions of voters in elderly and less formally educated groups. While direct data on MK voters is sparse, correlations of the local election data of 2009 with socio-economic variables suggest that MK did better in wards which have higher proportions of middle aged voters, lower socio-economic groups and those with no qualifications.[47] This preliminary finding implies that MK might be competing with Ukip in Cornwall for the 'left-behind' voter. If so, it is clearly failing at a parliamentary level, although its vote held up well in the face of the Ukip advance in the local elections of 2013.

However, viewing the potential source of demand for MK as merely a floating protest vote is insufficient. How far is there a potential constituency of support for core MK policies of devolution and recognition of Cornish interests? Testing for the salience of local over state-wide issues, John Ault surveyed four Cornish constituencies in 2008/09 and compared them with four others in England, four in Scotland and one in Wales, in all of which the Liberal Democrat vote was strong. He found that Cornish voters were as likely to emphasise local issues as the Scottish voters and slightly more likely than voters in the English constituencies. But while in Ceredigion local issues were felt to be more important by 51% to 47%, in Cornwall the difference (32%-55%) was not that dissimilar from the English constituencies (30%-63%). Moreover, Ault concluded that it was unclear whether the Liberal Democrats were tapping into a pre-existing territorial cleavage or whether party campaigning was helping to create that cleavage.[48]

This research suggests a limited role in Cornwall for the territorial cleavage. However, it is possible to point to other evidence for active support for MK's core demands. First, the 50,000 signatures raised between March 2000 and May 2001 in support of a Cornish Assembly indicated some level of support (and the ability of MK activists to organise this petition). Second, an opinion poll undertaken in advance of the 2015 general election in the Camborne-Redruth constituency found that 49% of those polled supported a 'Cornish Assembly with similar powers to those of

---

47 Bernard Deacon, 'Who is the Cornish voter? Social variables and party choice in Cornwall' (available at https://bernarddeacon.wordpress.com/publications/).

48 John Ault, *Liberal Democrats in Cornwall: Culture, Character or Campaigns?* (Penryn: Institute of Cornish Studies, 2015).

the Welsh Assembly ... such as control of the NHS and social welfare', with 31% opposed and 20% who didn't know or were neutral. Intriguingly, the pollsters found the highest support for a Cornish Assembly among those intending to vote Labour (59% in support) or Ukip (55%), despite neither of those parties favouring an Assembly.[49] That might suggest the territorial cleavage was far from the principal determinant for voters in Cornwall.

This limited evidence of support for a measure of devolution and a (slightly) greater salience of local issues on a micro-level implies a possible 'breeding-ground' for MK support. However, as Mudde points out, demand-side factors on their own do not automatically explain party success.[50] Potential support has to be mobilised. This is better explained at the meso-level, that of interactions at family, community, school and party level. At this level there is some evidence for an emerging potential pool of support for an ethnoregionalist party in the Pupil Level Annual Schools Census. Since 2006 that has included 'Cornish' among the ethnicity question options offered to the parents of primary schoolchildren and the secondary schoolchildren themselves who complete the census. The proportion opting for a Cornish ethnicity has doubled from 24% in 2006 to almost 50% at the most recently available census of 2015.[51]

MK emerged in the 1950s from a wider sub-cultural movement oriented to preservationism and the revival of the Cornish language. Since that time, this cultural revival has expanded in the size and range of its activity, particularly in the fields of music and dancing. Meanwhile, the Cornish language was recognised by the UK Government under the European Charter for Regional or Minority Languages in 2003 and is much more visible than in the mid-twentieth century, for example in revived Cornish signage and other domains such as company names. The enhanced visibility of a Celtic language and the wider appeal of what is seen as Cornish culture acts to remind people of their heritage and helps to sustain and invigorate a sense of popular Cornishness that might be viewed as more residual, resting on traditional, but now shrinking, domains, or fast disappearing cultural contexts.[52] This may help to explain the growth of expressions of Cornish ethnicity in recent years, as reflected in the schools census.

In addition, in 2001 the ONS gave the Cornish a census ethnicity coding, although in the census of that year there was no provision of an explicit

---

49 'How the West was won', http://htwww.org/2014/11/26/our-survation-poll-says-camborneredruth-too-close-to-call-and-good-news-for-pro-devolutionists/ (Accessed 12 May 2015).
50 Mudde, *Populist Radical Right*, 2007, p.230.
51 Pupil Level Annual School Census, 2006-2015.
52 Neil Kennedy, *Cornish Solidarity; Using Culture to Strengthen Communities* (Portlaoise: Evertype, 2016).

tick-box for the Cornish, as was the case for the Welsh. Nonetheless, 6.8% of people in Cornwall went to the length of describing themselves as Cornish (a process somewhat counter-intuitively involving rejecting a 'British' tick-box).[53] This compared with 14.4% in Wales who wrote in a Welsh identity, although the Welsh Assembly publicised the option. In 2011 the numbers expressing a Cornish identity doubled to 13.8%. In Wales, which now had an explicit tick-box, the proportion leapt to 65.9%.[54] This strongly implies that, had such a tick-box been available for Cornish, the proportion expressing a Cornish identity would have been between 30% and 50%. This evidence of a growing willingness to express a Cornish identity has not however been reflected in MK's vote share at a state level. Clearly, the party has so far been unable to mobilise growing expressions of Cornish identity or the demand for devolution. In order to explain that, we need to move from demand-side to supply-side factors.

External supply-side factors
These equate to the commonly used 'political opportunity structure', which in turn contains institutional, political or cultural dimensions.[55] The structural constraints for smaller parties of state-wide first past the post electoral systems are well known.[56] While a geographical concentration of support can overcome the disproportionate nature of plurality voting systems, such systems create greater barriers against an initial electoral breakthrough. In MK's case these barriers are compounded by Cornwall's size and the official refusal to recognise Cornwall as a region in its own right. Thus, although contesting all six Cornish constituencies at the 2010 and 2015 general elections, MK was denied televised party political broadcasts. The BBC ruled that these were only available to parties contesting a minimum of one-sixth (or 89) of the seats in England, which effectively debars MK from this type of television coverage despite contesting all the seats in its target territory. Similarly, Cornwall comprised just a tenth of the large regional constituency used in the European elections. Although in Cornwall in 2009 it gained well above the 2.5% of the vote required to save the £5,000 deposit for standing in this election, MK lost its deposit because the party's vote across the whole constituency was only 1.0%. Even at a local level the drive to establish a unitary

---

53 2001 Census, Table C0235; Husk, 'Ethnic group affiliation and social exclusion in Cornwall; analysis, adjustment and extension of the 2001 England and Wales Census data', (unpublished doctoral thesis, University of Plymouth, 2012), p.269.
54 2001 Census, Table KS06A; 2011 Census, Table KS202EW.
55 Tarrow, *Power in Movement*, 1994, pp.32-33 and 85.
56 Mudde, *Populist Radical Right*, 2007, p.233.

authority in 2009 closed off electoral possibilities for MK. This is because it resulted in the abolition of the lower-tier district councils and their amalgamation into one single Cornwall-wide authority. Many of the wards at district council level were multi-member, which offered more opportunity for MK than the single seat wards of Cornwall Council elections. Two years after the party increased its representation at district council level from five to seven councillors in 2007 and in some parts of west and mid-Cornwall appeared close to a major breakthrough, that tier of local government was abolished.

The core level for ethnoregionalist parties is the region.[57] However, Cornwall has no regional level and the usual dividend available to ethnoregionalist parties is therefore unavailable. In fact regionalization between the 1990s and 2010 from MK's perspective was viewed as a further centralization of governance, transferring functions (such as strategic planning) upwards from local government. Regionalization in this context merely highlighted Cornwall's absence of regional status and contradicted the perceived benefits of recognition as a European region. Yet, even in its limited English version, multi-level governance could affect MK's policies on the centre-periphery cleavage. The formation of the unelected Regional Development Agency in the 1990s led MK to support the cross-party and no-party Cornish Constitutional Convention (CCC), which demanded a Cornish Assembly. In doing so, it re-branded its familiar demand for 'internal self-government' to take advantage of a wider, although ultimately unsuccessful, movement for democratic regional government in England.[58]

As critical, if not more critical, than the electoral system is the system of party competition. Tronconi found that the disproportionality of electoral systems, the volatility of the vote, the level of polarisation between state-wide parties and the clarity of government/opposition divides, and therefore the importance of any given election in changing a government, all have effects on regionalist parties.[59] Since Tronconi's intervention, there has been a flurry of studies of inter-party competition. Many of these are influenced by Meguid's 'Position, salience and ownership theory' of party competition. This concentrates more directly on the strategies adopted by other parties

---

57 Anwen Elias and Filippo Tronconi, 'From protest to power: autonomist parties in government', *Party Politics* 17 (2011), 505-524.
58 Mark Sandford, *The Cornish Question: Devolution in the South-West Region* (London: The Constitution Unit, UCL, 2002); Joanie Willett and Arianna Giovannini, 'The uneven path of UK devolution: Top-down vs. bottom-up regionalism in England – Cornwall and the North-East compared', *Political Studies* 62 (2014), 343-360.
59 Filippo Tronconi, 'Ethnic identity and party competition. An analysis of the electoral performance of ethnoregionalist parties in Western Europe', *World Political Science Review* 2 (2006), 137-63.

when explaining the differential performance of minor parties in Europe since the 1970s. In doing so it combines a focus on party competition with the strategic manoeuvrings of agents and claims to be more alert to changes in party performance over time. For Meguid the crucial agents are not the 'niche' parties themselves but the mainstream parties, which adopt strategies that affect minor party support, by either accommodating, ignoring or opposing them.[60]

In this context it is interesting to note how the Liberals toyed with devolutionist politics in Cornwall from a very early stage. As early as 1952 prominent Cornish Liberals were expressing support for Cornish home rule, on the grounds that the 'Cornish people were a separate nation'.[61] In 1959 all five Liberal parliamentary candidates supported a regional assembly. Significantly, this was at a time when MK was still a pressure group allowing dual membership, and Liberal activists, including Members of Parliament, were prominent members. In 1968, two years before MK's first foray into a parliamentary election, Liberal constituency associations in Cornwall were reported to be 'investigating the political and economic implications of independence' and considering a bill demanding independence for Cornwall.[62] In MK's case, the emergence of the party into the electoral arena did not trigger greater radicalism on the centre-periphery cleavage from regional branches of state-wide parties. In contrast, its transition from pressure group to political party post-dated expressions of support for Cornish devolution from Liberal Party activists in Cornwall. This timing was critical. Unlike Wales and Scotland, where nationalist parties began to contest elections before the Liberal revival of the 1960s, in Cornwall that revival preceded MK's entry into electoral politics. Local Liberals' accommodative strategy challenged MK's ownership of the devolution issue and closed down the available political space, suppressing potential support and siphoning off activists. The most prominent of these was the Liberal Democrat MP for St Ives from 1997 to 2015, Andrew George, a former MK member. MK's electoral difficulties in the face of an accommodative Liberal Democrat party echoes the situation in Brittany, where a regionally orientated Socialist Party played a similar role in the 1980s vis-à-vis the UDB, attracting both potential voters and activists.[63]

---

60 Bonnie Meguid. *Party Competition between Unequals: Strategies and Electoral Fortunes in Western Europe* (Cambridge: Cambridge University Press, 2008).

61 *Cornish Guardian*, 8 May 1952.

62 Garry Tregidga, '"Bodmin Man": Peter Bessell and Cornish politics in the 1950s and 1960s', in Philip Payton (ed.), *Cornish Studies: Eight* (Exeter: University of Exeter Press, 2000), 161-181.

Elias et al. add other possibilities to Meguid's positioning of mainstream parties. They argue that mainstream parties can also adopt 'vague, contradictory or ambiguous' policies when facing niche party competition, thus blurring the issue.[64] Another mainstream party blurring strategy is to adopt, whether deliberately or not, different strategies at different levels. The Liberal Democrats' presence at multiple political levels enables them to do this. For example, in 1997 when Lib Dem MPs were tabling early day motions calling for a Cornish Assembly, the majority of Lib Dem County Councillors were voting against a Cornish Development Agency and refusing to back an explicit call for a Cornish Assembly.[65] Ambiguity might also be seen in the Conservative Party's use of the rhetoric of 'localism' and 'devolution deals' since 2010, combined with actual policies of centralisation, for example in planning or as the result of austerity politics. There is yet another possibility. Mainstream parties can also subsume territorial issues within their own core dimensions. Thus calls for a Cornish Assembly are met by arguments from all three mainstream parties in Cornwall that stress the 'unacceptable' costs involved at a time of austerity. This re-packages the constitutional issue in an economic/financial discourse where neo-liberal assumptions about the 'costs' of democracy predominate.

Finally, we have the cultural opportunity structure. The academic literature is sketchier here. It might devote space to the attitudes of the media but tends to skate quickly over longer-term factors in the territory's historical context. This would be a mistake in this case as historical and cultural structures play a large part in explaining the paradox of persistence without performance in Cornwall.

The media can frame a party positively or negatively, or ignore it. In MK's case, while receiving occasional coverage, the media in general bestow little coverage on the party. Part of the reason for that is the ownership structure and territorial organisation of the media in Cornwall. Apart from the local newspaper press and BBC Radio Cornwall, the daily regional press in the shape of the *Western Morning News* is published just outside Cornwall in Plymouth and adopts a Devon and Cornwall, or 'West Country', stance on political issues. As does television local news - both BBC and ITV - which are organised on a wider south west regional basis. It is not that MK receives particularly negative framing, although the media tend to simplify its description to 'the Cornish nationalist party', which fails

---

63 Michael Keating, 'The rise and decline of micronationalism in mainland France', *Political Studies* 33 (1985), 1-18.

64 Anwen Elias, Edina Szöcsik, and Christina Zuber, 'Position, selective emphasis and framing: How parties deal with a second dimension in competition', *Party Politics*, 21 (2015), 839-850.

65 *Cornish Nation* 6 (1993), p.10; *Kernow* 34 (1996), p.19.

to capture the nuances of the party's position or its civic nationalist stance, or its position on secondary dimensions. It is more that the party is starved of publicity. In its post-election analysis in 1997 MK 'found it very hard going. It was almost impossible to generate any publicity'.[66] If any publicity is good publicity then MK suffers from its lack of visibility in the media.

More indirectly, the media are important in affecting the salience of an issue. The regional media operating in Cornwall do not emphasise the issue of devolution. When it is covered, it is either subsumed in a broader discussion of devolution to the 'south west' of England, or there is confusion between a Cornish Assembly with regional powers and Cornwall's unitary local authority, both reflecting and consolidating the low level of understanding found within mainstream parties in Cornwall. Given its size, comprising around 1% of the UK, Cornwall does not get regular coverage in the state-wide media. When it does it tends to be seen through the prism of leisure and holidaying. Issues such as second homes or the poverty that lie hidden behind a holiday image might receive attention but devolution more rarely does, although the level of trivialisation does appear to have decreased in recent times.[67]

The role of the media and external publicity is supposedly more pronounced in facilitating or preventing electoral breakthrough.[68] A relative lack of coverage in the media might therefore be a factor when explaining the case of MK. However, there is a further cultural supply-side factor, the effect of which may be more positive. We have seen how the presence of the Cornish language remains a symbol of Cornish cultural difference and helps to feed a vigorous sub-cultural movement. This in turn can act as an opportunity for MK, creating a reservoir of potential support. If the burgeoning activity in various Cornish cultural fields raises confidence in Cornish identity then MK, which claims that 'ours is the politics of identity', looks potentially set to benefit.[69]

Yet a sense of Cornishness can find other outlets. As well as the Lib Dems' rhetorical support for a measure of Cornish devolution and repeated demands for a 'fair deal' for Cornwall, Cornwall's cultural legacy also supplies a political tradition of electing Independent councillors at a local level. Preliminary research on correlations between social variables and voting behaviour at ward level found that the most significant correlation between expressions of Cornish identity and party vote was in relation to

---

66   *Cornish Nation* 6 (1997), pp.8-9.
67   For examples see 'Behind sea and surf: thousands of children living in poverty', *Guardian*, 24 Aug 2016; 'Corxit? Yorxit? Brexit fires up Cornwall and Yorkshire independence movements', *Daily Express*, 2 Aug 2016.
68   Mudde, *Populist Radical Right*, 2007, p.253.
69   *Cornish Nation* 47 (2008), p.2.

Independent candidates (and not MK).[70] In Cornwall in the early twentieth century a political tradition of Independent candidacies was institutionalized in local government as Conservatives and Liberals eschewed overt party politics at this level. It is significant that those MK candidates who do best tend to be well rooted locally and able to tap this available 'Independent' vote.[71] In such cases, the party appeals not primarily because of its green, left of centre and decentralist ideology but because of valence issues in the case of sitting councillors and because it is viewed as a credible defender of local interests, acting as a local tribune.

In a local electoral context where an 'Independent' tradition is well entrenched and unusually dynamic, MK could indeed be viewed as a somewhat more 'Cornish' wing of the Independents. Indeed, this role as a local tribune party might suggest that the most relevant comparator is not the French microregionalist parties, let alone the successful ethnoregionalist parties of the UK or Spain or the ethnic fringe and populist parties of northern Italy. Instead, its rootedness in the local terrain resembles the *Fryske Nasjonale Partij* (FNP) in Friesland. That party was formed in 1962 and first contested Dutch provincial elections in 1966, about the same time that MK began to venture once more into the electoral arena. After an initial peak in the early 1970s, the FNP's vote rose again in the 1990s and has stabilised since the turn of the century at around 10%, mirroring the rise in the local MK vote. However, the FNP is unlike MK in two ways. First, it does not contest elections to the Dutch House of Representatives. Second, its ideology is pragmatic rather than left of centre.[72]

Both elements of Cornwall's cultural legacy, its revivalist sub-culture and its Independent political tradition at a local level offer opportunities for MK. Although these have not been sufficient to contribute to a breakthrough, where the institutional and political constraints are more profound, they help explain the persistence of the party in the absence of electoral success.

To more fully grasp how this combination of longevity yet marginality has arisen and persists we have to adjust our lens of analysis to a wider focus. The external contextual factor of Cornwall's cultural legacy can be linked to a broader external supply-side factor, the result of the way the modernization process has impacted upon Cornwall. This is the demographic regime. Since the 1960s the population of Cornwall has risen

---

70 Deacon, 'Cornish voter'.
71 See for example the by-election victory of Tom Tremewan at Perranporth in 1994 (*Kernow* 28 (1994)).
72 Piet Hemminga, 'The Fryske Nasjonale Partij: Frisian and federal in the Netherlands', in De Winter et al. (eds), *Autonomist Parties*, 2006, vol 2, 141-160.

relatively rapidly. From 1961 to 2011 it grew by 57% in comparison with a 21% growth in England and 15% in Wales. Such a high level of growth was driven entirely by inwards migration, as counter-urbanisation flows set in and deepened, fuelled by the popularity of Cornwall as a tourist destination.[73] This provided both a problem and an opportunity for MK. It is a problem in that the population turnover introduces voters who are unaware of Cornwall's history and cultural legacy or Cornish claims to more than county status. Awareness of large-scale population growth partly explains MK's recurring emphasis on being an open and inclusive party open to all residents of Cornwall, regardless of origin.[74] Conversely, the levels of in-migration stimulated a cultural reaction among the long-term population, as people attempted to root themselves in their Cornish credentials. In short, mass in-migration has paralleled growing performances of Cornishness rather than erased that Cornishness, as was the fear in the 1970s.[75] There is also some evidence that the greater recent visibility of the Cornish language and 'Celtic' symbols has had a more general impact. In 2012 the Cornwall Visitor Survey found that 58% of visitors to Cornwall in 2011 were aware of the local Cornish/Celtic culture and 40% expressed an interest in finding out more about it.[76]

There is an even broader supply-side cultural factor that structures the attitudes of new residents, natives and non-residents alike. This flows from Cornwall's place in the spatial consciousness of British society. Basically, Cornwall has not been institutionalised as a region. Paasi directs our attention to the process through which regions are created. During this they gain their identity partly through the condensation of everyday practices into an indigenous consciousness but also through the images of a region held by both insiders and outsiders.[77] Adopting Paasi's insights, we can detect very different regional discourses operating in the south-west corner of the British Isles. Within one of these Cornwall is an English county, merely one local government administrative unit within a seven-county South West region. From this perspective, MK might well appear logically as a Cornish version of a local residents' association. From the other

---

73 See Ronald Perry, Ken Dean and Bryan Brown (eds), *Counterurbanisation: Case studies of urban to rural movement* (Norwich: Geo Books, 1986), pp.30-126 for an early study of the phenomenon.

74 *Cornish Nation* 34 (2004), p.4.

75 Charles Thomas, *The Importance of Being Cornish in Cornwall* (Redruth: Institute of Cornish Studies, 1973).

76 Visit Cornwall, *Cornwall Visitor Survey 2011* (Truro, 2012), p.72.

77 Anssi Paasi, 'The institutionalization of regions: a theoretical framework for understanding the emergence of regions and the constitution of regional identity', *Fennia* 164 (1986), 105-146.

perspective Cornwall becomes a nation or region in its own right. Yet attempts to gain special treatment for Cornwall, whether devolved regional powers, respect for its historic boundaries or the right to enter sporting competitions on a par with the other nations of the British Isles are met with puzzled incomprehension and the rebuff that 'Cornwall is no more than an English county'.[78] Cornwall is left in the position observed by Tom Nairn in his excoriating polemic *After Britain*, 'simply ignored by traditional all-British political reflection - too insignificant to figure, as it were, in its dazzling image of greatness and global reach'.[79]

Cornwall's small size in relation to the UK state consolidates its location as an English county and reinforces such perceptions and furthermore poses formidable obstacles for MK to overcome (for example in obtaining party political broadcasts). In early 2016 MK's National Executive Committee called on the Westminster political parties to make 2016 the 'year of Cornish recognition'.[80] Given the way Cornwall has been institutionalised, this was easier demanded than delivered. That said, the recognition of the Cornish as a national minority by the coalition government in April 2014 under the terms of the Framework Convention for the Protection of National Minorities offers a new tool for demanding equality of treatment with Scotland and Wales.[81]

Studies of French micronationalist parties tend to focus on more traditional, cultural explanations. For example Shrijver emphasises the subjective identity of the regional inhabitants as the key factor explaining the relative weakness of Breton and Alsatian nationalism when compared with Corsica. While Massetti and Sandri relate the weakness of the *Ligue Savoisienne* to a weak regional identity, cultural factors are also identified by Pasquier in his study of the Breton *Union Démocratique Bretonne* – the consensual identification of region and nation in Brittany. Yet he adds another three factors when discussing the UDB's relative failure. Like Hepburn, he notes problems of strategic and tactical choices but combines this with the electoral context within which the UDB operates and the disconnection of the party from the wider Breton cultural movement. Gurrutxaga's study of nationalism in the French Basque Country also combines a structural, cultural factor that resulted in a 'deep crisis of

78 Commonwealth Games Federation, cited in *Guardian*, 4 Jan 2006, in response to a campaign for Cornwall to enter a team in the Commonwealth Games of 2006.

79 Tom Nairn, *After Britain: New Labour and the Return of Scotland* (London: Granta, 2000), p.14.

80 *Cornish Nation* 72 (2016), p.3.

81 www.gov.uk/government/news/cornish-granted-minority-status-within-the-uk (accessed Sep 15 2016).

Basque identity' after the twentieth century world wars with 'internal factionalism' and ideological splits during the 1970s and 80s.[82]

Earlier explanations for ethnoregionalist party success more generally also emphasised the role of a regional identity, usually associated with the presence of linguistic difference or, as in the case of Ireland, longstanding religious and cultural traditions that sharpened ethnic boundaries. While the electoral and policy successes of parties such as the SNP and the Lega Nord demonstrate that a distinctive and widely spoken language is not a precondition for success, nonetheless some draw the conclusion that support for an ethnoregionalist party is positively related to a strong regional identity or sense of belonging. Reversing the direction of causality, there has been a tendency in relation to the Cornish case to read off the strength of the regional identity from the relative weakness of political nationalism. As the latter is weak then the regional identity must be weak.[83] This then completes a circular argument whereby the 'weakness' of identity becomes the reason for the electoral weakness of MK.

This is too simple. Instances from other regions would suggest that there is no clear link between cultural identity and the electoral performance of ethnoregionalist parties. For example, in Wales Elias notes the 'paradox of the 1990s', when Welsh nationalism appeared to become more credible, part cause and part effect of the narrow vote for a Welsh Assembly in 1997. Yet Plaid Cymru continued to fail to make an electoral impact in state-wide elections. Similarly, in Brittany the vitality of the cultural movement is accompanied by an 'emasculation of a genuine political regionalist movement'. Taking a wider view, Schrijver concludes that 'neither regional identities, nor preferences for regional autonomy are good indicators of the election results of regionalist parties'.[84]

---

82 Frans Schrijver, 'Electoral performance of regionalist parties and perspectives on regional identity in France', *Regional and Federal Studies* 14 (2004), 187-210; Massetti and Sandri, 'Francophone exceptionalism', 2012; Romain Pasquier, 'L'Union Démocratique Bretonne ou les limites de l'expression partisane autonomiste en Bretagne', *Pôle Sud*, 20 (2004), 113-32; Gurrutxaga, 'Nationalism', 2005.

83 Montserrat Guiberneau (ed.), *Governing European Diversity* (London: Sage, 2001), p.17.

84 Anwen Elias, 'From protest to power: Mapping the ideological evolution of Plaid Cymru and the Bloque Nacionalista Galego', *Regional and Federal Studies* 19 (2009), 533-557; Alistair Cole and A. and Jean-Baptiste Paul Harguindéguy, 'The Jacobin Republic and language rights. Ethnolinguistic mobilizations in France', *Regional and Federal Studies* 23 (2013), 27-46; Frans Schrijver, *Regionalism after Regionalisation: Spain, France and the United Kingdom* (Amsterdam: Amsterdam University Press, 2006), p.367.

There is no transparent or inevitable link between an ethnoregional identity and support for an ethnoregionalist party. Assertive expressions of Cornish identity can co-exist with support for mainstream parties. When interviewing political actors in Cornwall, none of whom were members of MK, Mols et al. discovered a willingness to express pro-Cornish sentiments. Local politicians, including Independents, Liberal Democrats and even one Conservative, articulated their feelings about the European Union by emphasising historic Cornish links to Europe within a discourse of trans-Celticism and a traditional Cornish openness to the rest of the world, in contrast to perceived English scepticism and xenophobic inwardness. However, these views were combined with support for existing state-wide parties.[85] What might appear to a nationalist as paradoxical behaviour might be explained by brief reference to the history of the Cornish identity.

A medieval compact between the crown, via the Duchy of Cornwall, and the institutions of Cornwall's principal industry of tin mining forged a close, if sometimes tense, relationship between commons and crown, with the crown appearing to guarantee the rights and liberties of the miners and helping to foster the growth of a particularistic local culture. In the early sixteenth century threats to traditional interests triggered rebellions against religious and political change. Their defeats in turn shaped a regional identity which, steered by the gentry in the seventeenth and the eighteenth centuries, became hyper-loyal and legitimist, reacting against the disastrous events of the sixteenth century and the taint of subversion.[86] These traditions then coloured the cultural nationalist movement that emerged at the end of the nineteenth century. Explicit Cornishness inherited a Blaverist and conservative tone, supporting the institutions of the centre, despite being culturally strongly 'Cornish' and continually seeking 'difference', even to the point of reviving the Cornish language.

The influence of this stream of thought partly explains MK's slow transition to a fully fledged political party before the 1970s. The organisation contained a legitimist and loyal but strongly culturally regionalist wing as well as activists inspired by ideas of Celtic nationalism. These traditions co-existed uneasily within the party until the late 1970s, when the move to a clearly left of centre position resulted in the departure of the more conservative elements. Nonetheless, a strategy of electoral

---

85   Frank Mols, Jolanda Jetten and S. Alexander Haslam, 'EU identification and endorsement in context: the importance of regional identity salience', *Journal of Common Market Studies* 47 (2009), 601-23.

86   Bernard Deacon, *Cornwall: A Concise History* (Cardiff: University of Wales Press, 2007), pp.95-99; Mark Stoyle, *West Britons: Cornish Identities and the Early Modern British State* (Exeter: University of Exeter Press, 2001), pp.157-180.

respectability and collaboration with non-nationalist organisations and individuals in campaigns for a Cornish Assembly and in defence of Cornish integrity since the 1990s might be seen to fit a temperate cultural tradition handed down by Cornish history. In this, reinvigorated memories of a 'Celtic' identity, historical narratives of non-Englishness and the presence of a non-English language provide the raw materials for a nationalist movement. But the actual, lived history of Cornishness has produced a more ambivalent and less confrontational attitude to centralised authority. Yet a cultural history that includes non-English and 'Celtic' tropes and representations helps to maintain the existence of MK and explains its persistence over time.

External supply-side factors in conjunction with demand facilitate party success rather than determine it.[87] For the final pieces of the jigsaw we have to investigate the internal supply side. This revolves around the factors of ideology or policy positioning, leadership and organisation. It remains a possibility that MK has just not done enough to mobilise the potential support for devolution in Cornwall.

Internal supply-side factors
A left of centre position on economic and social issues has been combined since the turn of the century with attempts to work with others in broader campaigns for a Cornish Assembly and a moderate stance that stresses the party's civic nationalism. In 2004 MK's leader Dick Cole emphasised the party was 'positive and inclusive' and campaigning for 'all the people of Cornwall'. An awareness of valence issues also underpinned the party's declaration in 2009 after the first elections for the new unitary local government authority that the three MK councillors were 'not part of the [Conservative and Independent] ruling administration but, at the same time, do not consider ourselves to be in opposition'. Despite those efforts to enhance the party's credibility, Dick Cole also admitted in 2015 that the party had a 'major credibility issue with voters when it comes to Westminster elections' as electoral breakthrough once again proved elusive.[88]

While policy consistency might be expected to enhance MK's credibility, its positioning as a left of centre party could be seen as putting it at odds with the political values of Cornish society. Despite an academic preoccupation with Cornwall's Liberal and radical tradition,[89] since the

87 Mudde, *Populist Radical Right*, 2007, p.253.

88 *Cornish Nation* 34 (2004), p.4; *Cornish Nation* 52 (2009), p.3; *Cornish Nation* 70 (2015), p.5.

89 Payton, *Making*, 1992, pp.155-158; Garry Tregidga, *the Liberal Party in South West Britain since 1918: Political Decline, Dormancy and Rebirth* (Exeter:

early twentieth century Cornwall's politics have for long periods been dominated by the Conservative Party. In parliamentary elections since 1950 the Conservatives have taken over 60% of the seats in Cornwall, with Liberals/Liberal Democrats winning 30% and Labour 9%. Only in the period from 1997 to 2005 did this dominance falter. In this respect, Cornwall has similarities with the other Atlantic regions of Brittany and Galicia, both of which traditionally voted on the right in the mid-twentieth century. Furthermore, in both those regions the main ethoregionalist party – the UDB in Brittany and the BNG in Galicia between 1993 and its catastrophic break-up in 2012, were explicitly socialist parties. In Brittany especially, but also in Galicia, there has been a long-term swing to the mainstream left. Faint echoes of this might have been observed in the greater success of Liberal Democrats at Cornish elections between 1979 and 2015, when they won a more competitive 45% of Cornish seats, compared with 51% for the Conservatives. On the other hand, in the two most recent general elections in 2015 and 2017 the Conservatives swept up all six Cornish seats.

If MK's positioning has arguably made it more difficult to appeal to the majority conservative sensibilities of the Cornish electorate, its position on Europe has also proved to be unreflective of popular opinion in Cornwall. By 1989 MK had rejected its earlier anti-European stance to declare that 'Cornwall's future lies in Europe'. The party's participation in the European Free Alliance, it said, 'finally dispels the myth ... that we are insular and parochial'.[90] The party remained strongly pro-European despite growing misgivings from some other ethnoregionalist parties about the neo-liberal and intergovernmentalist direction of the EU in the 2000s.[91] The European level indeed provided a useful tool in a multilevel and more flexible campaigning strategy after the late 1990s. It played a critical role in the ultimately successful campaigns to implement the Charter for Regional and Minority Languages for Cornish and to gain recognition for the Cornish under the Framework Charter for the Protection of National Minorities, as petitioning and lobbying at a European level complemented campaigning at Westminster and Truro. Yet the efficacy of multi-level campaigning contrasted with a growing euro-scepticism on the part of the Cornish electorate, despite large scale European grant aid. This was viewed as merely involving vanity projects and benefiting a peripatetic project class rather than the local population directly. A failure of MK, and the

---

University of Exeter Press, 2000; Ault, *Liberal Democrats*, 2015.

90 *Kernow* 3 (1989), p.13.

91 Anwen Elias, 'From Euro-Enthusiasm to Euro-Scepticism? A Re-Evaluation of Minority Nationalist Party Attitudes Towards European Integration', *Regional & Federal Studies* 18 (2008), 557–581.

mainstream parties, to convince voters of the benefits of EU membership led to Cornwall voting 56.5% for Brexit in 2016, compared with the 53.3% Brexit vote in England.[92]

MK was also strategically wrong-footed by the issue of unitary local government for Cornwall. In 1994 a press release declared that the majority of MK activists supported a single unitary authority 'that could one day evolve into a full, legislative Cornish Assembly'.[93] This merely repeated the unfounded claims of the Liberal Democrats. The party's desire to retain a governmental institution based on the historic territory of Cornwall blinded it to a recognition of the longer term consequences of allowing unitary local government to occupy the same spatial template as a Cornish Assembly. This made it more difficult to distinguish the party's call for a Cornish Assembly from the Liberal Democrat position and compounded the confusion surrounding the relationship between local and regional government in Cornwall.[94]

The second supply-side factor – leadership – is difficult to assess. Mudde usefully distinguishes between external charismatic leadership and internal practical leadership.[95] The former is more crucial for the electoral breakthrough phase while the latter is critical for maintaining the party's organisation. In 1997 Dick Cole was elected party chairman and has retained that position since, becoming the longest serving leader in MK's history. Over that time, there has been more focus on Cole as party leader, with *Cornish Nation* in 2007 noting that 'under Dick's leadership, Mebyon Kernow has undergone a period of growth and increased professionalisation', with a three-fold growth in candidates and a rising number of elected councillors.[96] While the role of the party leader has become more important, Dick Cole fits the description of an internal practical leader better than external charismatic leader. His influence lies in overseeing some organisational changes within the party and ensuring it remains more focused on an election-fighting strategy.

At various points since attaining the threshold of representation at a local level MK has claimed a greater professionalism. At the 1998 AGM Dick Cole described the party as undergoing 'continuing professionalisation'. In 1995, before his leadership commenced, new committee structures were put

---

92 Electoral Commission, 'EU Referendum results',
    http://www.electoralcommission.org.uk/find-information-by-subject/elections-and-referendums/past-elections-and-referendums/eu-referendum/electorate-and-count-information (accessed August 13, 2016).

93 *Cornish Nation* 1 (1995), p.2.

94 For example *Cornish Nation* 70 (2015), p.8.

95 Mudde, *Populist Radical Right*, 2007, p.260.

96 *Cornish Nation* 45 (2007), pp.8-9.

in place to cover administration and election campaigning following the decision to re-enter the parliamentary electoral arena. In 2000 new party structures were adopted, although changes were modest. The party conference remained the highest authority, but the management body of the National Executive Committee was slimmed down, with each member holding a particular policy brief, mimicking the shadow cabinets of mainstream British political parties. Later, a Leadership Team emerged, operating with an Administration and Publicity Team to direct party activities in the day to day arena.[97] Those changes allowed the party to reproduce itself and the revised party structures introduced a greater level of complexity. However, the branch structure based on district council areas in the 1990s and then parliamentary constituencies, reflected the party's variable presence on the ground with pockets of local activity co-existing with areas with no activity. Similarly, despite more organisational complexity, the party has been unable to afford to pay full time officers and in that sense remains amateur.

But does a relatively unsophisticated organisational capability explain the lack of electoral success or does the lack of success explain the organisational level? Research on other parties and party families tends to find no clear relationship. Indeed, it suggests that organisational strength is more important for electoral consolidation after breakthrough.[98] In MK's case the organisational changes since the mid-1990s are more useful for explaining why the party persists, despite its failure to achieve an electoral breakthrough at the state level.

Conclusion

This study has expanded the membership of the ethnoregionalist party family through examining the previously neglected case of Mebyon Kernow. While MK's performance has been comparable to that of most French micronationalist parties, it has signally failed to mobilise significant electoral support beyond second-order local and European elections. Although crossing the threshold of representation at a local level in the 1990s and establishing itself as a regular, though minor, player on the Cornish political scene, MK is far from making an electoral breakthrough at the state level. Its policy impact has also been muted, although gains made in recent years in relation to the revived Cornish language and the more important recognition of the Cornish in 2014 under the Framework Convention for the Protection of National Minorities stem from a greater

---

97 *Cornish Nation* 12 (1998-99, p.3; *Cornish Nation* 16 (2000), p.4; *Cornish Nation* 64 (2012), p.4.

98 Matt Golder, 'Far right parties in Europe', *Annual Review of Political Science* 19 (2016), 477-497.

role of the Cornish identity in regional politics. MK's persistence and durability over half a century has been a critical, albeit indirect, contributory factor in allowing that identity agenda to enjoy a greater legitimacy.[99]

Unlike the Psd'A however, where strategic miscalculations and ideological inconsistency were identified as major factors in its decline,[100] MK's ideological positioning has been consistent since the 1980s, if not earlier. Its failure to achieve electoral success (and its relative organisational weakness) is better explained by structural constraints that put limits on its strategic behaviour.[101] In many ways the political opportunity structures of the political scientists become political constraint structures when considering MK.

On the demand side, the ambiguous legacy of the Cornish identity means that enhanced confidence in that identity does not automatically translate into support for an ethnoregionalist party, particularly at the state level. This is compounded by external supply-side factors, especially party competition and the long-term structural location of Cornwall in wider spatial consciousness. MK faces a major problem in challenging a Liberal Democratic Party that shares ownership of the centre-periphery cleavage in Cornwall, having adopted an accommodationist strategy since before MK even crossed the threshold of declaration in the 1960s. It will not easily dislodge the Lib Dems from their position as the main repository for Cornish regional sentiment.

These underlying historical and cultural systemic contexts both reinforce Cornwall's institutionalisation as an English county and part of a wider 'region' rather than a region in its own right and shape the political space available in Cornwall for ethnoregionalism. As a result there is room at the local level but MK's prospects of electoral success and policy impact are severely curtailed at the state level. The party appears trapped in a fundamental paradox. The political invisibility of Cornwall and the reluctance by government and opinion-formers to give practical recognition to the national status of the Cornish erect substantial structural barriers to MK's breakthrough. Yet without such a breakthrough, Cornwall fails to be seen as somehow equivalent to Scotland and Wales and thus deserving of national recognition and similar special treatment. Unlike most ethnoregionalist parties in western Europe MK has to fight for a basic recognition of Cornwall's status as a region, a definition denied by the central state and even by many in Cornwall itself. An 'English county' discourse combines with the institutional constraints imposed by a political

---

99 Willett and Tredinnick-Rowe, 'Fragmentation', 2016.

100 Hepburn, 'Explaining failure', 2009.

101 cf. Jan Rovny, 'Riker and Rokkan: Remarks on the strategy and structure of party competition', *Party Politics* 21 (2015), 912-918.

system that lacks a democratic regional level.[102] These external structural constraints compound the difficulties posed by a disproportional electoral system and media that give little importance to the issue of Cornish devolution.

Nonetheless, MK has confounded the predictions of Pedersen's lifespan model and persisted for more than half a century. It has not withered away or disappeared, despite some uncertain moments in the late 1980s and early 1990s. Moreover, unlike some other small parties, it has not succumbed to factionalism since the early 1980s. Its durability also rests on long-term structural factors, notably the presence of enduring non-English cultural imaginings and a sense of difference that generates a potential demand for devolution in Cornwall. These have been enhanced by internal organisational changes since the early 1990s that have maintained its electoral competitiveness in the local arena. A non-English Celtic language, although marginal, and a history that can be interpreted as a struggle against incorporation into the central state, provide a usable past and the raw material for political nationalism.

Finally, what, if any, lessons does the experience of MK offer English regionalist parties? The structural limits of Cornwall's institutionalisation suggest that the Yorkshire Party and the North East Party will have to transcend the status of 'mere English counties'. Both might more easily be able to do this as they encompass a wider territory than just one current administrative county. In addition, their emergence could add weight to the pressure for changes in the rules on party political broadcasts and potentially in turn benefit MK. However, MK's persistence feeds off a longstanding non-English and 'Celtic' positioning. This is not available to the northern English regionalist parties and it remains to be seen how they might be able to replace this factor with equally effective means of delivering a durability approaching that of MK.

---

102 The role of this discourse in containing regionalist campaigns is not new, operating in the late nineteenth century – see Bernard Deacon, 'Regional identity in late nineteenth-century England; discursive terrains and rhetorical strategies', *International Journal of Regional and Local History* 16 (2016), 59-74 and chapter 7 above.

Index

www.ingramcontent.com/pod-product-compliance
Lightning Source LLC
LaVergne TN
LVHW051626080426
835511LV00016B/2199